The End of the Line

THE END OF THE LINE

*Essays on Psychoanalysis
and the Sublime*

NEIL HERTZ

COLUMBIA UNIVERSITY PRESS
New York

Library of Congress Cataloging in Publication Data

Hertz, Neil.
  The end of the line.

  Bibliography: p.
  Includes index.
  1 Psychoanalysis and literature—Addresses,
essays, lectures.   I. Title.
  PN56.P92H4 1985   801'.92   84-23081
  ISBN 0-231-05708-3 (alk. paper)
  ISBN 0-231-05709-1   (pa.)

Columbia University Press
New York   Guildford, Surrey
Copyright © 1985 Columbia University Press
All rights reserved
Printed in the United States of America

CONTENTS

PREFACE

The essays collected here were written for various occasions over a period of years: if they go together it is in the way that tokens of a preoccupation go together. I have slightly rearranged the order in which they appear, bringing related texts or topics together, and I have added an Afterword, in which I have tried to spell out some of their common concerns.

I am grateful to the editors and publishers of the periodicals and collections in which these articles first appeared for granting me permission to reprint them here. Specifically: to Editions du Seuil and the University of Chicago, for "A Reading of Longinus," which first appeared in French in *Poétique* (1973) 15 and in English in *Critical Inquiry* (1983) 9; to Boston University for "Wordsworth and the Tears of Adam," *Studies in Romanticism* (1967) 7; to the Johns Hopkins University Press, for "The Notion of Blockage in the Literature of the Sublime" in Geoffrey H. Hartman ed., *Psychoanalysis and the Question of the Text* (Baltimore and London, 1978) and for "Recognizing Casaubon" in *Glyph 6* (1979); to *Diacritics* for "Flaubert's Conversion" (Summer 1972) and "Dora's Secrets, Freud's Techniques" (Spring 1983); to the Cornell University Press for "Freud and the Sandman" in Josué V. Harari ed., *Textual Strategies: Perspectives in Post-Structuralist Criticism* (Ithaca, N.Y., 1979); to Yale University for "Two Extravagant Teachings" in Yale French Studies no. 63, *The Pedagogical Imperative,* ed. Barbara Johnson (1982); and to the University of California for "Medusa's Head: Male Hysteria under Political Pressure" and "More about 'Medusa's Head'" in *Representations* (Fall 1983) 4. Thanks, too, to Catherine Gallagher and Joel Fineman for kindly allowing me to reprint their contributions to the exchange on "Medusa's Head."

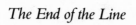

The End of the Line

1.
A READING OF LONGINUS

IT BECAME CUSTOMARY in the eighteenth century to praise Longinus in ways that mimicked one of his own favorite turns of thought—to identify enthusiastically two elements that would more commonly be thought of as quite distinct. To say, with Boileau and Pope, that Longinus "is himself the great Sublime he draws," or to profess to doubt, as Gibbon did, "which is the most sublime, Homer's Battle of the Gods or Longinus' apostrophe . . . upon it," is knowingly to override certain conventional lines of demarcation—between writers and their subject matter, between text and interpretation—very much in the manner of Longinus overriding the distinction between Homer and his heroes, between sublime language and its author ("sublimity is the echo of a noble mind"), or between sublime poet and his audience ("we come to believe we have created what we have only heard").[1] Longinus' admirers, struck by the force of the treatise, are usually willing to release him from the strictures of theoretical discourse and allow him the license of a poet; they are likely to appreciate his transgressions of conventional limits without ever calling them into question. It has been left to more skeptical readers, wary of Longinus' "transports," to draw attention to his odd movements of thought: W. K. Wimsatt, for example, is unsympathetic but acute when he accuses Longinus of "sliding" from one theoretical distinction to another, a slide "which seems to harbor a certain duplicity and invalidity."[2] Wimsatt is right: something one might want to call a "slide" is observable again and again in the treatise, and not merely from one theoretical distinction to another. One finds in the treatise

I

a rhetorician's argument conducted with great intelligence and energy, but one also discovers that it is remarkably easy to lose one's way, to forget which rhetorical topic is under consideration at a particular point, to find oneself attending to a quotation, a fragment of analysis, a metaphor—some interestingly resonant bit of language that draws one into quite another system of relationships. I want to attempt to follow that movement here, to hold it in mind and to question its implications. I will look closely at a number of passages in which Longinus interweaves language of his own with that of the authors he admires—for it is here, out of the play of text with quotation and of quotations with one another, that the most interesting meanings as well as the peculiar power of the treatise are generated.

I

Consider first a sequence of illustrations characterizing the sublime poet as in some sense godlike. They occur in chapter 9, in a discussion of what Longinus takes to be the most important source of sublimity, nobility of mind.

Great thoughts spur men to great language, he argues, and among such thoughts are those dwelling on the power of the gods: Longinus first sets down a medley of lines from the *Iliad,* then cites that most telling instance of mimesis, Moses' repetition of God's *fiat lux:*

> Similarly, the lawgiver of the Jews, no ordinary man—for he understood and expressed God's power in accordance with its worth—writes at the beginning of his *Laws:* "God said"—now what?—"Let there be light," and there was light; "let there be earth," and there was earth. [9.9]

There was clearly no need for further comment here, and Longinus makes none; instead, with an air of diffidence—rather like Proust writing about Flaubert—he turns to another text:

> Perhaps it will not be out of place, my friend, if I add a further Homeric example—from the human sphere this time—so that we

2

can see how the poet is accustomed to enter into the greatness of his heroes. Darkness falls suddenly. Thickest night blinds the Greek army. Ajax is bewildered. "O Father Zeus," he cries,

"Deliver the sons of the Achaeans out of the mist,
Make the sky clear, and let us see;
In the light—kill us."   [9.10]

The sentences that follow comment on the truthfulness of these lines as a representation of Ajax's feelings, yet they make nothing of what is most striking about the juxtaposition of these two fragments: that they are both calls for light—one, on the part of a god, associated with the creative act; the other, on the part of a mortal, at the risk of his own destruction. Yet the point—that heroes may mimic the speech of the gods, but at their peril—is nevertheless quietly enforced by the next quotation but one, this time from the *Odyssey*. Nestor is speaking:

There lies warlike Ajax, there Achilles,
There Patroclus, the gods' peer as a counsellor,
And there my own dear son.

Typically, Longinus proceeds in just this way. One quotation will suggest another but not necessarily because each illustrates the rhetorical topic at issue; both might, but the effective links between them seem at once flimsier and subtler than that. A single word— "light" or "Ajax"—will provide a superficial connection between passages that then turn out to be suggestively resonant. Here in chapter 9 a series of analogies for sublime language is produced: it is like God's creative word or perhaps only like Moses' echo of that utterance; it is like a heroically risky prayer to Father Zeus; it is like a father's elegiac naming of his dead son. We are made to feel that somewhere among these versions of the godlike we are entitled to locate the poet's own language. But where? Between the two quotations about Ajax, Longinus has placed another, this time not to illustrate his argument but to praise Homer. Alluding to the lines on Ajax's prayer, he writes:

In this passage, it is the real Homer, the gale of whose genius fans the excitement of battle; the poet

3

Rages like Ares, spear-brandishing, or the deadly fire
Raging in the mountains, in the thickets of the deep wood.
Foam shows at his mouth.   [9.11]

It is characteristic of Longinus that these lines both do and don't identify Homer with a god: literally they refer not to Ares but to the raging feelings of Hector, as he charges down on the Greek ships in *Iliad* 15. We are left with an excited and giddy feeling but with our question still unanswered. If Homer's language can be felt to participate in godlike power and godlike violence, it does so at one remove, by way of a heroic simile, "in a manner of speaking."

These problems and the linked motifs out of which they emerge are recurrent ones in the treatise, and they draw to them other elements as well: reading along one has the sense of moving through a verbal medium increasingly rich in repetitions and glancing analogies, the thematic equivalent of slant rhymes. The next chapter ostensibly turns to take up a new topic, the selection and organization of material, but its two chief illustrations glance back at the previous pages: another simile describing Hector's onslaught in *Iliad* 15, and Sappho's famous ode ("phainetai moi"), in which the throes of passion are presented in language that echoes the heroic idiom. Yet if Longinus is aware of this allusiveness, he says nothing about it; instead his discussion of Sappho provides the occasion for still another link, one which will bring the motifs of violence and risk and death into touch with the rhetorician's theory that the effective poem is an organic unity. For Sappho is introduced as an example of a poet selecting and composing elements so as to "organize them as a single body" (10.1).

The comparison goes back to the *Phaedrus,* where Socrates speaks of the ideal discourse as "constructed like a living creature, with its own body, as it were," and it is certain that Longinus takes the doctrine seriously (264c).[3] He will refer to it several times as the treatise goes on: "the removal of a syllable," he warns, discussing the rhythms in the prose of Demosthenes, "at once curtails and mutilates the grand effect" (39.4). Or again:

> I come now to a principle of particular importance for lending grandeur to our words. The beauty of the body depends on the

way in which the limbs are joined together, each one when severed from the others having nothing remarkable about it, but the whole together forming a perfect unity. Similarly great thoughts which lack connection are themselves wasted and waste the total sublime effect, whereas if they co-operate to form a unity and are linked by the bonds of harmony, they come to life and speak just by virtue of the periodic structure. [40.1; the last phrase—"auto to kuklo phonēenta ginetai"—is rendered by Grube as "in the rounded structure of the whole they find their voice"]

But here in chapter 10 the conventional analogy is made to take on a bizarre and intriguing appropriateness, for the elements that Sappho is bringing together into the body of her poem are precisely the names of the fragments of her natural body, seen as the debris of a shattering erotic experience that had brought her, in the words of the ode, "only a little short of death." Longinus cites the poem and then asks:

> Do you not admire the way in which she brings everything together—mind and body, hearing and tongue, eyes and skin? She seems to have lost them all, and to be looking for them as though they were external to her. [10.3; in Grube's translation, "as if they were scattered elements strange to her"]

Rarely has the doctrine of organic unity been presented with fewer wistful overtones. It is clear that Longinus admires the poem because when it becomes "like a living creature" and "finds its voice," it speaks of a moment of self-estrangement in language that captures the *dis*organized quality of the experience. It would seem to be the moment itself that fascinates Longinus, the point where the near-fatal stress of passion can be thought of as turning into—as indistinguishable from—the energy that is constituting the poem. Any doubts we might have about this are removed by the analysis of a passage from Homer that follows in chapter 10, where the emphasis falls less on the selection and arrangement of materials (still the topic under discussion) than on the violence with which they are worked into shape and the relation of that shaping power to the force inherent in the materials themselves. "A similar point," Longinus writes in a casual, terse, transitional sentence, "can be

5

made about the description of storms in Homer, who always picks out the most terrifying aspects." The passage he has in mind is one likening Hector to a storm at sea:

He [Hector] fell upon [the Greeks] as upon a swift ship falls
   a wave,
Huge, wind-reared by the clouds. The ship
Is curtained in foam, a hideous blast of wind
Roars in the sail. The sailors shudder in terror;
They being carried away from under death, but only just. . . .
[10.5]

Probably it was the last stanza of Sappho's poem—

Cold sweat pours off me; shivering grips me all over;
I am paler than grass; I seem near to dying.

—that brought the last lines of Homer's simile to mind. In any case, it is there that Longinus directs his comments:

> Notice also the forced combination of naturally uncompoundable prepositions: *hupek,* "away from under." Homer has tortured the words to correspond with the emotion of the moment, and expressed the emotion magnificently by thus crushing words together. He has in effect stamped the special character of the danger on the diction: "they are being carried away from under death."
> [10.6]

The singling out of that condensed prepositional phrase is one of the critical strokes that justifies Longinus' reputation. For the phrase catches in miniature the same moment that he had been drawn to in Sappho's ode, the turning away from near-annihilation, from being "under death" to being out from under death. This is, characteristically, the sublime turn (compare Wordsworth's "my mind turned round / As with the might of waters"), and it is rightly seen here as bound up with a transfer of power (or the simulation of such a transfer) from the threatening forces to the poetic activity itself: it is now Homer who is said to "force" or "torture" or "crush" his language.

This reversal is so crucial to the treatise that it is worth dwelling a bit longer on how it has been made to take place. The logic of it becomes apparent if we think of chapter 10 as composed of a series of transitive relationships, couplings of active and passive elements. Schematized, it would look something like this:

Passion	breaks down and scatters	the elements of Sappho's body, making her shiver close to death
Sappho	joins together	the names of these elements
Hector	charges	the Greeks
The wave	batters	the ship, making the sailors shudder, close to death
Homer	forces	his propositions
	tortures and crushes	his words
	stamps	his diction with the special character of the danger

Laid out in this way, the analogies are plain enough: all the subjects of these sentences are assimilated to one another, even though not all act with the same degree of ferocity (Sappho's skillful craftsmanship belies its power); all the objects being acted upon are likened as well, so that the elements of Sappho's body are made to seem not only like the nouns in her poem which represent them but also like the words in Homer's sentences; and her trembling, like that of the sailors, becomes the expressive sign of the force that is bearing down on her, in this respect the equivalent of the signs of peril ("the special character of the danger") that Homer has "stamped" on his diction. But notice that the turn itself, the transfer of power, can take place only if some element can shift its position from one side of the scheme to the other; it is here that we can see how Sappho's ode serves Longinus' purposes. For it is not simply a poem of passion and self-division but one which dramatizes, in a startlingly condensed fashion, the shift from Sappho-as-victimized-body to Sappho-as-poetic-force. As such it serves as a figure for both a certain disjunction and a certain continuity: we are made to feel, by analogy, that Homer has experienced the same stress, that he has ("as it were") survived the violent onslaught of Hector and is now not merely representing those energies but taking them over. By placing Homer's lines in touch with Sappho's, Longinus has deep-

ened his analysis of the similarities between poets and godlike heroes, a comparison that at certain points in the treatise can seem
merely wishful or glib. The grounds for comparison are now seen
to be not the grandeur of the hero's calling but its ambivalent connections with both violent action and the pathos of self-loss.
Wordsworth's paradoxical description of the poet as "weak, as is a
breaking wave," is a simile which brings together the chapter's
themes of power and disintegration in a turn Longinus could appreciate.

II

I hope by now I have conveyed some sense of what I take to be at
work in the treatise: the movement I follow is clearly not linear; it
does not run in tandem with the progress of the rhetorical argument from topic to topic but is in certain ways cumulative—that is,
at certain points one becomes aware of a thickening of texture.
These are pages where, challenged by an aspect of his theme or by
the strength of a quotation, Longinus seems to be working harder
at locating his discourse close in to the energies of his authors. At
those moments, he too is drawn into the sublime turning, and what
he is moved to produce is not merely an analysis illustrative of the
sublime but further figures for it. Chapter 10 seems to me one such
passage; another is the much-praised analysis of a text of Demosthenes in chapter 16. There, because he is dealing not with a poet—a
maker of acknowledged fictions—but with an orator, Longinus is
obliged to take up more carefully the question of language's power
to deceive. I want to move toward that section now by tracing first
the rapid and, I think, deliberately giddy build-up of quotations
that precedes it.

Chapter 15 is devoted to the topic of imagination, in the limited
sense of *phantasia,* the making of images. Longinus begins by distinguishing the orator's imagination from the poet's, then qualifies
that distinction, and then apparently ignores it altogether while he
puts together a sequence of short texts, mostly from Euripides. The

8

first two are fragments of outbursts by Orestes—the desperate imaginings of a parricide:

Mother, I beg you, do not drive them at me,
The women with the blood in their eyes and the snakes—
They are here, they are here, jumping right up to me.

Or again:

O, o! She'll kill me. Where shall I escape?

The commentary then goes on to make the bold, although by now predictable, connection: "The poet himself saw the Erinyes, and has as good as made his audience see what he imagined." Are we meant to feel that both Orestes' imagination and his guilt are somehow shared by Euripides? The next half-page suggests that we are. "Though not formed by nature for grandeur," Longinus writes of the dramatist, "he often forces himself to be tragic. When the moment for greatness comes, he [in Homer's words] 'whips flanks and buttocks with his tail / And drives himself to fight.'" Then, in still another passage from Euripides, we are told of Phaeton, driving his father's horses: "he whipped the flanks of the winged team, and let them go," although the emphasis now is ominously on the voice of Phaeton's father, directing and admonishing him. Again Longinus make the explicit identification: "May one not say that the writer's soul has mounted the chariot, has taken wing with the horses and shares the danger?"[4]

But the point is not simply that to force one's talent past its natural limit, as Euripides is said to have done, is a transgression equivalent to Phaeton's. Rather, I think, that the authenticity of the father's language—and it is appropriate here that the father is Helios—can be attained only by means of a sacrificial act: in this instance, by a common displacement, it is Phaeton who is sacrificed to the imaginative needs of his poet. For Euripides to emulate Helios he must first identify himself—and fall—with Phaeton. And indeed, only a little further along, four lines from *Seven Against*

9

Thebes strengthen the associations of powerful language with sacrifice:

Seven men of war, commanders of companies,
Killing a bull into a black-bound shield,
Dipping their hands in the bull's blood,
Took oath by Ares, by Enyo, by bloodthirsty Terror—

"They pledged their own death, showing themselves no mercy," Longinus adds. But what is the status of such an oath? It could be said to occupy an equivocal middle ground, somewhere between the transgressions of the son and either the admonitions or the creative word of the father. It can be seen as the mortal's attempt to capture for his language some of the prestige and stability of the divine by placing limits on his actions or binding himself (the Greek word for oath, *horkos,* derives from *herkos,* the word for an enclosure or wall); hence the oath's connection with sacrifice, invariably a figure for self-sacrifice, a gesture in the direction of one's own death. Ajax's prayer is such a gesture—closer to an oath than it is to the *fiat lux*—but so is Sappho's poem and so are the lines from Euripides' *Phaeton.*[5]

Yet because oaths (and their analogues in literary language) are never more than merely attempts at divine stability, there is always the risk that they will turn into—or turn out to be—merely a fancier form of transgression. Longinus will address himself to that risk in chapter 17, but for the moment he moves along, clustering together, in a rather breathless way, more quotations and allusions to the tragedians. Two more or less distinct series can be traced: on the one hand, oaths, fatherly admonitions, the divine portents Oedipus hears as he prepares for his own burial, the divine punishment that pursues Orestes—versions of authenticity or its approximations; on the other hand, the madness of Orestes, the daring flight of Phaeton, two instances of Bacchic frenzy, finally another wild cry from Orestes—versions of excess and transgression (15.2–15.8). Then, with all this confusedly present in his mind, the reader is confronted again with the (temporarily forgotten) question of oratory:

10

What then is the effect of rhetorical visualization [i.e., *phantasia*]? There is much it can do to bring urgency and passion into our words; but it is when it is closely involved with factual arguments that it enslaves the hearer as well as persuading him [as in this passage of Demosthenes]: "Suppose you heard a shout this very moment outside the court, and someone said that the prison had been broken open and the prisoners had escaped—no one, young or old, would be so casual as not to give what help he could. And if someone then came forward and said 'This is the man who let them out,' our friend would never get a hearing; it would be the end of him." [In Grube's translation: "he would be killed at once, before he had a chance to speak."] There is a similar instance in Hyperides' defense of himself when he was on trial for the proposal to liberate the slaves which he put forward after the defeat [at Chaeronea]. "It was not the proposer," he said, "who drew up this decree; it was the battle of Chaeronea." Here the orator uses a visualization actually in the moment of making his factual argument, with the result that his thought has taken him beyond the limits of mere persuasiveness. Now our natural instinct is, in all such cases, to attend to the stronger influence, so that we are diverted from the demonstration to the astonishment caused by the visualization, which by its very brilliance conceals the factual aspect. This is a natural reaction: when two things are joined together, the stronger attracts to itself the force of the weaker. [15.9–15.11]

I have quoted this passage at length in order to convey some sense of its bewildering assault on the reader. In no immediately recognizable relation to the quotations that preceded it, it offers some new resonances of its own, turning on a number of motifs that had not been prominent in the earlier sections of the treatise but which will become increasingly important from this point on: slavery, prison, freedom, and the Battle of Chaeronea. Here they seem brought together in an enigmatic connection, as overlapping figures teasingly out of alignment. But the relations among the motifs in this passage turn out to be rigorously controlled. Demosthenes and Hyperides are both caught in the act of "enslaving" their listeners by drawing attention away from the possible weaknesses, the possible falsity, of their arguments, with a striking image. But what Hyperides is on trial for is wishing to free the slaves; it is this wish that his reference to the Battle of Chaeronea is intended to conceal. And, strangely, what Demosthenes is talking about is someone with a similar wish—the man whom he imagines freeing the prisoners—and that man, were he once recognized, would be killed on the spot, "before he had a chance to speak"—that is, before he had a chance to argue his case like Hyperides and perhaps to conceal successfully the fact that it was he who had transgressed in this way. Given the chance—and it is important that he *not* be given the chance, Demosthenes suggests—he too might blame it all on something like the Battle of Chaeronea. Were he to find a figure striking enough, he too might "enslave" his audience. He would seem to be altogether too close to Demosthenes and Hyperides for comfort, and that is no doubt why—in the economy of Longinus' text—he is killed off. He functions here as a propitiatory sacrifice: for Longinus is about to devote the next section to the praise of Demosthenes, focusing on the magnificent oath he introduced into his speech "On the Crown," an oath designed to conceal from his audience that the Battle of Chaeronea was a defeat for Athens and, implicitly, for the policies of Demosthenes himself.

The analysis of the Marathon oath is taken up in chapter 16, where Longinus addresses himself, he announces, to an entirely new topic, that of figures (*schēmata*). Indeed, he seems particularly intent on distinguishing this section from what precedes it: the last words of chapter 15 gather up some (although, oddly, not all) of the main strands of the first half of the treatise in what sounds like a conclusive fashion ("This will suffice for an account of sublimity of thought produced by greatness of mind, imitation, or visualization" [15.12]), and then chapter 16 begins in an equally decisive tone ("The next topic is that of figures").[6] The effect of this pause is to draw attention back to the manifest argument of the treatise and away from the articulations of language we have been following. Yet what Longinus goes on to write takes up precisely where he left off at the end of chapter 15:

> Here is Demosthenes putting forward a demonstrative argu-
> ment on behalf of his policy. What would have been the natural
> way to put it? "You have not done wrong, you who fought for the
> liberty of Greece; you have examples to prove this close at home:
> the men of Marathon, of Salamis, of Plataea did not do wrong."

12

> But instead of this he was suddenly inspired to give voice to the oath by the heroes of Greece: "By those who risked their lives at Marathon, you have not done wrong!" Observe what he effects by this single figure of conjuration, or "apostrophe" as I call it here. He deifies his audience's ancestors, suggesting that it is right to take an oath by men who fell so bravely, as though they were gods. He inspires the judges with the temper of those who risked their lives. He transforms his demonstration into an extraordinary piece of sublimity and passion, and into the convincingness of this unusual and amazing oath. At the same time he injects into his hearers' minds a healing specific, so as to lighten their hearts by these paeans of praise and make them as proud of the battle with Philip as of the triumphs of Marathon and Salamis. In short, the figure enables him to run away with his audience. [16.2][7]

This is another instance of Longinus' talent for the stunningly apt citation, in this respect like his choice of Sappho's ode; or, rather, since the Marathon oath was much admired in antiquity and frequently cited by rhetoricians, this is an instance of Longinus' talent for selecting and arranging his own materials so as to bring them into interesting juxtaposition, for what Demosthenes is here being praised for is a reversal similar to that enacted by Sappho. Demosthenes is speaking after the defeat of the Athenian forces by Philip of Macedon—that is, after the moment that was traditionally considered the end of Greek liberty, the moment Werner Jaeger refers to as "the death of the city-state."[8] His audience, then, is in a rather peculiar relation to his language: it is as if they were hearing a dead man deliver their corporate funeral oration; they had already, that is, crossed the line into an imaginative relation to the natural body of Greek unity. This metaphor, taken from Longinus' chapter 24, illustrates how one can figuratively draw a plurality of things under a singular noun; he quotes once again from "On the Crown"— "The whole Peloponnese was divided"—then from Herodotus— "When Phrynicus produced *The Capture of Miletus* the theatre burst into tears"—and then comments that to "compress the separate individuals into the corresponding unity produces a more solid effect" (the final phrase here translates the Greek *sōmatoeidesteron:* "more solid" or "more like a body"). The Peloponnesus united in opposition to Philip was the natural body of Greek unity; that unity—such as it was—disintegrated at Chaeronea; and Demos-

13

thenes, in conjuring up its spirit, is offering in its place a fictional body to an audience that may be united again by that fiction, but only in the way that the audience at *The Capture of Miletus* was united when "the theatre burst into tears." Demosthenes' audience is estranged from itself by a military defeat that is the equivalent of Sappho's near-death, and it is precisely this defeat that underwrites Demosthenes' fiction.

The subtlety of Longinus' position may be seen more clearly if we compare him with the modern critic whom he most resembles, Walter Benjamin. Both would seem, at moments, to be writing out of a deep nostalgia directed ambiguously toward certain great literary works and toward the traditional culture out of which they sprung—Longinus, writing in imperial Rome, recalling the Golden Age of Athens; Benjamin, writing in Europe in the 1930s, recalling a Europe that existed before some not-too-clearly defined catastrophe. Each finds a word richly equivocal enough to locate the peculiar quality of the texts he admires in relation to something beyond literature: so Longinus' word for the sublime, *hupsos,* is linked, in certain suspiciously eloquent passages (e.g., 35.2–35.4), with cosmic Nature itself, just as Benjamin's *aura* is made to participate in the ritual values of a lost culture.[9] But then, strangely, each is drawn to texts that bear the marks of the disintegration of order: Longinus' fondness for the Chaeronea speech is in this respect analogous to Benjamin's praise of the "Spleen" poems of Baudelaire, poems which he reads as expressing "the disintegration of the aura in the experience of shock."[10] The comparison suggests that we cannot take either the critics' nostalgia or their structurings of history at face value; each evokes a catastrophe, yet each seems equally concerned with a recurrent phenomenon in literature, the movement of disintegration and figurative reconstitution I have been calling the sublime turn. This movement is not unrelated to their own method of writing, which consists in the more or less violent fragmentation of literary bodies into "quotations," in the interest of building up a discourse of one's own, a discourse which, in its turn, directs attention to passages that come to serve as emblems of the critic's most acute, least nostalgic sense of what he is about. "Quotations in my works," Benjamin wrote, "are like robbers by the roadside who make an armed attack and relieve an idler of his convictions."[11]

III

To return to the comparison between Sappho's ode and the speech "On the Crown," there are differences between the two which, for one important reason, are worth considering. The lyric poem, even though seemingly autobiographical, does not raise the question of its truth in quite the way Demosthenes' speech does. The orator is, after all, defending his political actions and in very unfavorable circumstances. Longinus realizes this and doesn't attempt to conceal the ways in which Demosthenes is cleverly misleading his audience:

> Because he was faced with the possible objection "your policies brought us to defeat—and yet you swear by victories!" he brings his thought back under control and makes it safe and unanswerable, showing that sobriety is needed even under the influence of inspiration: "By those who *risked their lives* at Marathon, and *fought in the ships* at Salamis and Artemisium, and *formed the line* at Plataea!" He never says *conquered;* throughout he withholds the word for the final issue, because it was a happy issue, and the opposite to that of Chaeronea. [16.4]

Yet by making this explicit, Longinus has brought the notion of the sublime into dangerously close relation to that of the deceptive. His sense of this danger would seem to have prompted him once more to deepen his argument. In the next chapter he approaches the question of deception in what had become the conventional way— in terms of the commonplace that art must be used to conceal art— but he gives the argument an unusual twist of his own.

There is a reciprocal relation between figurative language and sublimity, he begins: they naturally reinforce each other. How can this be so? He goes on to explain:

> Playing tricks by means of figures is a peculiarly suspect procedure. It raises the suspicion of a trap, a deep design, a fallacy. It is

15

to be avoided in addressing tyrants, kings, governors or anybody in a high place. Such a person immediately becomes angry if he is led astray like a foolish child by some skillful orator's figures. He takes the fallacy as indicating contempt for himself. He becomes like a wild animal. Even if he controls his temper, he is now completely conditioned against being convinced by what is said. A figure is therefore generally thought to be best when the fact that it is a figure is concealed.

Thus sublimity and emotion [*hupsos kai pathos*] are a defense and a wonderful aid against the suspicion which the use of figures engenders. The artifice of the trick is lost to sight in the surrounding brilliance of beauty and grandeur [*tois kallesi kai megethesi*], and it escapes all suspicion. [17.1–17.2]

Longinus' general position here is the traditional one. The standard justification for why art should be used to conceal art was commonly put in prudential terms: one did so, so as not to arouse the suspicion of one's audience.[12] But it is Longinus' way of characterizing that audience here that seems interestingly excessive: the four nouns (judge, tyrants, kings, governors), where one would have served his purpose, the lingering on the imagined reaction of that eminent leader (his fear that he will be outwitted "like a foolish child," his personal touchiness, the possibility of his savage exasperation), where all that was necessary was to note that if he became suspicious he would be hard to convince. Instead we are presented with a theatrical sketch, the outlines of an Oedipal confrontation, the figure of authority threatened by a cunning would-be usurper, a situation that was hinted at by Aristotle when he commented that "if fine language were used by a slave or a very young person it would be hardly becoming," but which is here elaborated with an odd insistence.

But the Oedipal structure is not the only one informing this imagined scene, nor need we take it as the most fundamental. Notice that the eminent leader fears not that his possessions will be appropriated but that the tables will be turned on him, that the young man will outwit the old man, the son will make the father look like a child. What is figured here is another version—in some ways a parody—of the sublime reversal. We have already seen that reversal operating with other pairs of antithetical terms: divine and

16

human, natural and unnatural, living and dead, master and slave, victory and defeat; here father and son are drawn into that play. We may still be tempted to think that we've arrived at an end point, however: some recent theorists of the sublime would stop with the Oedipal figure and describe the vibratory activity of sublime turning as a mode of ambivalence.[13] But that act of identification may be premature. Consider the passage before us. It contains still another figure of reversal, suggested in the opening lines: "At this point, my friend, I feel I ought not to pass over an observation of my own. It shall be very brief: figures are natural allies of sublimity and themselves profit wonderfully from the alliance. I will explain how this happens. Playing tricks by means of figures . . ." etc. It is this reciprocal play—between figurative language and *hupsos*—that the chapter sets out to explain. The angry confrontation Longinus proceeds to imagine may be a diversionary movement, a way of domesticating a relationship still more bizarre, still more loaded, than that of fathers to sons. Can we pursue that relationship more carefully? I think we can by dwelling on the idea of concealment.

"For how did Demosthenes conceal the figure in that passage?" Longinus asks after he has established that figures should indeed be concealed (17.2). The answer he gives is itself a figure, a simile using the language of light and darkness: "By sheer brilliance of course. As fainter lights disappear when the sunshine surrounds them, so the sophisms of rhetoric are dimmed when they are enveloped in encircling grandeur." The sentence allows one to visualize the more abstract formulation of concealment that preceded it by a few lines: "sublimity and emotion [*hupsos kai pathos*] are a defense and a wonderful aid against the suspicion which the use of figures engenders. The artifice of the trick is lost to sight in the surrounding brilliance of beauty and grandeur [*tois kallesi kai megethesi*], and it escapes all suspicion." Surrounded by brilliance, the lesser light (the artifice) disappears from sight. But what is it that disappears? Not the particular figure, of course, but "the fact that it is a figure"—its figurativeness, so to speak. And what is it that hides the figurative? The passage offers two slightly different answers: at one point a combination of sublimity and pathos but immediately thereafter a combination of sublimity and beauty. The change of diction would seem trivial, but it has nevertheless puzzled Longinus' editors since 1694, when one proposed replacing the word for beauty (*kallesi*) with one for passion, so as to keep Longinus' pairings in this sentence consistent; but "beauty" is now accepted in the most authoritative texts.[14]

One result of the word's location in chapter 17 is to bring the language of this discussion into close touch with that of chapter 43, in which Longinus cautions against the use of trivial and sordid diction, diction which could be, he warns, a blot or disfigurement on the style. Here again the word "beauty" appears in relation to the notion of concealment and in a very suggestive context:

> It is wrong to descend, in a sublime passage, to the filthy and contemptible, unless we are absolutely compelled to do so. We ought to use words worthy of things. We ought to imitate nature, who, in creating man, did not set out private parts [*ta apporeta*] or the excretions of our body in the face, but concealed them as well as she could, and, as Xenophon says, made the channels of these organs as remote as possible, so as not to spoil the beauty of the creature as a whole [*to tou holou zoou kallos*]. [43.5]

"The beauty of the creature as a whole": the beauty of the organically unified natural body would be marred by—and hence conceals—the "private parts." But *ta apporeta* can refer to more than just "those unmentionable parts": in the singular, the noun can mean that which is forbidden, the unspeakable, a state secret, hence something mystical and sacred; it is one of those richly ambivalent nouns, like Freud's *das Unheimliche* or perhaps like *hupsos* itself. Yet if my analogy holds—the analogy between the concealed genital crevices and the concealed figures of speech—what is literally "unspeakable" is not the shame of sexuality or of Oedipal desire but the figurativeness of that shame; that is, the figurativeness of every instance of the figurative, including those figures that inform our sexual imaginings. What Longinus has allowed us to read is that when figurative language is concealed it may sustain the truthful, the natural, the masterful, and so on; but when it is revealed, it is always revealed as false. Worse yet, because more unsettling, what is revealed is not the language's flat-footed falsity but its peculiar agility in moving between the two poles, whether these be named the divine and the human, the true and the false, the position of the father and that of the son, or whatever. This is what is both "natural" and "wonderful": "figures are natural allies of sublimity and themselves profit wonderfully from the alliance" (17.1). It is when a literary text provides us with a powerful apprehension of this phenomenon that we are drawn to characterize it as "sublime."

A final example will show Longinus once again discerning this power in language but this time (in chapter 38) characterizing it in derogatory terms, as its power to "turn into its opposite." Although there are some pages missing at the beginning of the chapter, it is certain that the topic being discussed is hyperbole. Longinus, in language that is intended to recall that of chapter 17, is warning against hyperbole's improper use:

> The important thing to know is how far to push a given hyperbole; it sometimes destroys it to go too far; too much tension results in relaxation, and may indeed end in the contrary of the intended effect. Thus Isocrates' zeal for amplifying everything made him do a childish thing. The argument of his *Panegyricus* is that Athens surpasses Sparta in services to the Greek race. Right at the beginning we find the following: "Secondly, the power of speech is such that it can make great things lowly, and give grandeur to the trivial, say what is old in new fashion, and lend an appearance of antiquity to recent events." Is Isocrates then about to reverse the positions of Athens and Sparta? The encomium on the power of speech is equivalent to an introduction recommending the reader not to believe what he is told. I suspect that what we said of the best figures is true of the best hyperboles: they are those which avoid being seen for what they are. [38.1–38.3]

An eighteenth-century commentator had trouble with Longinus' illustration here: "The passage inserted by the critic from ISO-CRATES seems an ill-timed sentiment, rather than an hyperbole. Perhaps LONGINUS may be inclined to construe any sentiment forced, or unnaturally introduced, as deserving that title."[15] The editor of the Budé text agrees: "It is less a question of hyperboles than of procedures of argumentation and of style."[16] More recently still, a translator added this footnote: "We should note that Longinus uses the term hyperbole in a rather wide sense, for certainly this passage from Isocrates is hardly a hyperbole in the usual sense but at most an exaggeration."[17] And the editor of the definitive modern edition is similarly puzzled: "We may admit that Isocrates' love of antitheses has here led him to stultify his argument, but where precisely is the hyperbole?"[18] Where indeed? Unless this is one of those hyperboles which successfully elude our notice. More likely what annoys Longinus is that Isocrates is being insufficiently figurative about an important matter: this bland, overly explicit statement about the power of language affects Longinus as a collapsed hyperbole, a truth turned false. Isocrates, he suggests, is not to be trusted in this "childishness"; he must be dealt with severely, like the man in chapter 15 who would free the prisoners or the man whose ill-concealed figures provoked such exasperation in chapter 17. It is puerile of Isocrates to imagine that he—or anyone else—can ever quite let the cat out of the bag.

2.
WORDSWORTH AND THE
TEARS OF ADAM

THIS ESSAY on literary influence grew out of my bewilderment with one of the better-documented relationships in English poetry, that of Wordsworth to Milton. How was one to understand this case of influence? It was not just a theoretical problem but a puzzle, line by line, to the practical critic. Anyone who has tried to draw the lines of force between two poets, one in the more distant, one in the more recent past, will know what I mean: a reader quickly finds himself perplexed, conscious not only of the movement of the texts relative to each other but of the shifting, contingent quality of his own relation to either poet's work. Of course, this may be the case with any interpretive effort, but the study of influence has a way of bringing the point home with particular force. For what one finds, again and again, is that one's most interesting perceptions seem suspiciously anachronistic—as if it were really Wordsworth who was influencing Milton—or subjective—as if it were merely one's own interpretive acts that had become a source of fascination, a distracting influence from still another direction.

Yet it may be that both a sense of anachronism and of a certain kind of subjectivity are often signs that one is on the right track; for they may mean that the reader is moving into that order of time in which works of literature have their existence and in which the significant encounters between writers take place. In the pages that follow, since I would like to show what can be gained by ignoring

21

chronology, I shall begin by looking at a poem of Wordsworth's, then, with that in mind, turn to look backward toward a passage in *Paradise Lost,* then finally move forward again to consider "The Ruined Cottage." Fortunately, we are dealing with two writers who would find this approach congenial. Their works have traditionally raised questions about the nature of poetic subjectivity, and they are poets for whom anachronism holds no terrors, to whom phrases like "the child is father of the man" or "Adam the goodliest man of men since born his sons" were both meaningful and peculiarly satisfying. As such, it will not only be in their relation to one another, but in the encounters that take place within their individual works, that Milton and Wordsworth can help us to understand the encounter of poet with poet.

I

Here, first, is a text in many ways typical of Wordsworth: the experience it records is characteristic, and Wordsworth rightly considered his rendering of it an example of his best blank verse. But there are two things unusual about it which make it, from my point of view, particularly interesting. We most frequently find Wordsworth, in his major poems, writing in the first person and engaged in the imaginative retrieval of events in the more or less distant past. He is, we know, the poet of the egotistical sublime, and he is the poet who, in his own words, was "unused to make a present joy the matter of a song." But here we shall find him offering a third-person account of an experience which we know from his note to have been his own, and which he turned into poetry almost immediately after it had occurred. What is surprising is how little these differences seem to matter: the poem remains perfectly illustrative of Wordsworth's recurrent concerns. To understand how this can be so is to learn something about the quality of Wordsworthian subjectivity and of Wordsworth's interest in the past. The poem is "A Night-Piece" (1798):

—The sky is overcast
With a continuous cloud of texture close,

22

Heavy and wan, all whitened by the moon,
Which through that veil is indistinctly seen,
A dull, contracted circle, yielding light
So feebly spread, that not a shadow falls,
Chequering the ground—from rock, plant, tree, or tower.
At length a pleasant instantaneous gleam
Startles the pensive traveller while he treads
His lonesome path, with unobserving eye
Bent earthwards; he looks up—the clouds are split
Asunder,—and above his head he sees
The clear Moon, and the glory of the heavens.
There, in a black-blue vault she sails along,
Followed by multitudes of stars, that, small
And sharp, and bright, along the dark abyss
Drive as she drives: how fast they wheel away,
Yet vanish not! the wind is in the tree,
But they are silent;—still they roll along
Immeasurably distant; and the vault,
Built round by these white clouds, enormous clouds,
Still deepens its unfathomable depth.
At length the Vision closes; and the mind,
Not undisturbed by the *delight* it feels,
Which slowly settles into peaceful calm,
Is left to muse upon the solemn scene.[1]

The poem traces the movement of a mind imaginatively engaged with the external world, a movement that could be charted in a number of ways. For example, we might notice how the moon is gradually realized as a powerful presence. At first totally de-naturalized ("a dull, contracted circle"), then "the clear Moon," she finally emerges, fully personified, in line 14. When that happens, the visible world is transformed: it no longer makes up a field for empirical observation. Instead it is reconstituted, under the presiding light of the moon, as a "Vision," a "solemn scene" which bears musing on, because it is now emblematic.[2]

Inseparable from this process is another, involving the transformation of the voice we hear telling the story. The speaker of the opening lines is calmly and rather distantly observing the scene: his language, in its neutral, faintly scientific accuracy ("continuous cloud," "texture," "contracted circle"), corresponds in want of feeling to the "dull" quality of the scene itself. Whoever this spectator may be, he is certainly *ab extra:* the "pensive traveller" only appears in the ninth line, and his "unobserving eye / Bent earthwards" is presumably not the eye that so carefully registered details of cloud and moonlight earlier. But as the moon is revealed, and the power and significance of the scene take possession of the traveller, the narrative voice is itself changed, moving from the (still uninvolved) notation of emotional response ("a pleasant . . . gleam / Startles the pensive traveller") to conventional hyperbole ("the glory of the heavens"), then to a more excited participation: "how fast they wheel away / Yet vanish not!"

In that exclamation, the speaker's response is indistinguishable from the traveller's. Both seem to have been brought alive by this silent and powerful manifestation. We can speak of their state as one of heightened subjectivity, but here we must note that characteristically in Wordsworth such heightening creates not a more highly individualized subject but a more impersonal and generalized one. So it is here: speaker and traveller no longer occupy distinct points of view, and it is because of this coalescence that the poem can end as it does, now no longer referring either to traveller or observer or even to a poet recollecting emotion in tranquillity, but inclusively to "the mind." Indeed, one measure of the poem's success is that the encompassing gesture implicit in saying "the mind" embraces the reader as well, for he too, as the last lines settle into a calm regularity of cadence, is made to participate in the mind that muses on the solemn scene.

Wordsworth's note to the poem[3] confirms what we may have suspected anyway, that the observer, the pensive traveller, and the writer of the poem were really one and the same; they are simply aspects of Wordsworth's self following one upon the other in time. But the poem Wordsworth chose to write does not take that continuity for granted: rather, he seems in this case to have gone out of his way, by writing in the third person, to insist on the disjunctive nature of the self. The note suggests why this maneuver may have seemed necessary to him. If the poem was, in fact, composed extempore, the entire experience—the visual revelation and its verbal repetition—would have had about it a specious feeling of personal continuity. The man who works into blank verse the exclamation "How fast they wheel away . . .!" at, say, 9:45 P.M. is very obviously—too obviously, for Wordsworth's purposes—the same man who, at 9:30, had initially exclaimed those words. No great effort of the imagination would seem necessary in order to recapture sensations so recently experienced. By writing in the third person, Wordsworth deliberately introduces into this apparently seamless experience a gap, a vacancy between aspects of the self that makes his account of this "present joy" identical in structure to the more familiar poetry of childhood remembered. Here are some lines from the second book of *The Prelude* (1805):

A tranquillizing spirit presses now
On my corporeal frame, so wide appears
The vacancy between me and those days,
Which yet have such self-presence in my mind
That sometimes when I think of them, I seem
Two consciousnesses—conscious of myself,
And of some other being.   [11.27–33]

These are the circumstances in which Wordsworth's finest poetry is written, and what "A Night-Piece" makes clear is how necessary it was for him to experience this doubling of consciousness. It was a state of mind that would come more or less naturally when he was musing on the almost-forgotten past, but in "A Night-Piece" we find him obliged to induce it quite deliberately, by manipulating the dramatic structure of his account. The result is to split the self into a poet existing in the present and "some other being" who acts as a mediating figure—often a childhood self, but in this case the mature man seen as a "pensive traveller." But this mediator is also involved in another powerfully resonant relation, usually with a natural object—as the pensive traveller is, here, with the moon—and it is precisely this relational moment that Wordsworth seeks to bring into connection with his present poetic activity. What he thus succeeds in creating is a chain of successive and analogous relations: the moon is to the pensive traveller as the pensive traveller is to the

poet as the poet is to the reader; or, to schematize the more frequently encountered sequence, Nature : child :: child : Poet :: poet :
reader. The intention of Wordsworth's major poetry is never essentially the re-creation of the past. When his imagination turns backward toward the original experience, it is in search of that "other
being"—neither poet nor reader—who will, when paired with the
poet, occupy the central position in the chain of relations I have just
described.

I want to linger on this metaphor of a chain because I believe it
will make it easier to bring into connection a number of aspects of
Wordsworth's thought. First, it suggests why a critic's interest in
Wordsworthian rhetoric (that is, the relation of reader to poet) is
inseparable from an interest in Wordsworthian memory (the relation of poet to child) and in Wordsworthian metaphysics (the relation of child to Nature). Second, it can give us an insight into the
peculiar quality of time encountered in Wordsworth's poetry, and
into the connection between that time and the kind of human consciousness—autonomous, subjective, and impersonal—that comes
into existence at certain moments in his poetry, moments like the
one we have observed toward the end of "A Night-Piece." There
we noticed that the center of subjectivity, "the mind," was inclusively that of the traveller, the poet, and the reader. Yet Wordsworth was insisting that there was a gap between poet and traveller
of the same sort that exists between poet and reader, and that that
gap may be bridged but is not thereby removed. As a result, the
poem testifies to a remarkable generosity, a willingness on Wordsworth's part to confer autonomy on prior moments in his own
existence and on the consciousness of the reader as well. But the
order of time in which this autonomous subjectivity is constituted,
in which the chain of relations is created, is not ordinary historical
time. If we ask when the exclamation "How fast they wheel away!"
takes place, we cannot localize it exclusively at the moment of the
traveller's original experience, nor can we place it at the moment at
which the poet repeats the words, nor yet at the moment the reader
encounters them. The chain exists in a mode of present time—call it
the narrative present—which is a creation of the language of the
poem, of the telling of the story, and in which traveller and poet

26

and reader mutually participate. Finally, the metaphor of a chain will be helpful when we turn to examine another relation, that of poet to poet, of Wordsworth to Milton, for it suggests that there might be a way of thinking about literary influence that honors the autonomy of both poets involved.

II

We can begin by raising the question of Milton's subjectivity, that is, of the quality of his presence in the work. That question no longer engages our attention as it once did that of the Romantics, probably because the whole issue was so badly confused during the 1930s. Then too much of the wrong sort of attention was paid to the ways Milton's personality made itself heard in *Paradise Lost,* usually on the part of critics who found him personally offensive and who were bothered by any signs of his intrusion. Attacks on his personality generally were accompanied by attacks on his idiosyncrasies as a stylist or as a thinker; so, in reply, recent students of *Paradise Lost* have taken pains to show that particular aspects of Milton's poetry are neither as strange nor as peculiar to him as they were once held to be. These later studies have generally been convincing, and together they have produced a more sophisticated sense of Milton's location in history. But one consequence of this emphasis has been a relative lack of interest in what Coleridge spoke of as the "subjectivity of the poet, as of Milton, who is himself before himself in every thing he writes."[4] The lines of Wordsworth's we have just considered can suggest the variety of ways in which a poet can be "before himself" as he writes, as well as the impersonal quality of the highest reach of poetic subjectivity; as such they can serve as a guide to a still-disputed and interesting section of *Paradise Lost.*

In the eleventh book, the Archangel Michael, sent to expel Adam from the Garden, first offers him a prophetic account of history, that is, of the long-range consequences of his Fall. The prophecy takes the form of a series of visions, each of which provokes a response from Adam—usually one of grief or dismay, for the scenes

Adam is shown are almost universally grim. Each of Adam's responses, in turn, elicits an explanation from Michael, and the tone of these explanations in general matches the visions, and sometimes even surpasses them, in grimness. Commenting on a group of sinners who appear to be enjoying themselves, Michael is made to say, with the air of a man clearly enjoying *him*self, that they

> now swim in joy,
> (Erelong to swim at large) and laugh, for which
> The World erelong a world of tears must weepe.   [11.625–27]

Critics have fastened on lines such as these as proof that there was something immoderately sour about Milton's view of history, imputing the edge in Michael's tone either to the personal bitterness the poet may be imagined to have felt after the Restoration or, in less flatly *ad hominem* terms, to the rigors of his later theology. "In this portion of the poem," one writer complains, "Milton's imagination seems to take wing only in delineating scenes of destruction."[5]

I have seen no defense of the eleventh book that directly confronts these *ad hominem* complaints. Instead, admirers of this section of the poem argue their case in more objective terms, locating Milton's imaginative investment either in his reworking a vein of Christian historiography that goes back to St. Paul, or in his careful plotting of the drama of Adam's education.[6] Both these interpretations are valid, although, like much educational dialogue, the exchanges of Adam and Michael constitute a rather lumbering "drama." But there is another dramatic movement discernible in book 11, one which involves Milton more directly in the fabric of his poem, and one which our Wordsworthian model puts us in a position to appreciate.

Late in the book, Milton's own voice interrupts the dialogue of Adam and the Angel; the poet breaks off his account of Noah's Flood in order to address his sympathy directly to Adam.

> How didst thou grieve then, *Adam,* to behold
> The end of all thy Ofspring, end so sad,

Depopulation; thee another Floud,
Of tears and sorrow a Floud thee also drownd,
And sunk thee as thy Sons; till gently reard
By th' Angel, on thy feet thou stoodst at last,
Though comfortless, as when a Father mourns
His Children, all in view destroyd at once. [11.754–61]

This far along in the poem, we have become accustomed to the constant and often subtle pressure Milton exercises to shape his reader's response to the story he is telling; and we are also accustomed to his sometimes turning away from his readers entirely, in prayer or invocation. What is rare—I count only three instances throughout the poem[7]—is for the poet to thus address himself to a character. Even more surprising is the quality of this address: the tenderness implicit in the repeated use of *thee* and *thou* and *thy,* and the powerful sense of loss these lines communicate. Tenderness, we know, has not been the dominant note of book 11, nor have we been led to expect Milton to grieve at the thought of sinners being swept away. Yet here it seems as if the act of imagining the Flood, far from providing a source of grim pleasure to Milton, has liberated in him a flow of compassion: "thee another Floud, / Of tears and sorrow a Floud thee also drownd."

"In the Paradise Lost," wrote Coleridge, "the sublimest parts are the revelations of Milton's own mind, producing itself and evolving its own greatness."[8] He was thinking of the Invocation to Light in book 3 when he wrote this, but signs of the same evolution may be observed in Book 11: it is possible to read this section as a dramatic development of the poet's consciousness, analogous to the movement of mind recorded in Wordsworth's "Night-Piece," and en route to the address to Adam. To read the passage in this way is to accept the imputations of *ad hominem* critics, to agree that Milton's personal resentment (along with other less damaging sentiments) may be heard in the voice of the Archangel; but it is also to carry the tonal analysis one step further, and to insist that the accents of personal resentment that we may catch in Michael's speech are no longer audible when Milton himself addresses Adam. Paradoxically, that moment when Milton speaks out in his own voice is among the least personal in the poem. It is worth considering how this might have come about, and what its implications are for a reading of the rest of *Paradise Lost*.

A good place to begin is with one of the lessons that Michael's account of history seems intended to teach: where there are multitudes, there is sin. Adam's Fall has put God's command to increase and multiply in a new and ironic light. The sequence of visions Adam is shown brings home the lesson, as each new scene is enlarged in scope and more confusingly populous. Counterpointing this association of sin with human multitudes is an increasing stress on the unique and isolated figure of the righteous man. This is less obvious in the opening vision of Cain and Abel, although Michael makes the point when he comments that "th'unjust the just hath slain" (11.455); but in the later visions of Enoch ("The onely righteous in a World perverse" [11.701]) and of Noah ("The one just Man alive" [11.818]) this Old Testament motif that had so long and so deeply engaged Milton's imagination is made quite explicit.

If we set out—as *ad hominem* critics do—to ground this dialectic in the actualities of Milton's life, it is easy enough to see how, in the 1660s, the figures of the citizen as the One Just Man or the poet as the severe but truth-telling Archangel would have been appealing images to Milton, stirring in him the bitter satisfactions of self-righteousness. Something of this sort is undoubtedly going on in book 11; but it soon becomes clear that the demands of Milton's imagination are not fully met by these mediators, and that his mind is moving beyond them toward a confrontation with what Wordsworth would call "some other Being," a figure who will mediate to him a truer sense of his poetic identity. That figure is Adam, not Adam seen as an archetype of innocence, but Adam after the Fall, surviving but mortal, and listening in tears to the sad tale of loss.

The turning point is the story of the Flood, which begins with an account of Noah testifying against the ways of the multitude and preaching "Conversion and Repentance":

But all in vain: which when he saw, he ceas'd
Contending, and remov'd his Tents farr off;
Then from the Mountain hewing Timber tall,
Began to build a Vessel of huge bulk.   [11.726–29]

This is the One Just Man in his finest hour, aloof but irre-proachably so. But now the mood of the poem changes as Milton turns for his text from the account in *Genesis* to the stranger poetry of Deucalion's flood in Ovid:

Meanwhile the Southwind rose, and with black-wings
Wide hovering, all the Clouds together drove
From under Heav'n; the Hills to their supplie
Vapour, and Exhalation dusk and moist,
Sent up amain; and now the thick'nd Skie
Like a dark Ceeling stood; down rushd the Rain
Impetuous, and continu'd till the Earth
No more was seen; the floating Vessel swum
Uplifted; and secure with beaked prow
Rode tilting o'er the Waves, all dwellings else
Flood overwhelm'd, and them with all thir pomp
Deep under water rould; Sea coverd Sea,
Sea without shour; and in thir Palaces
Where luxurie late reignd, Sea-monsters whelpd
And stabl'd. [11.738–52]

This is certainly Ovid moralized; the grotesque underwater de-tails illustrate the wages of sin, for Milton is still concerned with "*thir* pomp," "*thir* Palaces / Where luxurie late reignd." But the metamorphic power of these images and cadences, the sense of sea-change familiar to readers of "Lycidas," reaches out beyond the sinful multitudes—those others—to involve the consciousness of the righteous poet as well. As the scene is radically diminished in scope, the pathos of loss is suddenly the dominant feeling, mingled with a new sense of how fragile is the vessel in which righteousness survives: "of Mankind, so numerous late, / All left, in one small bottom swum imbarkt" (11.752–53). With this the transformation of the poet's voice is completed, and he can turn, in sympathy and in the recognition of kinship, to Adam.

But what are the grounds of this kinship? Adam's response to the vision turns out to be characteristically generous but, as usual, exaggerated, for it is based on a misapprehension. Moved by the scope of the disaster and ignorant of its outcome, he naturally assumes that all mankind did indeed perish, including Noah and his

family, whom he imagines finally dying of "Famine and anguish
. . . Wandring that watrie Desert" (11.778–79). Later, when Michael
enlightens him and goes on to describe the receding of the waters
and the renewal of the Covenant, Adam joyfully brings his feelings
into line with his new understanding of the event:

Farr less I now lament for one whole World
Of wicked Sons destroyd, then I rejoyce
For one Man found so perfet and so just.   [11.874–76]

Adam's self-correction has about it some of the same harsh zest
with which Milton, in a more famous passage in the poem—the
description of Mulciber's fall—suddenly reins in his own erring
imagination. The comparison is worth considering, for just as
there Milton had allowed his verse to linger affectionately over the
story as the Greeks told it before pulling himself up short to insist
on its falsity, so in directly addressing himself to Adam, in taking
Adam's interpretation of the scene so readily for granted, he has
lent himself to this error. To break into the texture of the poem at
this point is to imaginatively assume the burden of Adam's igno-
rance and of his innocence of Christian doctrine. It is as if Milton
had been moved by the compelling poetry of the Flood to momentarily suspend his sense of the certainties of his faith—moved back
beyond doctrine, beyond the hope of redemption, to an encounter
with Adam in the heart of loss.

This interpretation needn't obscure the Christian intention of
Paradise Lost or the presence of a redemptive pattern as a structural
element in the last two books. The poetry of the Flood takes its
place in that pattern, of course, for Michael's prophecy is intended
to serve as an object lesson for Adam in Pauline faith, in "the
substance of things unseen." So the lines that unfold the dimensions of Adam's loss may be read as part of his education, a negative
experience designed to detach his hopes from the wrong objects so
that they may fix themselves on the promised end. We have seen
what Adam learns from the first account of the Flood: it is to
"renounce a World of wicked Sons," to temper his hopes that blood
lineage can provide an alternative to the permanence he has for-

feited at the Fall. Later, there is another passage intended to teach him a related lesson, to purge him of any false hopes about the permanence of his dwelling place. It comes from Michael's speech after the vision of the Flood, and it is unusual in one respect: for it has not been Michael's practice, when commenting on the visions he produces, to get so caught up in their detail. Yet here he begins by interpreting the Flood and ends by vividly retelling the story. He has come of the point where Noah is commanded to "save himself and household from amidst / A World devoted to universal rack":

No sooner hee with them of Man and Beast
Select for life shall in the Ark be lodg'd,
And shelterd round, but all the Cataracts
Of Heav'n set op'n on the Earth shall powre
Raine day and night, all fountains of the Deep
Broke up, shall heave the Ocean to usurp
Beyond all bounds, till inundation rise
Above the highest Hills: then shall this Mount
Of Paradise by might of Waves be moovd
Out of his place, pusht by the horned floud,
With all his verdure spoild, and Trees adrift
Down the great River to the op'ning Gulf,
And there take root an Iland salt and bare,
The haunt of Seales and Orcs, and Sea-mews' clang:
To teach thee that God attributes to place
No sanctitie, if none be thither brought
By Men who there frequent, or therein dwell.   [11.822–38]

The moral is clear and relevant, but it is not at all adequate to the full suggestiveness of this poetry. Nor can we really account for the length of this reprise or for its appearance at this point in the poem by reflecting on Michael's motives as a prophet or as a teacher. It is certainly Milton whose imagination is caught up in the story, and to understand the fascination that the Flood held for him, I think that, instead of looking further along in the poem for signs of the redemptive pattern, we should turn back to the poet's address to Adam.

  I have suggested that Milton, in addressing Adam, has achieved the same quality of impersonality that can be heard in Words-worth's voice in the climactic lines of "A Night-Piece": there are still other analogies between the two texts which I would like to pursue. Consider what it means for Milton to break into his narra-tive and speak to a character: it involves an odd—and, for the surprised reader, a very exciting—leap of the imagination in time. For if we ask when this address takes place, we must say it occurs neither in Adam's ordinary time—something between the Fall and the Expulsion—nor in Milton's—sometime in the 1660s. Chronol-ogy becomes misleading, and we must locate this point of imagina-tive contact in another order of time. This is the same situation we found ourselves in when we were considering "A Night-Piece," and asking when the exclamation "How fast they wheel away . . . !" occurs. In the case of Wordsworth's poetry, I have called that order of time the narrative present, and noted that it was a creation of the language of the poem, brought into being by the telling of a story, and hence available for the participation of the reader or the hearer of the tale. And that too may be said of this moment in *Paradise Lost*. For what moves Adam to tears is not an event in his immediate experience but the image of one that has not yet taken place, as it is summoned up for him, in a prospective vision, by the angelic narrator; and what moves Milton to compas-sion is not his witnessing the Flood itself, but his imaginative par-ticipation in Adam's subjective response to it. For an instant, Adam and Milton meet, not as eyewitnesses to a disaster, but as members of Michael's audience, and much of the poignancy of their encoun-ter is due to this. Like Milton's own audience, they are, in effect, listening to a story, one which will be perpetuated by successive retellings—Michael to Adam, Moses to the children of Israel, and so on. In fact, what Milton's audience is listening to is simul-taneously both the earliest and the most recent telling of the tale; for Adam was the first to hear it, and its latest rehearsal is here and now, as a story within the story of *Paradise Lost*.

This, of course, is true of the entire prophecy in books 11 and 12. But within that structure the story of the Flood is unique, not only because of its length or the generally high quality of its verse, but because so many elements in that section of the poem are brought into tight and resonant interrelation. The lines describing the drowning of the sinful are also the occasion of a symbolic drowning or transformation of the poet's voice, a movement from a self-righteous identification with the One Just Man, through a moment of self-loss, toward a compassionate identification with Adam fallen, who is now recognizable as a fellow-survivor, someone who has himself experienced, as he weeps for his descendants, a death-by-water. Finally these multiplied and interinvolved instances of loss are related to the most formal element in the encounter of Milton and Adam, the fact that its takes place through the mediation of a prospective vision or story. For listening to a story, regardless of its theme, is also an experience of self-loss, of the suspension of one's commitments in ordinary time in favor of an alternative sequence of events in narrative time. Yet here formal and thematic elements are inseparable: Milton's moving out of self-righteousness is concurrent with his moving through the poetry of the Flood into the story, into the time in which he can confront Adam. When that encounter takes place, a chain of relations is established similar to that created in Wordsworth's poem, for Adam, Milton, and Milton's reader as well have been brought into the narrative continuum: if we are moved by what we hear in these lines, then we find ourselves in a relation to the voice of their poet that is not identical with but analogous to the relation he is in to Adam, and that Adam bears to Michael's vision of his drowning sons.

What I would like to suggest is that this perpetuation of the story of the Flood provides Milton with an emblem of continuity which is as compelling to his imagination as is the perpetuation of faith in the redemptive process. Through the rehearsal of the story the encounter with Adam is brought about, and the poet led to an insight into the nature of loss and the nature of human subjectivity and the relation between the two. It is the firm—although fleeting—possession of that insight which underwrites the new note of generosity that can be heard in Milton's voice, a compassion that embraces, in Adam, mankind at large, the sinful and the righteous alike. For Milton to have arrived at that height of address is a sign that he has, in one sense, gone as far as he can go: the transformed voice no longer sounds in need of redemption. Perhaps this can help to explain the rather perfunctory treatment which the Redemption receives in book 12, as well as the relative inertness of the verse there when compared with these passages on the Flood.

There are other points in *Paradise Lost* where an analysis of the play of personal and impersonal accents in the poet's voice would produce very different conclusions: in the great invocations, for example, the means by which the voice arrives at its authority are quite consciously and traditionally Christian. But the poetry of the Flood both participates in the central Christian intention of the poem and enacts other Miltonic intentions which are, at best, tangential to Christian thought. This situation is not unique in Milton's poetry. The last eight lines of "Lycidas," for example, come as a surprise, after the totally convincing language of Christian apotheosis, by introducing a new speaker, one who detaches himself from the body of the poem and contemplates it at a distance. His doing so is not at all felt to be ironically destructive of the religious concerns of the poem, yet this movement of the imagination does not seem to have grown out of these concerns, nor does the cool, impersonal, but highly subjective voice to be heard in those last lines seem to draw its authority from Milton's faith. If it is possible to discriminate such distinct intentions in "Lycidas" or in *Paradise Lost* it is chiefly because the achievement of poets like Wordsworth has set the body of Miltonic poetry in a new light. I would like now to turn to a final Wordsworthian text, a poem which is at once an indication of his achievement and an illustration of what is most Miltonic about his imagination.

III

"The Ruined Cottage" was more or less completed in 1798, not long after Wordsworth composed "A Night-Piece," but it was not immediately published. It was put aside for a few years, taken up and revised during the winter of 1801-2, then finally printed as the first book of *The Excursion* in 1814. There it serves as an introduction to the character Wordsworth calls "the Wanderer," who functions as the poet's hero and spokesman throughout the long work.

In its final form, "The Ruined Cottage" begins with the poet moving "across a bare wide Common," toward a prearranged meeting with the Wanderer, a rendezvous set in a shady grove surrounding an abandoned and dilapidated cottage. Wordsworth comes in sight of the grove, but postpones his account of their meeting until he has described at length how the Wanderer had come to be as he is, an exemplary Wordsworthian man, aged, wisely passive, profoundly and serenely in touch with Nature. The description of the Wanderer's childhood could have been composed for the opening books of The Prelude, but Wordsworth avoids insisting on his likeness to the older man. Rather he admiringly sets the Wanderer off at a distance, in a realm of calm self-possession that the poet himself has yet to attain. This distancing provides Wordsworth with a principle of dramatic structure for the rest of the poem, which falls quite naturally into two roughly equal sections. The first describes the Wanderer's education, a model of the gentle and molding power of Nature; the second half of the poem obliquely echoes this process, for it is concerned with what is really an incident in the poet's education, although this time it is not Nature but the Wanderer's words that exercise the benign influence. Like Adam listening to Michael, Wordsworth is gradually led toward the truth, and toward the appropriate response to the truth, as he listens to the Wanderer tell a sad story, the history of the last occupants of the now-ruined cottage.

Characteristically the Wanderer insists that what he is telling is only "a common tale, / An ordinary sorrow of man's life" (11.636–37), but the accents in which he begins his story mark his intention as prophetic:

Thus did he speak. "I see around me here
Things which you cannot see: we die, my Friend,
Nor we alone, but that which each man loved
And prized in his peculiar nook of earth
Dies with him, or is changed; and very soon
Even of the good is no memorial left.   [11.469–74]

And that is the burden of the story which follows. A family disintegrates; the wife, Margaret, abandoned by her husband, gradually loses hope of his return, and allows one of her children to leave her for a distant farm, the other to fall ill and die. She herself finally dies, and her cottage and garden are now to be seen caught in the slow process of wasting back into the landscape. Like Milton's story of the Flood, the story of Margaret may be taken as an object lesson: the dead child, the overgrown garden, the ruined cottage speak of the same losses that Adam is made to feel as he learns that the Flood will sweep away his descendants and his dwelling place; and the play of Wordsworth's curiosity and grief against the wiser but not entirely impassive understanding of the Wanderer recapitulates the dialogue of Adam and the Archangel. There is even a Wordsworthian analogue of the redemptive process, for it is suggested that Nature herself, the Nature that ministered to the Wanderer as a child, is providentially overseeing this episode in human history. But it is chiefly in the telling of the tale, in the rehearsal in words of the truth of loss, that the poem asserts a saving continuity; the pathos of Margaret's history is given additional depth and poignancy because it comes to us as a story within a story, and, just as in *Paradise Lost,* a chain of mediations is established that brings the reader into the continuum, into the repetitive process by which reality is turned into truth.[9]

These structural and thematic resemblances would, in themselves, make us suspect that Wordsworth had meditated on Milton's story of the Flood. But they also can tell us more than that, for they point beyond the similarities of these particular texts toward a clue to Milton's influence on Wordsworth and, possibly, to the general nature of literary influence. In this particular case, influence is best understood not by picking up the echoes of specific bits of Milton's language or the reappearance of Miltonic themes, but by noticing the interrelation of theme and structure, of the theme of loss and the structure of narrative. The loss of human continuities is the burden of ordinary historical time; the creation of another order of time, in which that loss is confronted and acknowledged, is the achievement of narrative. Taken singly, both the poetry of the Flood and "The Ruined Cottage" embody these truths; taken together, they exemplify the kind of continuity with which each is concerned. For the encounter of poet with poet is analogous to that of Michael with Adam, or of Milton with Adam, or of Wordsworth with the Wanderer.

I would like to close with one more quotation, this time not from the poetry but from Dorothy Wordsworth's *Journal*. It is intended to illustrate once again the nature of the influence we have been considering, by bringing the relation of poet to poet more closely in line with that of reader to poet. In the early months of 1802, Wordsworth was at work revising "The Ruined Cottage," which by that time he had taken to calling "The Pedlar." Here is part of Dorothy's entry for Tuesday, February 2:

> The sun shone but it was cold. After dinner William worked at *The Pedlar.* After tea I read aloud from the eleventh book of *Paradise Lost.* We were much impressed, and also melted into tears.[10]

For a moment, the two orders of time we have been considering—historical time and the narrative present—meet here as Wordsworth listens to *Paradise Lost:* the tears he wept that afternoon are the same tears that Adam weeps in Milton's poem.

3.
THE NOTION OF
BLOCKAGE IN THE LITERATURE
OF THE SUBLIME

THERE IS, according to Kant, a sense of the sublime—he calls it the mathematical sublime—arising out of sheer cognitive exhaustion, the mind blocked not by the threat of an overwhelming force, but by the fear of losing count or of being reduced to nothing but counting—this and this and this—with no hope of bringing a long series or a vast scattering under some sort of conceptual unity. Kant describes a painful pause—"a momentary checking of the vital powers"—followed by a compensatory positive movement, the mind's exultation in its own rational faculties, in its ability to think a totality that cannot be taken in through the senses.[1] In illustration, Kant alludes to "the bewilderment or, as it were, perplexity which it is said seizes the spectator on his first entrance into St. Peter's at Rome,"[2] but one needn't go to Rome to experience bewilderment or perplexity. They are available in quantity much closer to home. Professional explainers of literature have only to try to locate themselves in the current intellectual scene, to try to determine what is to be learned from the linguists or the philosophers or the psychoanalysts or the political economists, in order to experience the requisite mental overload, and possibly even that momentary checking of the vital powers. It is difficult to speculate about literature just now without sounding either more assured or more confused than one really feels. In such circumstances, some remarks about the mathematical sublime, that is, about one version of the play between confusion and assurance, might prove useful. In particular, it may be useful to examine that moment of blockage, the "checking of the vital powers," to consider both the role it played in eighteenth- and nineteenth-century accounts of the sublime and the fascination it still seems to exert on contemporary historians and theorists of literature.

I

Consider first some paragraphs from a recent issue of *Studies in English Literature;* they express a scholar's fear that soon we shall all be overwhelmed by the rising tide of academic publication. The genre of this writing may be that of the omnibus review (Thomas McFarland is here reporting on a year's worth of literary studies), but tonally and thematically it can be grouped with the last lines of *The Dunciad,* with the "Analytic of the Sublime,"or with Wordsworth's dream of the Arab bearing the emblems of culture just ahead of "the fleet waters of a drowning world." First, the threat represented by the dimensions of the problem:

> It is not simply that there is no one—such is the exponential accumulation of secondary discussion—who can any longer claim to be competent to provide specialist commentary on more than a decade or two . . . . : it is, more complexly, that the burgeoning contributions call into question the use and purpose of culture as such. Just as the enormous increase in human population threatens all the values of individuality so carefully inculcated by centuries of humanistic refinement, so too does the flood of publication threaten the very knowledge that publication purports to serve.[3]

Notice that the population explosion is not brought into the argument literally, as yet another problem (one with a certain world-historical urgency of its own), but figuratively, as a thrilling comparison, a current topos of the mathematical sublime. We might suspect that other figures of scary proliferation may be at hand, and indeed they are:

What then will be the eventual disposition and use of most of these secondary studies? The answer seems clear: in due course their contents will be programmed into a computer, and, as time passes, will more and more be remembered by the computer and forgotten by men. And in a still further length of time, it will be possible not only to reproduce instantaneously any aspect of previous secondary work, but actually to produce new work simply by instructing the computer to make the necessary recombinations. The wheel will then have come full circle: computers will be writing for computers, and the test of meaningful publication will be to think and write in a way a computer could not.

Certain turns of phrase—the fine Johnsonian cadence of "remembered by the computer and forgotten by men," for example—suggest that McFarland may have taken a mournful pleasure in working up this fragment of science fiction, but we may suspect that he's also quite serious: this is something more than a reviewer's ritual groan. In fact, the statement of the problem is accompanied by a rapid and pointed analysis of its causes. McFarland sees that the justification for much scholarly activity is itself a fiction; one pretends a work is "needed" on, say, Shelley's life; in truth, as McFarland notes, "the need goes the other way. The student needs the doctorate; then needs an academic position; then needs recognition and advancement." Critical and scholarly writing proliferates as the energies of personal ambition are fed into an increasingly unwieldy and mindless institutional machine.

If one agrees with McFarland's analysis and shares his dismay, one reads on with certain ethical or political expectations, imagining that one is about to be told what ought to be done, or perhaps one is about to see something being done right then and there—the reviewer savagely but righteously clearing the field of at least a few unnecessary books. In fact, nothing of the sort develops. What follows this intense and, I assume, earnest indictment is a summary of nineteenth-century studies distinguished by its critical intelligence and knowledgeability but not in any other way out of the ordinary. It is written with a great deal of generosity and with no signs whatever that its writer is anything but content with his role: he has made a professional commitment to review these books and he is carrying it out in a professional fashion.

We seem to have come a long way from the mathematical sublime, but I believe we are still very much within its field of force. We have simply followed the reviewer to a point of blockage: he has written of the threat of being overwhelmed by too much writing, and it may not be possible to go beyond that—in writing. The appropriate corrective measures may still be taken elsewhere, and we can assume McFarland knows what they are: in his dealings with his students and colleagues, in the pressure he applies to publishers and to the makers of university, foundation, and government policy, he can still wield varying degrees of influence on the politics of literary scholarship. If he nevertheless sounds thwarted, it may not be chiefly because the dimensions of the political problem are out of proportion to his own practical force, but rather because he has run his sense of the problem to the point where he can glimpse another sort of incommensurability. That, at least, is what I gather from another paragraph in the review, one that may be read as a gesture beyond blockage, but that produces only a further occasion for bewilderment:

> The scholar, in Emerson's conception, is "man thinking." With the proliferation of secondary comment, he must necessarily become ever more something else: man reading. And yet, in a very real sense the whole aim of culture should be the integration of awareness—should be eventually to read less, not more. "The constant influx of other people's ideas," writes Schopenhauer, "must certainly stop and stifle our own, and indeed, in the long run paralyze the power of thought. . . . Therefore incessant reading and study positively ruin the mind. . . . Reading no longer anticipates thinking, but entirely takes its place."

In the face of "the proliferation of secondary comment"—plural, heterogeneous, dismaying—the reviewer posits an ideal, "the integration of awareness," and the human, if abstract, embodiment of that ideal, the figure of "man thinking." But if McFarland would enjoin us, and himself, to read less, why has he gone on to cite Schopenhauer, when Schopenhauer is saying much the same thing that he has just thoughtfully set down himself? Why wasn't once enough, especially for someone who is insisting that enough is enough?

43

I don't think a serious answer to that question can be framed either in terms of personal psychology or in terms of institutional structures: those vocabularies of motivation have been left behind by the language of the paragraph. Its rhetorical heightening (its invocation of Emerson and Schopenhauer, the urgency we hear in phrases like "in a very real sense"), its insistence that thinking is to be distinguished from reading just when, paradoxically, it is displaying what looks like an unavoidable contamination of the one by the other—all this suggests that the reviewer has led us, willy-nilly, into the region of the sublime. In a scenario characteristic of the sublime, an attempt to come to terms with plurality in the interest of an "integration of awareness" has generated a curiously spare tableau: the mind blocked in confrontation with an unsettling and indeterminate play between two elements (here called "man thinking" and "man reading") that themselves resist integration. We can better understand the logic of this scenario if we turn back to some of its earlier manifestations.

II

The moment of blockage is a familiar one to readers of Wordsworth, who repeatedly represents himself as, in his phrasing, "thwarted, baffled and rescued in his own despite,"[4] checked in some activity—sometimes clearly perverse, sometimes apparently innocuous—then released into another order of experience or of discourse: the Simplon Pass episode and the encounter with the Blind Beggar are but two of the most memorable of such passages in *The Prelude*. If the experience seems to us both very Wordsworthian and perfectly natural, that may be in part a tribute to the persuasiveness of Wordsworth's poetry, in part a way of acknowledging how commonplace the scenario (if not the experience) had become by the end of the eighteenth century. Kant's "Analytic of the Sublime" (1790) offers the most rigorous philosophical account, but the staging of blockage had been blocked out much earlier. Samuel Monk finds it already informing Addison's description of the imagination's pleasurable dealings with greatness, "its

44

aspiration to grasp the object, the preordained failure, and the consequent feeling of bafflement, and the sense of awe and wonder."[5] "Various men," Monk comments, "were to use this pattern with varying significance, but it is essentially the sublime experience from Addison to Kant." In fact, it was his noticing the continuity of this pattern that allowed Monk to organize his history of what he refers to as the "chaos" of esthetic speculation in the eighteenth century. His book opens with a careful paraphrase of Kant because, as he says, "it would be unwise to embark on the confused seas of English theories of the sublime without having some ideas as to where we are going";[6] it concludes with a long citation from the sixth book of *The Prelude*—the lines on the Simplon Pass—which Monk reads as the "apotheosis" of the eighteenth-century sublime.

Because the task of the historian—the reduction to narrative order of a large, sometimes seemingly infinite mass of detail—resembles the play of apprehension and comprehension, of counting and organizing, associated with the mathematical sublime, it might be worth dwelling for a moment on Monk's introductory remarks about his history. "Theories of beauty," he writes, "are relatively trim and respectable; but in theories of the sublime one catches the century somewhat off its guard, sees it, as it were, without powder or pomatum, whalebone and patches." What people are led to call "chaos" sometimes strikes them as the confused seas on which they must embark; here, in a figure equally traditional, chaos is a woman out of Swift or Rowlandson, in disarray and déshabille, slightly all over the place, not yet fit to be seen. There is a *soupçon* of blockage about this fondly misogynistic turn, but Monk's mind recuperates its powers and reestablishes its forward movement: "Indeed, the chief problem has been the problem of organization. The necessity of imposing form of some sort has continually led to the danger of imposing a false or artificial form." If raw heterogeneity—the world without whalebone and patches—is a danger, so is sheer willfully cosmetic unity, "artificial form"; we are led to expect an image of synthesis or integration, and we are not disappointed: "I have therefore grouped the theories together loosely under very general headings in an effort to indicate that there is a progress, slow and continuous, but that this progress

is one of organic growth. . . . The direction of this growth is toward the subjectivism of Kant."[7]

Monk's book was written over forty years ago, when historians
of eighteenth-century literature and philosophy were not afraid of
using the word "preromanticism" or of picturing the century tele-
ologically, as if it were en route to writers like Wordsworth or
Kant, or to concepts like that of the Imagination. That mode of
historical argument has been sufficiently challenged so that Monk's
narrative may seem dated. Yet a recent theoretical study of the
sublime, a splendidly intelligent book by Thomas Weiskel,[8] still
finds its organizing figures in Kant and Wordsworth, and more
particularly, in their accounts of the mind's movement, blockage,
and release. Is the moment of blockage, then, simply a *fact* about
the experience of the sublime, attested to by one after another
eighteenth-century writer, available for the subsequent generaliz-
ing commentary of historians like Monk or literary theorists like
Weiskel? I think not; rather, a look at the provenance of the notion
of blockage will reveal a more interesting development.

Eighteenth-century writers do not use the word "blockage";
they use verbs like "baffle" and "check" or nouns like "astonishment" or "difficulty." Here, for example, is Hume on the reason
we venerate "the relicts of antiquity": "The mind, elevated by the
vastness of its object, is still farther elevated by the difficulty of the
conception; and being oblig'd every moment to renew its efforts in
the transition from one part of time to another, feels a more vig-
orous and sublime dispositon."[9] "Difficulty," Hume had just written, "instead of extinguishing [the mind's] vigour and alacrity, has
the contrary effect, of sustaining and encreasing it." Language such
as this—and there is much similar talk throughout the century of
the tonic effects of opposition or sheer recalcitrance—language
such as this is easily enough assimilated to the pattern of motion
and blockage, but it is worth noticing that it is not saying quite the
same thing: here the mind is braced and roused but not absolutely
(even if only for a moment) checked. This may sound trivial, a
mere difference in degree, but such differences, between the absolute and the not-so-absolute, often take on philosophical and narrative importance. When Saul, on his way to Damascus, was

thwarted, baffled, and rescued in his own despite, the Bible does not report that he merely faltered in his purpose, slumped to his hands and knees, then rose at the count of nine. The example can serve as a reminder that the metaphor of blockage draws much of its power from the literature of religious conversion, that is, from a literature that describes major experiential transformation, the mind not merely challenged and thereby invigorated but thoroughly "turned round."

As for the notion of difficulty, Angus Fletcher has shown that it too has a religious origin, although it is associated not with the act of conversion but with the more commonplace—and continuous—activity of interpreting the figurative language of Scripture, of working out the sense of what had come to be known as "difficult ornament." I quote from Fletcher's discussion in his book on allegory:

> "Difficulty" implies here a calculated obscurity which elicits an interpretive response in the reader. The very obscurity is a source of pleasure, especially to the extent that the actual process of deciphering the exegetical content of a passage would be painfully arduous and uncertain. Obscurity stirs curiosity; the reader wants to tear the veil aside. "The more they seem obscure through their use of figurative expressions," says Augustine, "the more they give pleasure when they have been made clear."[10]

The citation of Augustine can remind us that discussions of religious conversion and of biblical exegesis are not entirely irrelevant to one another, the intermediate notion, as Fletcher indicates, being that of an ascesis of reading:

> Augustine is pointing to a cosmic uncertainty embodied in much of Scripture, in response to which he can only advocate an interpretive frame of mind, which for him becomes the occasion of an *ascesis*. The mixture of pain and pleasure, an intellectual tension accompanying the hard work of exegetical labor, is nothing less than the cognitive aspect of the ambivalence which inheres in the contemplation of any sacred object. Whatever is *sacer* must cause the shiver of mingled delight and awe that constitutes our sense of "difficulty."

47

Augustinian ascesis organizes reading so that it becomes a movement, albeit with difficult steps, down the line toward a pleasure that is also a guarantee of the proximity of the sacred object. I think we can find an equivalent of that in the eighteenth century's absorption of the rhetorical concept of difficulty into the experiential notion of blockage. This process is contemporary with the progressive loss of interest in Longinus' treatise, or rather, with the selective appropriation of elements of his rhetoric as modes of extraliterary experience. The two processes would seem to go together, although in ways I have not yet made clear. The translation of "difficulty" into "blockage" and the submersion of the rhetorical sublime so that its figures function as a sort of experiential underwriting both seem like strategies designed to consolidate a reassuringly operative notion of the self. A telling paragraph from an eclectic mid-century theorist, Alexander Gerard, can provide us with an illustration of the strategy at work:

> We always contemplate objects and ideas with a disposition similar to their nature. When a large object is presented, the mind expands itself to the extent of that object, and is filled with one grand sensation, which totally possessing it, composes it into a solemn sedateness, and strikes it with deep silent wonder and admiration: it finds such a difficulty in spreading itself to the dimensions of its object, as enlivens and invigorates its frame: and having overcome the opposition which this occasions, it sometimes imagines itself present in every part of the scene which it contemplates; and from the sense of this immensity, feels a noble pride, and entertains a lofty conception of its own capacity.[11]

Notions of "difficulty" and "blockage" are loosely accommodated by this prose, which draws on Addison and Hume as well as on Longinus. The mind, seeking to match itself to its object, "expands," and that "enlivens" and "invigorates" it; but when its capacity matches the extent of the object, the sense of containing the object, but also (with a hint of theological paradox) of being filled by it, possessed by it, blocks the mind's further movement and "composes it into a solemn sedateness," "strikes it with deep silent wonder." The *activity* of the mind may be associated with an enlivening sense of difficulty, but the mind's *unity* is most strongly felt when it is "filled with one grand sensation," a container practically indistinguishable from the one thing it contains; and it is precisely the mind's unity that is at stake in such discussions of the natural sublime. The "integration of awareness" thus posited is achieved by a passage to the limit that carries the notion of difficulty to the point where it turns into absolute difficulty, a negative moment but nevertheless a reassuring one.

III

Earlier, in considering Samuel Monk's introductory remarks, I assumed an analogy between the scholar's imagining himself heroically coming to grips with a chaotic heap of historical matter and the situation of the hero of one of Kant's sublime scenarios, that of the mathematical sublime. I wish now to look a bit more closely at Kant's "Analytic of the Sublime," this time in connection with the work of Thomas Weiskel. It is Weiskel's distinction to have seen that the poetic and philosophic language of the primary sublime texts could be made to resonate with two quite different twentieth-century idioms, that of psychoanalysis and that of the semiological writings of Saussure, Jakobson, and Barthes. Weiskel's fine responsiveness to poetry, along with the patience and lucidity with which he elaborates a complex argument, make his book a difficult one to excerpt or to summarize, but my own understanding of the sublime requires me to come to terms with at least some elements of it, to question it at certain points and to explore the ways it locates itself in relation to its material. I shall be chiefly concerned with his discussion of the mathematical sublime, more particularly still with his attempt to bring Kant within the explanatory range of Freudian metapsychology.

Partly to satisfy the internal necessities of the Critical Philosophy, partly in response to an observable difference in accounts of sublime experience, Kant divides his consideration of the sublime into two sections, depending on whether the feeling is generated by the mind's confrontation with a seemingly overwhelming natural force (this is the dynamical sublime, the sublime of waterfalls, hurricanes, earthquakes, and the like) or else by the disturbances of cognition I described in the first section of this essay. This latter is the sublime of magnitude, the mathematical sublime, and it is of this mode that Kant writes: "For there is here a feeling of the inadequacy of [the] imagination for presenting the ideas of a whole, wherein the imagination reaches its maximum, and, in striving to surpass it, sinks back into iself, by which, however, a kind of emotional satisfaction is produced."[12] This is, one senses, the intellectual's sublime (Weiskel calls it, appropriately, the reader's or hermeneutical sublime). Kant is seemingly evenhanded in his treatment of the two modes; he makes no attempt to subordinate the one to the other, but rather, he locates each in relation to the branching symmetries of his entire system. The mathematical sublime is associated with cognition and hence with the epistemological concerns of the *Critique of Pure Reason;* the dynamical sublime, because it confirms man's sense of his "spiritual destination," is referred to what Kant calls the faculty of desire and hence to the ethical concerns of the second *Critique.* But here an important qualification is introduced: the mathematical sublime too, it develops, shares this link with the ethical. For, as Kant presents this drama of collapse and compensation, the "emotional satisfaction" he finds there is taken to be an effect of the recognition that what the imagination has failed to bring into a unity (the infinite or the indefinitely plural) can nevertheless be *thought* as such, and that the agent of this thinking, the reason, must thus be a guarantor of man's "supersensible destiny." What is intriguing is that the drama seems to be available for two incompatible interpretations: we can think of it as the story of Ethics coming to the rescue in a situation of cognitive distress, or we can see that distress as slightly factitious, staged precisely in order to require the somewhat melodramatic arrival of Ethics. This is the sort of puzzle to which Weiskel addresses himself.

Weiskel's deliberate strategy is that of a translator. He would seek to understand the sublime by construing it, as he puts it, outside the presuppositions of idealism.[13] The drama of the imagination's collapse and reason's intervention, for example, looks as if it might allow itself to be restaged in modern dress and in a psychoanalytic vernacular. The delight in the mathematical sublime, Kant had written, is a feeling of "imagination by its own act depriving itself of its freedom by receiving a final determination in accordance with a law other than that of its empirical employment." "In this way," Kant continues, "it gains an extension and a power greater than that which it sacrifices. But the ground of this is concealed from it, and in its place it *feels* the sacrifice or deprivation to which it is subjected." Weiskel cites the passage, then wonders at its motivational structure: why can't the imagination share the mind's pleasure in reason? Why this talk of sacrifice and concealment? There is further, he notices, a hint that the imagination has been, in a way, entrapped, led into this disaster by reason itself and for reason's own ends. "The real motive or cause of the sublime," Weiskel suggests, "is not efficient but teleological; we are ultimately referred not to the failure of empirical imagination but to reason's project in requiring this failure. The cause of the sublime is the *aggrandizement of reason at the expense of reality and the imaginative apprehension of reality.*"[14]

Readers of Freud should have no trouble predicting the general direction of Weiskel's argument: the Kantian sublime, in both its manifestations, becomes "the very moment in which the mind turns within and performs its identification with reason. The sublime recapitulates and thereby reestablishes the oedipus complex," with Kant's reason taking the role of the superego, that agency generated by an act of sublimation, "an identification with the father taken as a model."[15]

What one could not have foreseen is the turn Weiskel's argument takes at this point. Throughout his discussion of the mathematical sublime, he has had to come to terms with the question of excess; for the theme of magnitude, of that which resists conceptualization, was bound to raise the problem. Until now, to the extent that both the mathematical and the dynamical sublime could be rendered as affirmative of reason—that is, of the superego—it had been possible to think of excess in terms of Freud's discussion of excessive identification, of that supererogatory strength of investment that turns the superego into a harsher taskmaster than the father on whom it is modeled. But there may be other forms of excess associated with the mathematical sublime that are not so easily accounted for: is it possible that there is excess that cannot, in Jacques Derrida's phrase, be brought back home to the father? Weiskel takes up the question in a section that begins with what sounds like a scholar's twinge of conscience about his own sublime operations of mind: "Have we not," he asks, "arrived at [this] model by pressing one theory and suppressing a multitude of facts for which it cannot account?" This qualm, intensified by a further look at some of the lines from *The Prelude,* leads Weiskel to suspect that the "anxiety of the sublime does not ultimately result from the pressure of the super-ego after all . . . that the oedipus complex is not its deep structure."[16] What follows is an intensely reasoned and difficult four pages, as Weiskel works to integrate this new discovery into the larger movement of his argument. This involves him in an exploration of the terrors and wishes of the pre-Oedipal phases, where he finally locates the motivating power of the mathematical sublime, then sees that as rejoining a secondary system that is recognizably Oedipal and more clearly manifested in the dynamical sublime. I quote his conclusion:

> We should not be surprised to find that the sublime movement is overdetermined in its effect on the mind. The excess which we have supposed to be the precipitating occasion, or "trigger," directly prompts the secondary anxiety in the case of the dynamical sublime of terror. In the mathematical sublime, however, the traumatic phase exhibits a primary system on which the secondary (guilt) system is superimposed. This situation explains an odd but unmistakable fact of Kant's analytic. Whenever he is generalizing about both versions of the negative sublime, the (secondary) rhetoric of power dominates. It is not logically necessary that the reason's capacity for totality or infinity should be invariably construed as power degrading the sensible and rescuing man from "humiliation" at the hands of nature. But though the sublime of magnitude does not originate in a power struggle, it almost instantaneously turns into one as the secondary oedipal system takes over.[17]

If we step back a moment, it may now be possible to state, in a general and schematic fashion, just where the fascination of the mathematical sublime lies and what sort of problem it represents for the historian or the theorist. Weiskel's scrupulosity in raising the question of excess, in wishing not to suppress "a multitude of facts" in the interest of establishing a theoretical model, parallels Samuel Monk's qualm lest he impose a "false and artificial form" on a chaotic mass of material. We might even see in Weiskel's invocation of the (maternal) pre-Oedipal phases, in his interpretation of them as constituting the deep (hence primary) structure of the sublime and yet as still only a tributary of the Oedipal system into which it invariably flows, a more serious and argued version of Monk's joking about the woman not fit to be seen. The goal in each case is the Oedipal moment, that is, the goal is the sublime of conflict and structure. The scholar's *wish* is for the moment of blockage, when an indefinite and disarrayed sequence is resolved (at whatever sacrifice) into a one-to-one confrontation, when numerical excess can be converted into that supererogatory identification with the blocking agent that is the guarantor of the self's own integrity as an agent.

I suggested earlier that something similar could be seen at work during the eighteenth century, as the notion of difficulty or recalcitrance was transformed, through a passage to the limit, into the notion of absolute blockage. This too would seem to have been the result of a wish, for although the moment of blockage might have been rendered as one of utter self-loss, it was, even before its recuperation as sublime exaltation, a confirmation of the unitary status of the self. A passage to the limit may seem lurid, but it has its ethical and metaphysical uses.

IV

At the beginning of this essay I proposed some paragraphs written by the scholar Thomas McFarland as a contemporary instance of the mathematical sublime. There, I suggested, we could trace a scenario that eighteenth-century theorists would have found familiar: the progress of the mind as it sought to take in a dismaying plurality of objects. If we look back at McFarland's text now, we should be able to bring its movement into clearer focus.

The mind is set in motion by a threat, the "exponential accumulation of secondary discussion," the "flood of publication," a threat directed not at the exterior intellectual landscape but at the inner integrity of the mind itself, that is, at the integrity of the individual scholar's mind. No single reader can "claim to be competent to provide specialist commentary on more than a decade or two," McFarland notes. And it is the ideal of a cultured—i.e., broadly competent—individual that McFarland would defend. Hence, McFarland makes no attempt to "totalize" or "integrate" the objects of his dismay, whatever that might mean in practice (perhaps a reorganization of literary scholarship along more efficient lines?). Setting such activity aside as impracticable and no doubt undesirable in any case, and therefore checked in its commerce with its objects, the scholar's mind, in Kant's phrase, "sinks back into itself," not without "a kind of emotional satisfaction": what is generated is a rhetoric of interior totalization, the plea for "the integration of awareness" and its embodiment in the figure of "man thinking." But at this point a further difficulty arises: for the scholar to contemplate the Emersonian description of "man thinking" is to be quite literally cast in the role of "man reading"; or, more accurately, to discern that one's thinking and one's reading are, in the best of scholarly times (and when would that have been? before what Fall?), hard to disentangle. In response to this puzzling recognition the figure of Schopenhauer is called up. He appears as McFarland's double, reiterating his dismay, seconding his call for an integration of awareness in still more authoritative tones. But the presence of his words within quotation marks serves as one more reminder that "other people's ideas" are as much the material of genuine thinking as they are a hindrance to it. Schopenhauer, we could say, is the name of that difficulty; he stands for the recurrent and commonplace difficulty of distinguishing thinking from reading, and he is conjured up here as an agent of sublime blockage, an eloquent voice at the end of the line.[18]

But why this thrust toward eloquence and confrontation? My discussion of the eighteenth-century sublime suggests one answer: that the self cannot simply think but must read the confirmation of its own integrity, which is only legible in a specular structure, a structure in which the self can perform that "supererogatory identification with the blocking agent." That, I believe, is what drives McFarland to summon up Schopenhauer from the grave, and it is the same energy that erodes the stability of that specular poise: the voice of Schopenhauer is replaced, in the next paragraph, by the fantasy of the computer. This grimly comic version is set in the future ("The wheel will then have come full circle; computers will be writing for computers") but it is an embodiment of a threat that has been present all along. The computer is the machine inside the ghost of Schopenhauer, the system of energies that links "thinking" to "reading" to "remembering" to "citing" to "writing." It serves here as a figure for what makes scholars run, when that process is felt to be most threatening to the integrity of individual awareness, a threat from which even "the strongest are not free."

Oh, blank confusion! true epitome
Of what the mighty City is herself
To thousands upon thousands of her sons,
Living amid the same perpetual whirl
Of trivial objects, melted and reduced
To one identity, by differences
That have no law, no meaning, and no end—
Oppression, under which even highest minds
Must labour, whence the strongest are not free.[19]

Bartholomew Fair, as it is imagined in the last lines of book 7 of *The Prelude,* was Wordsworth's computer, a city within the City, a scale model of urban mechanisms, designed to focus his fear:

Tents and Booths
Meanwhile, as if the whole were one vast mill,
Are vomiting, receiving on all sides,
Men, Women, three-years Children, Babes in arms.   [7.718-21]

The lines on Bartholomew Fair repeat, in a condensed and phantasmagoric fashion, what had been the burden of the earlier

accounts of London: the sometimes exhilarating, sometimes baffling proliferation, not merely of sights and sounds, objects and
people, but of consciously chosen and exhibited modes of representation. Book 7 is the book of spectacle, theatricality, oratory, adver-
tising, and *ad hoc* showmanship, not just the book of crowds. A
Whitmanesque passage from early in the book catches the mixture
as well as providing an instance of Wordsworth's own narrative—or
rather, *non*narrative—stance:

> Rise up, thou monstrous ant-hill on the plain
> Of a too busy world! Before me flow,
> Thou endless stream of men and moving things!
> Thy every-day appearance, as it strikes—
> With wonder heightened, or sublimed with awe—
> On strangers, of all ages; the quick dance
> Of colours, lights and forms; the deafening din:
> The comers and the goers face to face,
> Face after face; the string of dazzling wares,
> Shop after shop, with symbols, blazoned names,
> And all the tradesman's honours overhead:
> Here, fronts of houses, like a title-page,
> With letters huge inscribed from top to toe,
> Stationed above the door, like guardian saints;
> There, allegoric shapes, female or male,
> Or physiognomies of real men,
> Land-warriors, kings, or admirals of the sea,
> Boyle, Shakespeare, Newton, or the attractive head
> Of some quack-doctor, famous in his day.   [7.149–67]

These lines, so full of detail, are not exactly narrative; they conjure
more than they describe. And what they summon up is a different
order of experience from what we think of as characteristically
Wordsworthian. They resist the phenomenological reading that
seems so appropriate elsewhere in *The Prelude,* a reading attuned to
the nuanced interinvolvements of centrally Wordsworthian modes
of experience—seeing and gazing, listening, remembering, feeling.
Instead, they present a plethora of prefabricated items—trades-

men's signs, statuary—that are intended to be legible, not merely visible, and mix these in with sights and sounds, "men and moving things," in rapid appositional sequence until everything comes to seem like reading matter ("Face after face; the string of dazzling wares, / Shop after shop, with symbols, blazoned names . . .").

As the book goes on, the prodigious energy Wordsworth experiences in London is more and more made to seem a function of the tradesmen's and showmen's and actors' wish to represent and of the populace's complementary hunger for spectacle: representation comes to seem like the very pulse of the machine. And in a startling moment, too strange to be simply satirical, the showman's crude inventiveness and the audience's will to believe are brought into touch with the developing opposition between what can be seen and what can be read. Wordsworth is describing a performance of "Jack the Giant-killer" at Sadler's Wells:

> Lo!
> He dons his coat of darkness; on the stage
> Walks, and achieves his wonders, from the eye
> Of living Mortal covert, 'as the moon
> Hid in her vacant interlunar cave.'
> Delusion bold! and how can it be wrought?
> The garb he wears is black as death, the word
> 'Invisible' flames forth upon his chest.   [7.280–87]

I have offered these citations and have been teasing out thematic strands as a way of suggesting the drift of book 7 toward a sublime encounter, the episode with the Blind Beggar, who occupies what we might call the "Schopenhauer position" in the structure of the poem. Wordsworth himself has been drifting through the book, sometimes presenting his experience anecdotally, in the auto-biographical past tense ("I saw . . . ," "I viewed . . .") that we are accustomed to in *The Prelude,* more often presenting himself as poet-impresario of the great spectacle, in a generalized present tense ("I glance but at a few conspicuous marks, / Leaving a thousand others, that, in hall, / Court, theatre . . ."). Without forcing the poem, I think we can say that the difference between the subject of autobiographical experience and the poet-impresario is made to seem, in book 7 more than elsewhere in *The Prelude,* like the difference between seeing and reading. In London, more than in the country, everybody's experience is mediated by the semiotic intentions of others; in book 7, more than anywhere else in *The Prelude,* the poet adopts the showman's stance. I believe it is the developing confusion of these two roles, the odd slackening of the tension between them, as much as the accumulating overload of urban detail, that precipitates the critical scene with the Blind Beggar. I cite the episode in its earlier version, which is less elegantly worded but at one point more revealing:

How often in the overflowing Streets,
Have I gone forward with the Crowd, and said
Unto myself, the face of every one
That passes by me is a mystery.
Thus have I look'd, nor ceas'd to look, oppress'd
By thoughts of what, and whither, when and how,
Until the shapes before my eyes became
A second-sight procession, such as glides
Over still mountains, or appears in dreams;
And all the ballast of familiar life,
The present, and the past; hope, fear; all stays,
All laws of acting, thinking, speaking man
Went from me, neither knowing me, nor known.
                                   [1805 text, 7.594–606]

The last four lines of this passage, eliminated when Wordsworth revised the poem, tell of a moment, a recurrent moment, of thoroughgoing self-loss—not the recuperable baffled self associated with scenarios of blockage, but a more radical flux and dispersion of the subject. The world is neither legible nor visible in the familiar way; faces, which had earlier been associated with signs, are there but they cannot be deciphered, while visible shapes have taken on a dreamlike lack of immediacy. This loss of "ballast" is made to sound like the situation of "blank confusion" at Bartholomew Fair, when objects become "melted and reduced / To one identity, by differences / That have no law, no meaning, and no end": it is not that differences disappear, but that the possibility of interpreting them as significant differences vanishes. It may be, for instance, that seeing and reading are not that distinct, that as the possibility of interpreting differences diminishes, the possibility of distinguishing presentation from representation does too, and with it, the possibility of drawing a clear demarcation between the sub- ject of autobiography and the poet-impresario. Some remarkable effects can be generated by crossing that line (the famous instance would be the rising up of Imagination in book 6), but the line needs to be established in order to be vividly transgressed. These are the threats, this is the "ferment silent and sublime" (8.572), that inhere in these lines, and I believe it is in response to them that the Blind Beggar is brought into the poem:

> 'twas my chance
> Abruptly to be smitten with the view
> Of a blind Beggar, who, with upright face,
> Stood propp'd against a Wall, upon his Chest
> Wearing a written paper, to explain
> The story of the Man, and who he was.
> My mind did at this spectacle turn round
> As with the might of waters, and it seem'd
> To me that in this Label was a type,
> Or emblem, of the utmost that we know,
> Both of ourselves and of the universe;
> And, on the shape of the unmoving man,
> His fixèd face and sightless eyes, I look'd
> As if admonish'd from another world.   [1805 text, 7.609–22]

In one sense, the Beggar simply allows Wordsworth to reiterate his sense of bafflement. Earlier he had told himself "the face of every one / That passes by me is a mystery"; now he is faced with "an emblem of the utmost we can know." And in the play between the Beggar's blank face and the minimally informative text on his chest, the difference between what Wordsworth can see and what he can read is hardly reestablished in any plenitude: it is a fixed difference—the text won't float up and blur into the lineaments of the Beggar's face—but it is still almost no difference at all. However, it is precisely the fixity that is the point—a point softened in the direction of a more intelligibly humane reading by Wordsworth's decision to change "His fixèd face" (1805) to "His steadfast face" (1850). The encounter with the Beggar triangulates the poet's self in relation to his double, who is represented, for a moment, as an emblem of minimal difference fixed in relation to itself. The power of the emblem is that it reestablishes boundaries between representor and represented and, while minimizing the differences between them, keeps the poet-impresario from tumbling into his text. I would suggest that this is the common function of the moment of blockage in sublime scenarios.

4.
FLAUBERT'S CONVERSION

IN THE *Search for a Method*, in various interviews, and again in a brief preface, Sartre laid out clearly enough his reasons for writing *L'Idiot de la famille*.[1] To begin with, he sets himself an intellectual problem conceived in the most general terms: he would like to answer the question "What can be known about a man?"—that is, to what extent is it possible to construct a single, coherent and truthful account of a life, what Sartre calls a "totalization," out of the various kinds of data (socioeconomic, psychoanalytic, etc.) that can be gathered about any given person? Isn't there a risk, he asks in his preface, that no such totalization is possible, that at best all we can produce is a collection of "heterogeneous and irreducible layers of meaning"? Perhaps, but Sartre would forestall such scepticism, and in the next sentence he makes his project explicit, in language whose tone shifts slightly as one reads it from that of a modest working hypothesis to something more like that of a confession of faith: "This book attempts to prove that the irreducibility is only apparent and that each bit of information, once set in place, becomes a portion of a whole which never ceases buiding itself up [*la portion d'un tout qui ne cesse de se faire*]" (p. 7). The use of the reflexive in that last phrase is both metaphysically exciting and somewhat puzzling: what is this entity which never ceases building itself up? It cannot be either a person's actual life or his own comprehension of his life—in the case of Flaubert, at least, we can be sure that those ongoing totalizations have come to a halt. Is it then, perhaps, the "Life" we hold in our hands, a book that is both ample and as yet incomplete? I don't mean to worry a sentence in Sartre's preface, but I do want to call attention to the tinge of the absolute that colors his prose whenever he refers to the activity of totalizing, and to a certain ambiguity about the status and location of this totalizing agent or self-creating whole. For I believe that such moments of tonal heightening best reveal the connection between Sartre's most general formulation of his aims as a biographer and his choice of his particular subject, Flaubert.

Sartre would assert that in one sense the choice of a subject doesn't matter—anyone would do, provided we had a certain amount of information at our disposal—but he is thoroughly aware that he had his reasons for choosing Flaubert. In his preface he mentions a number of these: his well-known fascination with (and antipathy to) Flaubert, the fact that the novelist had already "objectified himself" in his works, the availability of so much material for interpretation in the early writings and in the correspondence, the centrality of Flaubert "at the crossroads of all our contemporary literary problems." But still another reason, the most strikingly worded Sartre produced, does not appear in the preface: it is to be found in his conversation with the editors of the *New Left Review:* why Flaubert? "Because he is the imaginary. With him, I am at the border, the barrier of dreams."[2] Here again the language rises, this time to a lyrical rendering of a moment of absolute confrontation across the threshold that divides two realms. The encounter between the biographer and the life he would rehearse and interpret, between Sartre and his subject, is figured here as an allegory of encounter between the real and the imaginary, because of the nature of this particular subject. Sartre takes this as a challenge that calls forth his efforts as a would-be totalizing biographer: one writes about Flaubert in order to understand the relation between the real and the imaginary. Yet there is something oddly static about that image of confrontation; it feels more like an end of the line than it does like the beginning of a work-in-progress. Perhaps even too much like an end of the line: for it could be taken as a figure for the impossibility of the sort of totalization Sartre desires. Seen in this light, *L'Idiot* would seem to be an attempt to deny the implications of that figure; the work's declared purpose—to prove that the "irreducibility" of "heterogeneous layers of meaning" is only apparent—becomes part of a more fundamental attempt to prove that the "real" and "imaginary" are not themselves heterogeneous and irreducible categories, that, in fact, the imaginary is reducible to the real. In the pages that follow I would like to consider one of the ways in which Flaubert both lends himself to this project—for the Flaubert of the letters, far from being Sartre's great antagonist, is in many ways in complicity with him—and, ultimately, frustrates it. I shall be concerned chiefly with the interpretation of Flaubert's collapse at Pont l'Evêque in January 1844, the event Sartre refers to as the novelist's conversion, and with the fictional representation of that event in the 1845 *Sentimental Education*.[3]

Flaubert himself was the first to take the incident at Pont l'Evêque as a key to the understanding of his life: two years later, in what has become a famous letter, he wrote that it marked the division between "two distinct existences," the moment when his "active life" ended and "something else" began. What did he mean by this? Sartre devotes the last 350 pages of *L'Idiot* to answering that question, and what he sets forth is not merely the most elaborate but in places the most convincing interpretation we have, a sustained analysis that is patient, tactful, and steadily shrewd. By locating his account of Pont l'Evêque at the turning point of his own narrative, he endorses Flaubert's sense of the event's unique importance; the first and second major divisions of *L'Idiot* have followed the novelist through his childhood and adolescence, tracing his development into what Sartre calls a "passive agent" and arriving with him at a dead end, where the contradictions inherent in his position are brought to bear, with intolerable pressure, on his life. On the last page of part 2 (p. 1766) the dilemma is formulated: Flaubert finds himself incapable of continuing his work as a law student but equally incapable of speaking out against his father's wish that he continue. What will he do? Sartre insists that he cannot "do" anything, yet that something had to be "done." Part 2 ends on this note of somewhat melodramatic suspense: when the narration is taken up again we are presented with a spare but no less melodramatic account of what took place at Pont l'Evêque:

63

One night in January '44, Achille and Gustave are returning from Deauville, where they had gone to look over the chalet. It is dark out, black as the inside of a furnace; Gustave himself is driving the cabriolet. Suddenly, somewhere near Pont l'Evêque, as a wagon overtakes them on the right, Gustave drops the reins and falls thunderstruck at his brother's feet. [p. 1771]

For Flaubert, Sartre claims, this was "a moment in which a life totalizes itself and realizes the destiny it has been bearing within itself" (p. 1799); the rest of part 3 will unfold the meaning of this totalization. Sartre proceeds by stages. First he considers the collapse as the epitome of Flaubert's neurosis—that is, as the conversion of the psychological into the somatic, a maneuver that allows the novelist to win his quarrel with his father without actually putting anything into words. For indeed the collapse and the subsequent milder seizures in the months that followed had the effect of absolving Flaubert of any further responsibilities as a law student, of focusing his family's concerned attention on him, and of leaving him free to read and write. Sartre sees in this Flaubert's "immediate, negative, and tactical response to an emergency." But now a further question arises: is there a fundamental and necessary relation between Flaubert's neurosis and his art? Sartre believes that there is, and sets out next to demonstrate that this tactical response, which a psychoanalyst would take as a symptom of "conversion hysteria," can be interpreted "*at the deepest level* as a strategic and positive response to . . . the necessity and the impossibility . . . of being an Artist" (p. 1920; the italics are Sartre's); to this aspect of the maneuver Sartre gives the name of "the conversion to optimism," using the word "conversion" now no longer in its psychoanalytic but in its religious or metaphysical sense (p. 1929).

Sartre is now in a position to reintrepret the collapse in the light of that principle of total compensation which he likes to call the *Qui perd gagne;* when Flaubert falls senseless at his brother's feet he is, according to Sartre, betting that "he who loseth his life shall find it" and thus placing himself in a tradition of Augustinian transformation. But what is it Flaubert hopes to gain, in return for his "active life"? Sartre uncovers two layers of intention. There is, first of all, the most obvious hope: that Flaubert will see his powers as

64

an artist emerge out of the wreckage of his life. This wish Sartre finds most fully elaborated in the last chapters of the 1845 *Sentimental Education,* chapters that were added to the novel in the months following Pont l'Evêque. But there is something a bit strident and schematic about the end of that novel, in which Flaubert's hero is abruptly transformed from a moody young man with conventional literary yearnings into someone we are told is now a serious writer; Sartre is led to suspect that the ease with which the hero is consolidated in his new role as Artist masks a certain uneasiness on his creator's part, and that the "real meaning of the '*Qui perd gagne*'" (p. 2013) may lie at a still deeper level. The final section of *L'Idiot* sets out in search of that "real meaning" and discovers it to be ultimately religious: despite his proclaimed and no doubt sincere agnosticism, "what the convert of Pont l'Evêque is trying to recover is that identification of the Father with God which once guaranteed his personal identity" (p. 2083).

This is but the barest account of the richly detailed and energetic interpretative activity at work in *L'Idiot de la famille;* what I hope to have suggested is that the structure (although certainly not the tone) of Sartre's book is basically that of a certain kind of hagiography: the narrative of a life whose meaning is disclosed through the progressively deepened understanding of a single, decisive moment of conversion. Sartre is anxious to insist both on the uniqueness of Flaubert's conversion as a moment in time (see pp. 1771 ff., where Sartre tries to fix the exact date of Flaubert's first seizure and to privilege it over its subsequent repetitions) and on its structural unity as a "fundamental and *single* conversion in which the tactical level and the strategic level reciprocally symbolize each other" (p. 1920). Why this insistence? I believe that it is because the conversion is meant to serve as that prior act of synthesis whose (real) existence underwrites the totalization Sartre aims at in his biography: the interpreter need no longer fear that he is faced with the merely tautological "unity" of an individual life if that life has already caught up on its own threads and, in effect, totalized itself. In this way Flaubert's letter serves Sartre's purposes: when the novelist writes of his "two distinct existences" and orders them in an irreversible sequence he is telling a story Sartre wants to hear, for it is a story whose burden is the possibility of totalization. Sartre may wish to introduce qualifications into his own rehearsal of that story—to catch Flaubert out in moments of self-mystification, to distinguish and stratify the levels at which the life discloses itself, etc.—but the unity of Flaubert's sense of his life, and, more important, its organization in time, leading up to and away from a point of conversion, is never seriously challenged in *L'Idiot de la famille*.

Yet there are signs that Flaubert himself had a more complex understanding of the meaning of Pont l'Evêque—not in the letters, which substantiate Sartre's view, but in those very last chapters of the 1845 *Sentimental Education* which Sartre reads as corroborating evidence. It is worth looking more closely at those chapters, for while they offer themselves to Sartre's interpretation, they also raise questions about that central link—between conversion and totalization—upon which Sartre's project seem to depend. We shall see that in order to interpret the novel as he does Sartre must ignore or minimalize the effect of this questioning.

No one is sure exactly how far along in his manuscript Flaubert had come before his seizure obliged him to put it aside, but it is certain that chapters 26 and 27 were not composed until sometime late in 1844. A radical change in tone and in conception is apparent in the opening lines of chapter 26, where one of the two main characters, Jules, is seen walking through the countryside; it is very quickly obvious that he is a much more interesting figure than he was when he last appeared in the novel. Some twenty pages earlier he was hardly more than a poet manqué; now we find him involved in a wavering but progressive and increasingly complex meditation. The language of these pages is often strongly articulated, the turns of thought are subtle, and the concerns very clearly Flaubert's own; there can be no doubt that he is writing out of the experience of Pont l'Evêque. What is at issue is precisely the question of totalization: the first of these chapters dramatizes Jules' attempts to locate himself in relation to his own past, to his conception of art, and to the world at large, and it moves toward two climactic moments, one presented as a sublime but fleeting vision of totality, the other as a grotesque complement to that vision, an uncanny encounter with a hideous dog. As a result of this encounter, we are meant to feel, Jules' life is transformed; in Sartre's account the meeting with the dog represents the "symbolic" equivalent of Pont l'Evêque, "the instant in which the convert, in fear and trembling, sees his life totalized, in all its ugliness . . ." (p. 1927). What follows, in chapter 27, is a lengthy and at times rhapsodic presentation of Jules in his new incarnation as Artist: "He has become a grave and great artist, whose patience is untiring and whose devotion to the ideal is no longer intermittent; by taking his form from a study of the masters, and by drawing out of himself the matter that it should contain, he found that he had naturally acquired a new manner, a real originality" (p. 281; *L'Idiot,* p. 1991).

Here a curious problem of interpretation arises. Sartre locates the moment of "definitive rupture," the dividing line between Jules' old and new lives, in the space between the last lines of chapter 26 and the beginning of chapter 27 (p. 1929). But, as I've already suggested, Jules is portrayed as a changed man even in the opening pages of chapter 26. He is first seen wondering at his own "serene immobility" (p. 223), a self-imposed "calm" which has succeeded in distancing him "so abruptly from his youth, and had required of him so harsh and so sustained an effort of will, that he had hardened himself to tenderness and had almost petrified his heart" (p. 224; *L'Idiot,* p. 1923). This self-discipline was intended to separate him not only from his past emotions but from his present feelings as well: "Even while stimulating his sensibility with his imagination, his mind worked to annul the effects of this, so that the importance of the sensation (*le sérieux de la sensation*) would vanish as rapidly as the sensation itself" (p. 224; *L'Idiot,* p. 1933). Despite certain "lapses and relapses" (p. 224), this program of "superhuman stoicism" (p. 225; *L'Idiot,* p. 1932) has, we are told, been a thorough, almost a too-thorough success: "if [Jules] hadn't felt each day obliged, as an artist, to study [his passions] and to seek them out in others, then to reproduce them in the most concrete and salient form . . . he might have come almost to despise them" (p. 225; *L'Idiot,* p. 1937). Jules' state of mind here is, it would seem, indistinguishable from what it will become after his encounter with the dog; if anything the language in these pages is more convincing, because considerably less inflated, than that of chapter 27. And

67

indeed Sartre, in the course of a discussion of how Jules is represented *after* his conversion, draws repeatedly on these earlier pages. Each of the quotations above reappears in *L'Idiot* side by side with passages from chapter 27, as if there were no compelling reason to differentiate the two moments in Jules' progress (see in particular p. 1932, where Sartre constructs a long quotation out of a medley of fragments from both sections of the novel; also pp. 1936–37, 1966–67). But if no such differentiation is necessary, what becomes of the notion of conversion, of that "definitive rupture" that Sartre would locate in the lives of both Jules and his creator?

Sartre does not raise the question as explicitly as this, but his interpretation of the novel suggests what his answer might be: Jules is indeed transformed at the *end* of chapter 26, he would insist, but he was "already well on his way to conversion" (p. 1927) before the episode of the dog. His movement along this path has been progressive but not steadily so: rather, it is spoken of as a series of humiliating falls (p. 225) from which Jules "rebounds" each time to a higher position, only to fall still deeper the next time. "The last and deepest" fall, Sartre notes, "evidently corresponds to the crisis of January '44" (*L'Idiot,* p. 1926 n. 2). This is a plausible account of the structure of these chapters, but I don't find it a convincing one. What Flaubert's text presents, it seems to me, is at once a subtler and a more equivocal temporal scheme, whose implications are richer than the overt pattern of Jules' conversion can quite deal with. Chapter 26 makes sense when it is seen to be organized around two distinct time schemes, one (Jules') moving forward to a "conversion" at the end of the chapter, the other (Flaubert's) looking backward to a "conversion" that had already taken place in January '44. Sometimes the two rhythms seem to be consonant, sometimes not, and out of this play there emerges a telling uncertainty. But it is not the uncertainty that Sartre finds in the novel, turning on the question of the "real meaning" of Pont l'Evêque; rather it is an uncertainty in Flaubert's understanding of what it means to invent (or to revive) a character named Jules, who can be made, more or less obliquely, to "represent" oneself at a moment of critical experience. The novel does not succeed in resolving this uncertainty, and if we look once more at the last chapters we can perhaps see why.

68

The "serenity" Jules experiences in the opening paragraphs of chapter 26 is not as "immobile" as he could wish; it soon dissolves into feelings of wonder and fear at the effects of his own detachment. Moving through a landscape that reminds him of various sentimental moments in his past, he finds himself unable to connect his thoughts and memories with one another; turning inwards he finds nothing but a painful "confusion, a whole world whose secret, whose unity, he could not understand" (p. 224). In Sartre's terms, we might say that Jules is confronted by all that is apparently "heterogeneous and irreducible" in his life. But within the space of a few intensely active paragraphs his thought begins to move into a more hopeful vein as he imagines the possibility that, through "art, pure art" (p. 226; *L'Idiot,* p. 1966), the scattered elements of his life might be arranged in a meaningful sequence, then that this ordering may correspond to some benign, though hidden, principle: "Perhaps, therefore, everything that he had felt, endured, suffered had come for purposes he knew nothing about, directed toward a fixed and constant goal, unperceived but real" (p. 226). And it is at this point that Jules is granted his vision of totality:

And then he thought that all that had once seemed to him so miserable might well have its own beauty and harmony; by synthesizing it and by bringing it back to first principles, he perceived a miraculous symmetry in the mere fact of the periodic return of the same ideas when confronted with the same things, the same sensations in the presence of the same facts; Nature lent itself to this concert and the entire world appeared to him, reproducing the infinite and reflecting the face of God; Art drew all those lines, sang out all those sounds, sculpted all those forms, seized their respective proportions and in unknown ways drew them to that beauty more beautiful than Beauty itself. . . .

He lifted up his head, the air was pure and penetrated with the scent of briars; he breathed it in deeply and something fresh and vivifying entered his soul; the cloudless sky was as white as a veil, the sun, which was setting, sent out no rays, showed its face, luminous and easy to contemplate. It seemed to him that he was emerging from a dream, for he felt the freshness that one experiences on waking, and the naïve surprise that takes hold of us on seeing again objects which seem to us new, lost as we were, just a moment before, in a world that has vanished. Where was he? in what place? at what time of day? what had he done? what had he

69

thought? He tried to get hold of himself and to reenter the reality
he had left behind. [pp. 226–27]

The first of these paragraphs describes a sublime moment of totalization; but the effect of all such moments is to suspend and dissimulate the powerful expansive pressures that have generated
them—like Wordsworth in "Tintern Abbey," Jules is "laid asleep"
so that "with an eye made quiet by the power of harmony" he may
"see into the life of things." Perhaps it would be more accurate to
say that Jules' activity is suspended and Flaubert's is dissimulated,
for it is out of that difference—between the author and his surrogate, however closely identified they may be—that the instability of
such passages is developed. The precariousness of the moment can
be felt in the shift from the first paragraph to the second, from "the
entire world appeared to him . . . reflecting the face of God" to
"the sun . . . showed its face, luminous and easy to contemplate," a
gentle shift that brings Jules back to a fuller consciousness just
before the vision is fading. His reappearance is evoked in language
that blends a sense of innocence and renewal with hints of imaginative imperialism: we are reminded that Jules' consciousness, like
Flaubert's, is both the scene of this vision and a supplementary and
disturbing element within that scene. And, significantly, Flaubert's
scene immediately darkens: Jules comes to himself to the sound of
the barking of a dog, and the rest of the chapter details the bizarre
encounter with an animal recurrently described as repulsively ugly
but in some horrid way fascinating.

Like the familiar details of the landscape in the chapter's opening
pages, the dog reminds Jules of his past—is this creature, he wonders bathetically, perhaps the same spaniel he had once given to the
woman he loved?—and he is again led into a meditative sequence,
although this time the rhythm of his thoughts is more desperate
and their content more lugubrious. Now the world appears to him
not as a vision of totaity or even as a confused series of impressions
but as sheer repetition: the dog keeps trailing him, barking steadily,
and Jules strains to interpret this literally inarticulate speech:

> Jules tried to discover some difference in the monotony of these
> furious, plaintive, and frenetic sounds; he forced himself to guess

at and seize the thought, the thing, the prognostic, the tale, or the complaint that they were trying to express; but his ear could hear nothing but the same vibrations, almost continuous, strident, always alike. [p. 231]

Into this void of meaning Jules' thought expands in morbid fantasy; he recalls suicidal broodings of his own, then fears that perhaps the dog's mistress killed herself, and then, in what can be read as a sketch for the end of *Madame Bovary,* conjures up an image of "her corpse, the mouth half-opened, the eyes shut" (p. 231). His thought is approaching a point at furthest remove from his earliest vision; from what had seemed at the moment like a poised reconciliation of his imaginative powers with a fresh and sunlit world he has been led to an encounter in which the dog figures those same powers, but now seen as alien and threatening. The presentation is Gothic, deliberately excessive:

> The clouds parted and . . . the moonlight lit up the accursed dog, who was still barking; . . . it seemed, in the night, as if two threads of fire were issuing from its eyes and coming straight toward Jules' face and meeting his gaze; then the beast's eyes suddenly grew larger and took on a human form, a human feeling palpitated within them, issued from them, out of them poured a sympathetic effusion which grew and grew, always increasing and invading you with an infinite seduction . . . .
>
> There were no more cries; the beast was mute and did nothing but widen that yellow pupil in which it seemed to Jules that he could see his reflection. Astonishment was exchanged, they confronted each other, each asking of the other things that cannot be spoken. Quivering at this mutual contact, they were both terrified, they were frightening each other; the man trembled under the gaze of the beast, in which he believed he could see a soul, and the beast trembled under the gaze of the man, in which it saw, perhaps, a god.
>
> Enlarging more rapidly than flame, Jules' thought had turned into doubt, the doubt into certitude, the certitude into fear, the fear into hatred. "Then die!" he screamed, shaking with anger and smashing the dog's face with a violent and sudden kick: "Die! die! get out of here! leave me alone!" [p. 232]

"He is the imaginary. With him, I am at the border, the barrier of dreams." Sartre's characterization of Flaubert is to the point; Jules could properly say the same thing of the dog, another figure of "the imaginary" as a projected creature of the self. The encounter, in this case, is experienced as a moment of mad expansiveness and uncertain exchange, followed by panic: Jules' thought tailspins into murderous action. Yet his fall is simply an accelerated and lurid sequel to the milder declension we noticed earlier, when the image of the world reflecting the face of God was displaced by one of Jules gazing easily at the sun. I have suggested that the instability of that moment of plenitude and totalization was not accidental but inherent, a function of the difference between an imagining self and whatever it seeks to totalize. What is presented in the episode of the dog is someone experiencing that difference as madness and seeking to reduce it by violence. Jules calms down, but his next act—his "conversion"—is no less a domestication: it is still another attempt to reduce the anxious, vibratory temporality that is figured so melodramatically in his exchange of glances with the dog, this time not by eliminating the dog but by orienting his own life in a time scheme that offers a clear and reassuring sense of "before" and "after." This is what gives the novel the linear structure Sartre finds there. There is no doubt that he is in touch with one of Flaubert's intentions when he places Jules' conversion at the end of chapter 26 and sees in it a representation of Pont l'Evêque, for Flaubert himself has a stake in imagining Jules' life in these reassuring terms.

But Flaubert is also responsible for constructing the chapter in such a way that this linear pattern is blurred and cast in doubt. Jules may already be "saved" in its opening pages; if so, we see him fall again and again experience a conversion; conversion comes to seem less an act of totalization than what one repeatedly does when in despair of totalization. The crucial difference comes to seem not that between an old life and a new one—whether Jules' or Flaubert's—but that between Jules and Flaubert. And the discovery of the novel may be that that relationship is both irreducible and perpetually subject to disorientation. Flaubert's reaction to Jules— that is, to an imagined self—is as shifty, as open to dislocating fantasy, as is Jules' to the dog.

Or as Sartre's to Flaubert, for that matter, if we turn and read L'Idiot de la famille in the light cast by the 1845 Education. To say that

Flaubert "is" the imaginary is to grant him the prestige of an object of absolute ambivalence, by turns repulsive and seductive, like Jules' dog. The biographer then sets out to totalize that figure. The hope is not simply that another man's life, with all its contingent differences, will be truthfully interpreted, or even that the possibility of such a totalization will be vindicated, but that a more radical difference will be reduced. There is a passage in *The Words*[4] that shows Sartre at work on this project at an early age:

> The dining-room would be bathed in shadow. I would push my little desk against the window. The anguish would start creeping up again. The docility of my heroes, who were unfailingly sublime, unappreciated and rehabilitated, would reveal their unsubstantiality. Then *it* would come, a dizzying, invisible being that fascinated me. In order to be seen, it had to be described. I quickly finished off the adventure I was working on, took my characters to an entirely different part of the globe, generally subterranean or underseas, and hastily exposed them to new dangers: as improvised geologists or deep-sea divers, they would pick up the Being's trail, follow it, and suddenly encounter it. What flowed from my pen at that point—an octopus with eyes of flame, a twenty-ton crustacean, a giant spider that talked—was I myself, a child monster; it was my boredom with life, my fear of death, my dullness and my perversity. I did not recognize myself. No sooner was the foul creature born than it rose up against me, against my brave speleologists. I feared for their lives. My heart would race away; I would forget my hand; penning the words, I would think I was reading them. Very often things ended there: I wouldn't deliver the men up to the Beast, but I didn't get them out of trouble either. In short, it was enough that I had put them in contact. I would get up and go to the kitchen or the library. The next day, I would leave a page or two blank and launch my characters on a new venture. Strange "novels," always unfinished, always begun over or, if you like, continued under other titles, odds and ends of gloomy tales and cheery adventures, of fantastic events and encyclopedia articles. I have lost them and I sometimes think it's a pity. If it had occurred to me to lock them up, they would reveal to me my entire childhood.

L'Idiot takes its place in that series of "strange 'novels' . . . continued under other titles" which Sartre accurately names as perpetually displaced versions of autobiography. The final encounter with the Beast, the ultimate totalizing moment, is deferred, perhaps for reasons that may be more respectable than Sartre believes them to be. Flaubert's fascination is partly that of the Beast, but partly that of another writer, one who has, at certain points in his work, made it clear that he has understood the entire project more thoroughly than Sartre and who thus threatens Sartre with the possibility that both the melodrama and the wistfulness that suffuse this childhood memory are somewhat unnecessary.

5.
RECOGNIZING CASAUBON

ABOUT HALFWAY through *Middlemarch,* after having described one more manifestation of Mr. Casaubon's preoccupying self-concern, the narrator goes on to add a more general reflection:

> Will not a tiny speck very close to our vision blot out the glory of the world, and leave only a margin by which we see the blot? I know no speck so troublesome as self. [p. 307][1]

The remark is characteristic of George Eliot in a number of ways, most obviously in its ethical implications: egotism in her writings is almost always rendered as narcissism, the self doubled and figured as both the eye and the blot. But equally typical is the care with which a particular image is introduced and its figurative possibilities developed. The speck blots out the glory of the world: that in itself would have enforced the moral. But the trope is given a second turn: the glory of the world illuminates the margin—the effect is of a sort of halo of light—but only so as to allow us all the better to see the blot. The intelligence at work extending a line of figurative language brings it back, with a nice appropriateness, to the ethical point. This is an instance of the sort of metaphorical control that teacher-critics have always admired in *Middlemarch,* the sign of a humane moral consciousness elaborating patterns of action and imagery with great inventiveness and absolutely no horsing around. Many a telling demonstration—in print and in the classroom, especially in the classroom—of the extraliterary value of formal analysis has been built around passages like this.

But what about that blot and its margin? Is the figurative language here so firmly anchored in a stable understanding of the moral relations of the self that it can't drift off in the direction of other margins and other blots?

I have in mind two specific citations, both associated with Mr. Casaubon early in the novel. At one point George Eliot's heroine, Dorothea, is seen in her library "seated and already deep in one of the pamphlets which had some marginal manuscript of Mr. Casaubon's" (p. 28); at another, Casaubon's pedantically accurate memory is compared to "a volume where a *vide supra* could serve instead of repetitions, and not the ordinary long-used blotting-book which only tells of forgotten writing" (p. 19). It might be objected that the blot we've been considering is clearly not an ink-blot, the margin clearly not the margin of a printed page; that indeed it is only by ruling out those meanings as extraneous to this particular context that we can visualize the image at all—this image of vision, of obstructed vision, of some small physical object coming between one's eyes and the world. Of course: the image, to remain an image, must restrict the range of figurative meaning we allow to the words that compose it. And, given that restraining function, it seems all the more appropriate that the image here is operating to clarify an ethical point about the self, just as it is appropriate that the tag "the moral imagination" has been so popular a way of referring to George Eliot's particular powers as a writer.

And yet, between themselves, those words *blot* and *margin* work to encourage just such a misreading of the image they nevertheless define and are defined by: *blot* helps us hear a rustle of paper in *margin, margin* makes *blot* sound just a bit inkier. And both, as it happens, are easily drawn out of their immediate context by the cumulative force of a series of less equivocal allusions to handwriting, printing, writing in general, all clustered about the figure of Casaubon. One character refers to him as a "sort of parchment code" (p. 51), another wisecracks "Somebody put a drop [of his blood] under a magnifying glass, and it was all semi-colons and parentheses" (p. 52), his own single lugubrious attempt at a joke turns on "a word that has dropped out of the text" (p. 57), and there are more serious and consequential allusions of the same sort. Earlier in their acquaintance, when Dorothea is most taken with her husband-to-be, Eliot writes: "He was all she had at first imagined him to be: almost everything he had said seemed like a specimen from a mine, or the inscription on the door of a museum which might open on the treasure of past ages" (p. 24). Later, in Rome, after the first quarrel of their marriage, Dorothea accompanies him to the Vatican, walking with him "through the stony avenue of inscriptions" and leaving him at the entrance to the library (p. 150). Back in England, in their own library, after another quarrel, Mr. Casaubon tries to resume work, but "his hand trembled so much that the words seemed to be written in an unknown character." (p. 209).

In the past, when critics have directed attention to such passages it has been either to comment on the general appropriateness of these images to Mr. Casaubon—who is, after all, a scholar—or on the particular finesse with which one image or another is adjusted to the unfolding drama of the Casaubons' marriage. More recently Hillis Miller, citing a pair of similar passages, both about Dorothea's wildly mistaken first impressions of her husband, has stressed the nondramatic value of these allusions: Casaubon, he notes, "is a text, a collection of signs which Dorothea misreads, according to that universal propensity for misinterpretation which infects all the characters in *Middlemarch.*"[2] Miller is right about Casaubon, but the point he would make is still more inclusive: he is arguing for a reading of the novel that would see every character as simultaneously an interpreter (the word is a recurrent one in *Middlemarch*) and a text available for the interpretations (plural, always partial, and often in conflict) of others. It is with reference to Lydgate, he could have pointed out, and not to Casaubon, that George Eliot writes that a man may "be known merely as a cluster of signs for his neighbors' false suppositions." (p. 105).

Miller's argument is persuasive, and the reading of the novel he sketches is a bold and attractive one: he takes *Middlemarch* to be simultaneously affirming the values of Victorian humanism which it has been traditionally held to affirm—for example, a belief in the consistence of the self as a moral agent—and systematically under-

77

cutting those values, offering in place of an ethically stable notion of the self the somewhat less reassuring figure of a focus of semiotic energy, receiving and interpreting signs, itself a "cluster of signs" more or less legible. Miller's movement toward this poised, deconstructive formulation, however, is condensed and rapid, and may still leave one wondering how those two notions of the self are held in suspension in the novel, and what the commerce is between them. In the pages that follow I propose to take up that question by dwelling on the figure of Casaubon, and by asking what it might mean, if *all* the characters in *Middlemarch* may be thought of as texts or as clusters of signs, for the signs of textuality to cluster so thickly around one particular name. Or, to put it another way, why is Mr. Casaubon made to seem not merely an especially sterile and egotistical person, but at moments like a quasi-allegorical figure, the personification of the dead letter, the written word? Personifications exist somewhere in the middle ground between realistically represented persons and configurations of signs: that would seem to be ground worth going over. But I want to approach it obliquely, by first considering some passages where it is not Casaubon, but George Eliot herself—not the blot but the eye— around whom are clustered the signs of egotism and of writing.

I

Reading through Eliot's early letters one comes across—not on every page, but often enough to catch one's attention—a particular kind of apology. In one, for example, written when she was nineteen, she concludes with these lines:

> I have written at random and have not said all I wanted to say. I hope the frequent use of the personal pronoun will not lead you to think that I suppose it to confer any weight on what I have said. I used it to prevent circumlocution and waste of time. I am ashamed to send a letter like this as if I thought more highly of myself than I ought to think, which is alas! too true. [1:23–24][3]

And then, beneath her signature, as a second thought, a postscript:

> In reading my letter I find difficulties in understanding my scribble
> that I fear are hopelessly insurmountable for another. [1:24]

Typically, apologies for what she fears may seem like egotism are accompanied by apologies for her handwriting:

> I . . . hope that you will be magnanimous enough to forgive the
> trouble my almost indecipherable letter will give you. Do not,
> pray, write neatly to me, for I cannot undertake to correspond
> with any one who will not allow me to scribble, though this
> precious sheet has, I think, an extra portion of untidiness . . . .
> [1:8]
>
> I have written an almost unpardonably egotistical letter to say
> nothing of its other blemishes . . . . [1:52]
>
> Tell me if you have great trouble in making out my cabalistic
> letters: if you have, I will write more deliberately next time. [1:134]

The feeling behind these apologies need not be either particularly strong or particularly sincere: often they are perfunctory, or positively comical, as in this passage, where jokes about handwriting oddly prefigure the language that will be associated with Casaubon thirty years later:

> You will think me interminably loquacious, and still worse you
> will be ready to compare my scribbled sheet to the walls of an
> Egyptian tomb for mystery, and determine not to imitate certain
> wise antiquaries or antiquarian wiseacres who "waste their pre-
> cious years, how soon to fail?" in deciphering information which
> has only the lichen and moss of age to make it more valuable than
> the facts graphically conveyed by an upholsterer's pattern book.
> [1:64]

What's curious is the stress not simply on the messiness of what she calls her "scribble," but on its cabalistic or hieroglypic inde-cipherability. The point might be that language turns opaque and resistant when it is too purely in the service of self, when self-expressive scribbles replace legible communicating signs. In that case these apologies for sloppy handwriting might be read as slight nervous displacements of the apologies for egotism they accompany. But there is more going on here than that: writing, like the self-doubling of narcissism, is disturbing not simply because it may seem "self-centered" but because it is both that and self-dispersing at once.

When handwriting is legible it becomes not only available to others but transparent—and attractive—as self-expression, seemingly adequate in its relation to whatever it is the self would exteriorize. At such moments one's sense of the distance between one's self and the signs one produces can be cheerfully ignored or even enjoyed. And in fact an instance of just such enjoyment—narcissistic through and through, and thoroughly engaging—can be discerned in what is, by a happy accident, the earliest bit of Eliot's writing to have survived. It is to be found on the cover of a school notebook she used when she was fourteen, a notebook which contains some arithmetic exercises, an essay on "affectation and conceit," the beginnings of a story in the manner of Sir Walter Scott, some poems she'd copied out, some drawings, and so forth. But on its cover, in a large, flourishing, ornate script, is a date—"March 16th 1834"—and a name: "Marianne Evans." It is her signature, but not quite her name, for she was christened Mary Anne, not Marianne. Gordon Haight, who reprints parts of the notebook in an appendix to his biography,[4] remarks that she was learning French at the time, as well as being trained, as was the custom in girls' schools, in elegant penmanship: the combination seems to have produced this striking emblem of a writer's beginnings, the schoolgirl's slight, slightly romantic alteration of her name, written out large and with care, there to be contemplated on the cover of her book, the space of musing reverie opening up between herself and her signature, a space in which a certain play of transformation becomes plausible.

Sometimes that space is welcomed as a "breathing-space," or, in a favorite image of George Eliot's, as "room" into which she can "expand"; at those moments the writing that structures that space stops being "scribble" and becomes what she likes to call "utterance," drawing on the Pentecostal associations of that word:

> It is necessary to me not simply to *be* but to *utter,* and I require
> utterance of my friends . . . . It is like a diffusion or expansion of
> one's own life to be assured that its vibrations are repeated in
> another, and words are the media of those vibrations. How can
> you say that music must end in silence? Is not the universe itself a
> perpetual utterance of the One Being? [1:255]

But these moments of expansive utterance, where neither the
distance between the self and its signs nor the difference between
selves is felt as a problem, are commonly followed in George Eliot's
texts by moments of anxious "shrinking" and remorse:

> I feel a sort of madness growing upon me—just the opposite of the
> delirium which makes people fancy that their bodies are filling the
> room. It seems to me as if I were shrinking into that mathematical
> abstraction, a point—so entirely am I destitute of contact that I am
> unconscious of length and breadth. [1:264]

This alternation between exuberance and apology, expansion and
shrinking, utterance and scribble, was to govern Eliot's literary
production throughout her life: she lived it as a rhythm of fluctuat-
ing excitement and discouragement while she was working on her
novels, followed by deep gloom when each was completed. More
interestingly, she inscribed that alternation into her novels, but curiously transformed. At a number of climactic moments the play of
expansion and shrinking reappears, but the rhythm is broken, lifted
out of the interior life of a single character and distributed to a pair
of characters, one of whom is seen expanding in loving recognition
of the other, who is commonly figured as shrunken or shrinking
from contact. Late in *Middlemarch,* for example, when Mrs.
Bulstrode, humiliated by the revelations of her husband's past, but
loyal to him nevertheless, goes to join him, we are told that "as she
went towards him she thought he looked smaller—he seemed so
withered and shrunken" (p. 550). Elsewhere in the novel, where
Dorothea touches her husband's arm, only to be horrified by his
unresponsive hardness, the narrator adds: "You may ask why, in the
name of manliness, Mr. Casaubon should have behaved that way.
Consider that his was a mind which shrank from pity" (p. 312).
These are instances of a distribution of attributes operating

81

within the fictional world of the novel: images that we have seen
George Eliot, in letters, applying to her own inner life are attached,
as in a medieval psychomachia, to separate characters in her narratives. But at times this distributive activity may be seen operating
across the boundary that separates the lives of the characters—the
ways they conduct themselves and engage with one another—from
the sensed activity of an author, the ways Eliot conducts the plotting of her novels. For example, Dorothea's loving acknowledge-
ment of her husband is followed, after not too long an interval, by
his death; or again, when Mrs. Bulstrode goes to her husband's
side, he is a permanently broken man. Within the world of
Middlemarch, neither Dorothea nor Mrs. Bulstrode can be held responsible for the turns of fate that crush their husbands, but it is
nonetheless true that certain recipients of moral generosity don't
fare well in that world. Seeking an explanation, a critic might wish
to read such scenes as unwittingly playing out their author's preoccupation in some wishful and compensatory fashion. Richard
Ellmann, for example, has found in the language associated with
Casaubon echoes of images linked, in an early letter, with the novelist's fears of her own erotic fantasizing. "The severity with which
Casaubon is treated," Ellman speculates, "would then derive from
her need to exorcise this part of her experience . . . . To berate
Casaubon, and to bury him, was to overcome in transformed state
the narcissistic sensuality of her adolescence."[5] To seek an author's
personal allegory behind the realistic surface she has woven is often
as unrewarding as it is methodologically dubious, but in the case of
George Eliot's works, because they are explicitly about the imagining of others—about the status of the image of one person in the
imagining mind of another—the play between the imaginer and the
imagined, between author and character, and the possibility of a
narcissistic confusion developing between the one and the other,
has already been thematized and made available for interpretations
such as Ellmann's. If anything, his claims are too modest: what he
presents as a contingent psychobiographical detail—an author's uneasiness about her own "narcissism"—may be read as neither contingent nor primarily biographical, but as part of a sustained and
impersonal questioning of the grounds of fiction. Nowhere is that

questioning more energetically in evidence than in the pages (in chapters 20 and 21) that recount the Casaubons' experience in Rome. If we turn to them now, beginning with the final paragraphs of chapter 21, we shall find another instance of the bifurcated activity characteristic of Eliot's writing:

> Today she has begun to see that she had been under a wild illusion in expecting a response to her feeling from Mr. Casaubon, and she had felt the waking of a presentiment that there might be a sad consciousness in his life which made as great a need on his side as on her own.
>
> We are all of us born in moral stupidity, taking the world as an udder to feed our supreme selves: Dorothea had early begun to emerge from that stupidity, but yet it had been easier for her to imagine how she would devote herself to Mr. Casaubon, and become wise and strong in his strength and wisdom, than to conceive with that distinctness which is no longer reflection but feeling—an idea wrought back to the directness of sense, like the solidity of objects—that he had an equivalent centre of self, whence the lights and shadows must always fall with a certain difference. [pp. 156–57]

These lines have been rightly admired, both as a powerful presentation of Dorothea's experience and as an epitome of the moral imagination at work, a text exhibiting the links between generous conduct, literary creation, and the reading of novels. For Dorothea's exemplary action would seem to be easily assimilated to the activity of a novelist and to that of a reader: to conceive Mr. Casaubon as different from oneself, and to do so "with that distinctness which is no longer reflection but feeling," sounds like a display of the same imaginative power that created the character of Casaubon in the first place, and the same power that *Middlemarch* would quicken in its readers. And indeed this view of the novel, and of the use of novels generally, was one that Eliot had already endorsed: "A picture of human life such as a great artist can give," she wrote, "surprises even the trivial and selfish into that attention to what is apart from themselves, which may be called the raw material of moral sentiment."[6] We shall want to pause to ask where Mr. Casaubon fits into this set of beliefs about literature and conduct, other than as the passive (and not altogether grateful) object of Dorothea's (and Eliot's, and the reader's) regard. But first, let us look more closely at how Eliot elaborates this view of the moral imagination. The notion that literature calls attention to unnoticed aspects of life, to its intricacies or simply to its variety, is certainly not peculiar to her; more characteristic, however, is the stress she places on the reader's (or the character's) reluctance to attend: in the sentence just quoted, it is the element of surprise that counts—even "the trivial and selfish" are to be shocked into noticing what is apart from themselves. Typically her plots present someone jolted into the consciousness of others, with the jolt all the more forceful because of the resistance encountered, a resistance which is generally figured as a powerful narcissistic investment in an image of the self, the blot that obscures the glory of the world. Or—still more generally—an investment in *some* image, for the notion of narcissism in these novels is deepened to include other sorts of imaginative fascination.

Thus the "moral stupidity" which Dorothea must emerge from can be presented as a clinging to a mistaken idea of her marriage: "Today she had begun to see that she had been under a wild illusion in expecting a response to her feeling from Mr. Casaubon . . . ." Later in the novel, echoing the encompassing turn of phrase of the earlier passage—"We are all of us born in moral stupidity"—Eliot writes, "We are all of us imaginative in some form or other, for images are the brood of desire" (p. 237). She is writing there of the old miser Featherstone, who never emerges or even begins to emerge from what she names "the fellowship of illusion." But the repetitions of syntax and cadence suggest an equivalence: to be born in moral stupidity is to be born imaginative; and it is against the inertia of this mode of imaginative activity, the narcissistic dwelling on and in an image, that the moral imagination has both to define itself and defend itself.

Define itself first, for the differences between these two kinds of imagination—one supposedly turned outward and hence moral, the other self-enclosed and narcissistic—may not, under scrutiny, be all that clear. Both activities, whatever their outward effects, would seem to originate within the same enclosure: it becomes important to be able to distinguish them at their source, and not merely in terms of their consequences. George Eliot is here engaging the same problem that led Romantic theorists like Coleridge to insist on a sharp and essential difference between the mental activities they named Imagination and Fancy, and her solution—if we now look back at the paragraph on moral stupidity—will be seen to resemble theirs. For what is most remarkable in that passage is the fact that Dorothea's exemplary action, the acknowledgment of an irreducible difference between persons, is accompanied by—is accomplished in—the flashing reduction of another sort of difference, that between "reflection" and "feeling," "idea" and "sense." To recognize Casaubon as possessing "an equivalent centre of self, whence the lights and shadows must always fall with a certain difference" is, for Dorothea, to overcome not merely her own egotism but also what another Eliot has called a "dissociation of sensibility," a troublesome interior difference. And, oddly, what she achieves is made to sound very much like what Mr. Casaubon, at another point in the novel, is pitied for having never experienced, that "rapturous transformation of consciousness" into "the vividness of a thought, the ardour of a passion, the energy of an action" (pp. 206–7). If we now ask what Mr. Casaubon is doing in this scene, we can see that he is presented both as a character, another person, the object of Dorothea's recognition, and as a figure, an exteriorized embodiment of a mode of imagination threateningly antithetical to hers—and to George Eliot's. For Dorothea to recognize him "as he is" is, for the author, to cast out what he may be taken to represent.

But what, exactly, may he be taken to represent? At times he would seem to be the personification of the written word, at others the personification of the narcissistic imagination; the connection between the two can be made in a more systematic way in terms of an economy of anxiety, by suggesting that the dislocation implicit in narcissism, the doubling of the self into an eye and an image, an eye and a blot, is a more manageable and comforting fiction than the more open and indeterminate self-dispersion associated with a plurality of signs or with the plurality of interpretations that writing can provoke. In chapters 20 and 21 of *Middlemarch* one can follow a movement toward the more reassuring fiction. They begin with the superb paragraphs in which Mr. Casaubon is associated with a vision of Rome as "stupendous fragmentariness" (p. 143), an unintelligible plurality that baffles Dorothea with "a glut of confused ideas" (p. 144); they then move through a complicated and uncertain grappling—on George Eliot's part—with the threat of narcissism, the threat that her own imaginative activity is nothing but narcissistic, to the exteriorization of that disturbing possibility in the figure of Casaubon, a personification now no longer of "writing" but of "narcissism" who can be "recognized" and banished from the novel. We shall follow that movement in chapter 20 more closely in a moment, but first we should take note of some texts that bear on another mode of imagination commonly attributed to George Eliot and held to be at work in the paragraphs on Rome, the "historical imagination."

II

In 1856, in a review entitled "Silly Novels by Lady Novelists," George Eliot commented on the current vogue for historical fiction in language that reads like a program for the writing of *Romola:*

> Admitting that genius which has familiarized itself with all the relics of an ancient period can sometimes, by the force of its sympathetic divination, restore the missing notes in the "music of humanity," and reconstruct the fragments into a whole which will really bring the remote past nearer to us, and interpret it to our duller apprehension,—this form of imaginative power must always be among the very rarest, because it demands as much accurate and minute knowledge as creative vigour.[7]

Her own work on *Romola,* which she began five or six years later, involved her in months of painstaking research in reconstructing the fragments of Renaissance Florence. But the emphasis on "accurate and minute knowledge" in this passage is common to most of the essays and reviews she wrote in the 1850s, just before she turned to fiction. Knowing the names of things, getting things right becomes, for an intellectual journalist, a criterion of success

86

and a moral criterion as well: the attention to detail required by research into any subject, but particularly into historical questions, is referred to as an escape from self, a salutary counter to the narcissism implicit in a vague and wishful relation to the things around one. Yet here a characteristic problem asserts itself: it is in the nature of historical research, even of the most rigorous and self-effacing kind, that the energies caught up in it are far from disinterested. Curiosity about the past, a wish to reconstruct the fragments into a whole, may indeed be a move beyond a casual, lazy, or provincial self-complacency, but it draws its powers from a more fundamental wish to reconstruct an original mirror of the self, a totalization of history which will be a history of one's own origins. In a bizarre scene in *Romola* George Eliot's sense of the willfulness informing attempts at historical reconstruction is dramatized in a striking and pertinent way.

Romola is both a Victorian humanist's effort to reconstruct a moment in the past and a story of a similar effort, that of the Florentine humanists, to piece together the fragments of classical civilization. One of the characters, Baldassare, is presented as someone who has been betrayed by his son into captivity and the loss of his fortune; as a result of his sufferings, we learn, he has lost his memory too, and with it his ability to read Greek. Making his way to Florence, he attempts to rehabilitate himself and to reclaim what's due him— to recapture his skills as a classical scholar and to avenge himself on his son. Eliot has constructed the plot so that these two motifs interlock in a peculiar scene. The son comes to visit Baldassare, who recognizes him and leaps at him with a dagger; but the dagger breaks, his son escapes him, and he is left alone, impotent to avenge himself and still incapable of making out the Greek text he had been puzzling over earlier:

> He leaned to take up the fragments of the dagger; then he turned towards the book which lay open at his side. It was a fine large manuscript, an odd volume of Pausanias. The moonlight was upon it, and he could see the large letters at the head of the page:

(and here George Eliot prints out the Greek capitals in a large open space on her own page before continuing):

87

ΜΕΣΣΝΙΚΑ. ΚΒ'

In old days he had known Pausanias familiarly; yet an hour or two ago he had been looking hopelessly at that page, and it had suggested no more meaning to him than if the letters had been black weather-marks on a wall; but at this moment they were once again the magic signs that conjure up a world.

Excitedly he takes up the book and reads, then goes out to walk about the city, feeling "the glow of conscious power":

> That city, which had been a weary labyrinth, was material that he could subdue to his purposes now: his mind glanced through its affairs with flashing conjecture; he was once more a man who knew cities, whose sense of vision was instructed in large experience, who felt the keen delight of holding all things in the grasp of language. Names! Images!—his mind rushed through its wealth without pausing, like one who enters on a great inheritance.[8]

The fragments of the dagger that had failed him are replaced by the no longer fragmentary Greek letters, once plural, discontinuous, and indecipherable—mere black marks—now capable of reconstruction into a text that is at once the mirror of Baldassare's reintegrated self (hence the excited exclamations: "Names! Images!") and the instrument of his vengeance. "The city, which had been a weary labyrinth"—like Casaubon's habitual setting—is now something Baldassare can subdue to his purposes: the mastery of language here, the reconstitution of the written word into significant clusters, is seen as thoroughly imperialistic, an emblem of the willed integrity of a wrathful father. There has rarely been a neater instance of what Jacques Derrida has called "ce qui revient au père": what literally comes back to this father is his memory, his identity and with it his power to dominate. What, then, are we to make of the historical novelist's wish to "restore the missing notes in the 'music of humanity'" and reconstruct the fragments into a whole? That no longer sounds like an utterly innocent project. With this in mind we can now turn to the paragraphs on Rome.

III

Chapter 20 opens with Dorothea in tears, with "no distinctly shapen grievance that she could state, even to herself" (p. 143). We

88

might wish to say that it soon becomes clear what is distressing her, that she has been hurt by her husband's cold and pedantic behavior, and overwhelmed by what she has seen of Rome, but that would be to travesty the experience of reading these paragraphs, to turn aside from the subtlety with which Dorothea's psychological state is rendered, as well as from the deft intermingling of the causes of her distress. From the chapter's third paragraph on, it becomes impossible to separate Dorothea's response to her husband from her response to the city, and just as impossible to allow the one noun—Casaubon—to stand in some flatly symbolic equivalence to the other noun—Rome. Certain likenesses are taken for granted: Casaubon is old, he is a historian and an interpreter, he is (to Dorothea, at least) a center of authority; but these paragraphs don't exactly dwell on this analogy or spell out its terms. Instead, the words associated earlier in the novel with Mr. Casaubon, the images that had been clustered around his name, are allowed to drift free of that center and to disperse themselves through the urban landscape: allusions to Mr. Casaubon himself, or to Dorothea's role as his wife, practically disappear. This disappearance, the withdrawal of Casaubon from the foreground of this prose, is marked by an odd figure, a sort of "dissolve" that displaces the couple's relations onto the seasons:

> Dorothea had now been five weeks in Rome, and in the kindly mornings when autumn and winter seemed to go hand in hand like a happy aged couple one of whom would presently survive in chiller loneliness, she had driven about at first with Mr. Casaubon, but of late chiefly with Tantripp and their experienced courier. [p. 143]

While Mr. Casaubon retires to the Vatican Library, Dorothea is left alone with Rome and her own life, and both are figured to her as enigmas: her confused and disorganized feelings are assimilated to the fragmentary nature of the scene around her, a scene now made up as much of the bits and pieces of language associated with Casaubon as of the "broken revelations of that Imperial and Papal city":

> The weight of unintelligible Rome might lie easily on bright nymphs to whom it formed a background for the brilliant picnic of Anglo-foreign society; but Dorothea had no such defence against deep impressions. Ruins and basilicas, palaces and colossi,

89

set in the midst of a sordid present, where all that was living and warm-blooded seemed sunk in the deep degeneracy of a superstition divorced from reverence; the dimmer yet eager Titanic life gazing and struggling on walls and ceilings; the long vistas of white forms whose marble eyes seemed to hold the monotonous light of an alien world: all this vast wreck of ambitious ideals, sensuous and spiritual, mixed confusedly with signs of breathing forgetfulness and degradation, at first jarred her with an electric shock, and then urged themselves on her with that ache belonging to a glut of confused ideas which check the flow of emotion. Forms both pale and glowing took possession of her young sense, and fixed themselves in her memory even when she was not thinking of them, preparing strange associations which remained through her after-years. Our moods are apt to bring with them images which succeed each other like the magic-lantern pictures of a doze; and in certain states of dull forlornness Dorothea all her life continued to see the vastness of St. Peter's, the huge bronze canopy, the excited intention in the attitudes and garments of the prophets and evangelists in the mosaics above, and the red drapery which was being hung for Christmas spreading itself everywhere like a disease of the retina. [pp. 143–44]

I have quoted this passage at length both in order to recall its intensity and to draw attention to its organization. The persistent emphasis on the scene's at once soliciting and resisting comprehension, linked to the rhythms in which these sentences accumulate layer on layer of plural nouns, until that accumulated charge is released in a "shock," a "glut of confused ideas which check the flow of emotion"—these elements mark Dorothea's experience as an experience of the sublime, in the specific sense that term took on in the writings of Kant or Wordsworth. I mention this not simply to identify a literary tradition—though I have enough of Casaubon in me to take an intense, bleak pleasure in interrupting a passionate moment with a scholarly gloss—but because to recognize the rhythm of the sublime in these sentences is to anticipate where the text might go from here, what one might expect to follow after that abrupt shock. At one point, for instance, Kant describes the feeling of the sublime as a pleasure that arises only indirectly, produced "by the feeling of a momentary checking of the vital powers and a consequent stronger outflow of them."[9] Elsewhere, explaining the "bewilderment or, as it were, perplexity which it is said seizes the spectator on his first entrance into St. Peter's in Rome," he writes: "For there is here a feeling of the inadequacy of his imagination for presenting the ideas of a whole, wherein the imagination reaches its maximum, and, in striving to surpass it, sinks back into itself, by which, however, a kind of emotional satisfaction is produced."[10] We might, with this model in mind, ask if there will be an outflow of vital powers in this passage or a sinking back of the imagination into itself. Or, if what we have in mind is the language of "Tintern Abbey," we might wonder if Dorothea will be released from "the burthen of the mystery," the "heavy and the weary weight of all this unintelligible world," and allowed to "see into the life of things." One way or another, a reader may be led to expect some resolution, and, indeed, these expectations are rewarded, although—and this too is characteristic of the sublime—not in quite the form anticipated.

For the movement of these pages seems to issue in not one but three moments that qualify as "resolutions," partly because of their position in the text, partly because of the level of their diction and the nature of the metaphors of which they are composed. One of these, the last in the sequence, I have already described in some detail: it is the paragraph with which chapter 21 concludes, the paragraph beginning "We are all of us born in moral stupidity." For if it is the "dream-like strangeness of her bridal life" that Dorothea is confronting in the opening pages of chapter 20, the baffling disparity between her sense of whom she was marrying and the realities of living with Mr. Casaubon, then her acknowledging that she had "been under a wild illusion" can be thought of as one response to the shock she registered in the previous chapter, a response that is deferred chiefly for reasons of dramatic verisimilitude, because it takes time to adjust to such new awareness. Here the sequence of sublime checking followed by some resolution underlies the ethical scenario we noticed earlier, where a character is jolted out of moral stupidity into the recognition of something apart from the self.

But the intensity of Dorothea's feelings, as they are presented in these opening paragraphs, as well as the scope of Eliot's rhetoric, are far in excess of anything that could be resolved dramatically: she has been shown attempting to come to terms not simply with her husband, but with the heterogeneous assault of Rome, with a collection of signs that may be summed up in a verbal formulation (e.g. "all this vast wreck of ambitious ideals") but which neither Dorothea nor the author is in a position to render as a totality. The resolution of *this* aspect of Dorothea's experience is to be found in the sentences immediately following those on the checking of the flow of emotion, and in one sense it is no resolution at all: it takes the form of a compulsively repeated set of images, fixed in Dorothea's memory for life and unexorcisable. The plurality of unmasterable fragments is converted into a repetitive series of painful tokens. This is a dark sublimity, beyond the pleasure principle for Dorothea, and sufficiently at odds with the values of Victorian humanism to be distressing to George Eliot as well. The later paragraph, in which Dorothea recognizes Casaubon, may be read as, quite literally, a domestication of the anxiety associated with the earlier moment.

If one wanted to demonstrate that *Middlemarch* offers a reader two incompatible systems of value, conflicting views of the interpretation of history, of the possibilities of knowledge, of the consistency of the self, few passages in the novel would provide better evidence. One could contrast the sublime of repetition with that of recognition, then read the first as an undermining of moral and metaphysical categories, the second as the recuperation of those same categories. But what, then, are we to make of still another moment in these pages that is bound to strike a reader as "sublime"? It is to be found in the paragraph immediately following the description of Rome, and it has been cited, admiringly, perhaps as much as any other passage in Eliot's works:

> If we had a keen vision and a feeling for all ordinary human life, it would be like hearing the grass grow and the squirrel's heart beat, and we should die of that roar which lies on the other side of silence. As it is the quickest of us walk about well wadded in stupidity. [p. 144]

We might begin by noticing that these sentences, although they share with the other "resolutions" a sense of high-powered epistemological confrontation, are not about Dorothea's response either to Rome or to Mr. Casaubon; they are, rather, about how "we"—the readers and the narrator—might respond to Dorothea, and indeed they come at the end of a paragraph that had begun with a slightly awkward wavering of tone, as the narrator seemed to back off from the intensities of Dorothea's experience:

> Not that this inward amazement of Dorothea's was anything very exceptional: many souls in their young nudity are tumbled out among incongruities and left to "find their feet" among them, while their elders go about their business. Nor can I suppose that when Mrs. Casaubon is discovered in a fit of weeping six weeks after her wedding the situation will be regarded as tragic.

One of Eliot's most acute contemporary readers, Richard Holt Hutton, was struck by the oddness of these lines, and bothered by what he heard as a "bitter parenthetical laugh" at the expense of those souls tumbled out "in their young nudity"[11] I think it *is* an odd moment, but that the tonal irony seems less directed at the "souls"—that is, at Dorothea—than it does at some imagined insensitive reader: the "Nor can I suppose" is somewhat heavyhandedly reminding her readers of their perception of the tragic, of the limits of those powers of sympathetic imagination which would enable them to discern the tragic in "the very fact of frequency." Still more puzzling, however, is the combination of this sardonic diction with the note of high assurance the narrator strikes in the sentences about "the roar . . . on the other side of silence."

What is going on in this passage makes more sense once we learn that it is dense with self-quotation, with allusions to George Eliot's earlier fiction. Those "souls in their young nudity," for example, "tumbled out" and left to "find their feet" would seem to be a rendering as a figure of speech of what was once, in a story called "Janet's Repentance" (one of the *Scenes of Clerical Life*), a piece of dramatic action: there the heroine is literally thrown out of her house by her drunken husband, and her situation is described in these terms:

> The stony street, the bitter north-east wind and darkness—and in the midst of them a tender woman thrust out from her husband's home in her thin night-dress, the harsh wind cutting her naked feet, and driving her long hair away from her half-clad bosom, where the poor heart is crushed with anguish and despair.[12]

93

Also to be found in "Janet's Repentance" are lines which echo in the squirrel's heartbeat:

> Yet surely, surely the only true knowledge of our fellow-man is that which enables us to feel with him—which gives us a fine ear for the heart-pulses that are beating under the mere clothes of circumstance and opinion. Our subtlest analysis of schools and sects must miss the essential truth, unless it be lit up by the love that sees in all forms of human thought and work the life and death struggles of separate human beings.[13]

In still another story, "The Lifted Veil," the hero discovers in himself a power that torments him and which he describes as a "diseased participation in other people's consciousness": "It was like a preternaturally heightened sense of hearing," he relates, "making audible to one a roar of sound where others find perfect stillness."[14]

The validity of the novelist's imagination of others, whether it is seen as a saving gift or as a curse, is what is at stake in the lines on the squirrel's heartbeat. Placed between Dorothea's failure to reconstruct the fragments of history and her success in recognizing her husband as someone with an "equivalent centre of self," this passage seeks language adequate to a slightly different task, that of stabilizing the incommensurable relation between an author conceived of as somehow "outside" (but uncertainly outside) her creation and a privileged (but fictitious) consciousness within that imagined world. The allusions to earlier works of fiction, the reappearance of those evocations of pathos or of imaginative power, are accompanied by the reversal of their original meanings: what had seemed pathetic reality in "Janet's Repentance" has been transformed into a metaphor, and the "fine ear for heart-pulses," the ability to hear "a roar of sound where others find perfect stillness"—these are precisely the faculties that a reader is now told he does not possess. The wavering, then steadying of tone in which the narrator addresses the reader may be read as one way of readjusting to the felt instability of the author's relation to her character, to the unsettled sense that it was through an intense identification with Dorothea's experience in Rome that the magnificent previous paragraph had been written, but that the burden of that paragraph

94

was the fictitiousness and the willfulness of such identifications. The sublimity of the image of the roar on the other side of silence emerges from this thoroughly negative insight.

Behind this language about the limits of perception is still another text, one with a long history in eighteenth- and nineteenth-century writing about the sublime: it is the passage in the *Essay Concerning Human Understanding* in which Locke praises the aptness with which the human senses are scaled to man's position in the hierarchy of creatures:

> If our sense of hearing were but a thousand times quicker than it is, how would a perpetual noise distract us. And we should in the quietest retirement be less able to sleep or meditate than in the middle of a sea-fight. Nay, if that most instructive of senses, seeing, were in any man a thousand, or a hundred thousand times more acute than it is by the best microscope, things several millions of times less than the smallest object of his sight now would then be visible to his naked eyes, and so he would come nearer to the discovery of the texture and motion of the minute parts of corporeal things: and in many of them, probably get ideas of their internal constitutions; but then he would be in a quite different world from other people: nothing would appear the same to him and others.[15]

Locke's language converts a scaled continuum into an opposition between the ordinary world of sensation and sociability and the "quite different world" in which the man with microscopic vision would find himself. To allude to that language in *Middlemarch* is to stress that particular discontinuity at the moment when the incommensurability between an author and the creatures of her pen is under consideration. Suppose, to draw out the turns of this figure, one *were* to hear the roar which lies on the other side of silence. Possibly one might not die of it; instead—and this may not be the preferable alternative—one might become like Locke's man, moving nearer to the discovery of the texture and motion of things, but in a quite different world from other people. If, for example, one were to bring a drop of Mr. Casaubon's blood into focus, one might see nothing but semicolons and parentheses. That is the possibility that is written into *Middlemarch* in the idiom of the sublime; it is clearly not a possibility to be steadily contemplated by a working novelist—it must be repressed if books like *Middlemarch* are to be written at all. One sign of that repression is the recognition and exorcism of Casaubon.

6.
FREUD AND THE
SANDMAN

For my old age I have chosen the theme of death; I have stumbled on a
remarkable notion based on my theory of the instincts, and now must read
all kinds of things relevant to it, e.g. Schopenhauer, for the first time. But I
am not fond of reading.

—Freud to Lou Andreas-Salomé, August 1919

"I INVENTED psychoanalysis because it had
no literature," Freud once remarked,[1] joking about what is now
lugubriously known as the Burden of the Past or the Anxiety of
Influence. "Literature," of course, meant the writings of other in-
vestigators in his field—his predecessors, the contemporaries he
saw as rivals, or more benignly, as disciples and colleagues—but we
have only to let the word drift a bit, until "literature" means just
"literature," for the joke to become still more suggestive. That, at
any rate, will be the drift of what follows: the question of "literary
priority" and the concerns that cling to it (the wish to be original,
the fear of plagiarism, the rivalry among writers) will be brought
into touch with some topics commonly grouped under the rubric
Psychoanalysis-and-Literature (the overlapping of the two fields,
the rivalry between them, the power of one to interpret and neu-
tralize the other). My chief text will be Freud's essay "The Uncanny"[2]—in particular the reading he offers there of E. T. A.
Hoffman's story "The Sandman," and the links he establishes between the sentiment of the uncanny and his newly elaborated the-

ory of the repetition compulsion—but I shall also be examining some recently published biographical material which suggests that the motifs of the uncanny, of repetition, and of literary priority were playing themselves out in Freud's relations with one of his younger colleagues at about the same time that he was bringing them into prominence in his writing. My hope is to quilt together these scraps of verbal material, each with a somewhat different feel to it—a work of fiction, a psychoanalytic account of its structure, the formulation of a metapsychological theory, some biographical anecdotes—and to comment on their power, collectively or when working at odds with one another, to fix and fascinate our attention.

Even the simple facts concerning the writing and publication of "The Uncanny" seem designed to raise questions about repetition. The essay came out in the fall of 1919, and a letter of Freud's (May 12, 1919) indicates that it was written in May of that year, or, rather, rewritten, for the letter speaks of his going back to an old manuscript that he had set aside, for how long isn't clear—perhaps as long as a dozen years. However old the manuscript, it is usually assumed that Freud was prompted to return to it by his reformulation, in March or April of 1919, of his understanding of the repetition compulsion, in the course of producing a first draft of *Beyond the Pleasure Principle*. I have seen no account of the contents of that draft, which may no longer exist, but it is customarily thought to have been a considerably less developed version of the text Freud finally published as *Beyond the Pleasure Principle* late in 1920. That it contained a new and powerful theory of repetition is a safe guess, since that theory was available for publication in "The Uncanny," but scholars have also reasoned that it made no mention of the other remarkable notion included in the published version, Freud's postulation of the death instincts (18:3–4). That notion, it is assumed, was what Freud was working his way toward in the summer of 1919, when he wrote the letter quoted above, a letter which mentions the "theme of death" and a "theory of the instincts," but in which the compound noun *Todestriebe* does not appear; according to the editors of the *Standard Edition,* the death instinct is not mentioned as such until February 1920. An interval, then, is generally imagined, during which the theory of an autonomous compulsion to repeat existed in Freud's mind and on paper, as yet ungrounded in any more fundamental metapsychological explanation; and it was in that interval, and rather early on, that "The Uncanny" was rewritten.

If one then asks what relationship the essay bears to the theory it announces, the customary answer is that it represents an application of a general explanatory principle to a particular, though by no means central, case. "In the famous 'compulsion to repeat,'" Philip Rieff writes, "Freud found the concept that was to give unity and truth to an essay which, without such a transfusion of theory, would have remained a relatively pale piece of erudition."[3] And that seems reasonable, until one looks more closely at the essay and at the theory. For the essay's "unity" is anything but patent—if it is there at all, it must be tracked down through a rambling and intriguingly oblique presentation[4]—and the theory of the compulsion to repeat is so strange that its explanatory power is not the first thing one is likely to respond to when one comes across it. The impulse to rewrite "The Uncanny" may have been Freud's wish to test the value of his theory, as Rieff suggests, but it might also have been his exclamatory response ("Unheimlich!") to the theory's strangeness.

If one follows the course of Freud's thinking about repetition, one finds him, in 1919, granting an oddly autonomous status, and an emphatic priority, to what had previously been thought of as a secondary and explainable element within the system of psychoanalytic theory.[5] From the first, Freud was bound to attend to a variety of repeated and repeating phenomena—the recurrence of infantile material in dreams and in neurotic symptoms, the rehearsal of behavior patterns that came to be known as "acting out," the revivification and transference of unconscious wishes that a patient experienced in relation to his analyst, and so on. The word "repetition" could be used to designate all of these without purporting to explain why any of them should occur; that, Freud believed, was the task of his two interacting principles of mental functioning—the pleasure principle, and its more sober partner, the reality principle. Even in 1914, when he wrote of a patient's "compulsion to repeat" certain forgotten, because repressed, material, the attribution of power implicit in the term "compulsion" was still relative and, above all, still explicable through reference to forces other than itself. In 1919, however, Freud felt obliged (compelled?) by certain new data to acknowledge the independence of the compulsion to repeat, and, for at least several months, to address himself to its apparently irreducible inexplicability. The repetition compulsion "itself"—or was it merely Freud's theory of repetition?—may then have seemed to its discoverer to have taken on an uncanny life of its own; indeed, the very uncertainty as to whether it was the force "itself" or its theoretical formulation that was claiming attention would contribute to the effect of strangeness.

How does one come to terms with a force that seems at once mobile and concealed in its operation? When, in *Beyond the Pleasure Principle,* Freud developed his more abstract conception of a compulsion to repeat and argued for the existence of "death instincts," the mythical *Triebe* (drives) underlying (constituting? informing?) the *Zwang* (compulsion), he was obliged to acknowledge that evidence for such an instinctive force was hard to find: the drive was, in his words, never "visible," it "eluded perception" except (he added in *Civilization and its Discontents* [21:120]) when it was "tinged or colored" by sexuality. The metaphor has been taken as a means of suggesting something about the nature of instinctual forces—that they were always encountered in some mixture with each other, never in a state of "purity." But, with only a slight shift of emphasis, it can also be read as a way of describing an epistemological difficulty: like certain substances that must be prepared before they can be examined under a microscope, it is only when stained that the death instinct can be brought into focus. Taken in this latter sense, the relation between the erotic instincts and the death instinct comes to sound very much like the relationship Freud described, elsewhere in *Beyond the Pleasure Principle,* between his own figurative language and the "bewildering and obscure processes" with which he was concerned:[6]

We need not.feel greatly disturbed in judging our speculations upon the life and death instincts by the fact that so many bewildering and obscure processes occur in it—such as one instinct being driven out by another, or an instinct turning from an ego to an object, and so on. This is merely due to our being obliged to operate with the scientific terms, that is to say with the figurative language, peculiar to psychology (or, more precisely, to depth psychology). We could not otherwise describe the processes in question at all, and indeed we could not have become aware of them. [23:60]

Freud sees his figurative language as a means of lending color to what is otherwise imperceptible. We may wish, later, to question the appropriateness of this analogy, but for the moment let us accept it and explore its possible elaborations: can we press the point and say that the figures of psychoanalytic discourse are "like" the erotic instincts, color codings of a sort that allow one to trace the paths of concealed energy? Or, alternately, that the visible signs of desire are "like" figures of speech? The interest of these questions will become apparent when we rephrase them in the terms of "The Uncanny," in which the invisible energies are thought of as those of the repetition compulsion, and the glimpses one gets of them are felt as disturbing and strange:

It must be explained that we are able to postulate the principle of a repetition-compulsion in the unconscious mind, based upon instinctual activity and probably inherent in the very nature of the instincts—a principle powerful enough to overrule the pleasure-principle, lending to certain aspects of the mind their daemonic character, and still very clearly expressed in the tendencies of small children; a principle, too, which is responsible for a part of the course taken by the analysis of neurotic patients. Taken in all, the foregoing prepares us for the discovery that whatever reminds us of this inner repetition-compulsion is perceived as uncanny. [17:238]

The feeling of the uncanny would seem to be generated by being reminded of the repetition compulsion, not by being reminded of whatever it is that is repeated. The becoming aware of the process is felt as eerie, not the becoming aware of some particular item in the unconscious, once familiar, then repressed, now coming back into consciousness. Elsewhere in the essay, Freud seems to be saying something easier to understand. When he quotes Schelling's formulation: "Everything is uncanny that ought to have remained hidden and secret yet comes to light" (17:224), or even when he describes the effect produced by "The Sandman" as bound up with the reactivation of a repressed infantile dread of castration it would seem to be the something-that-is-repeated that is the determining factor, not the reminder of compulsive repetition itself. Freud stresses the bolder and more puzzling hypothesis once more in *Beyond the Pleasure Principle:* "It may be presumed that when people unfamiliar with analysis feel an obscure fear—a dread of rousing something that, so they feel, is better left sleeping—what they are afraid of us the emergence of this compulsion with its hint of possession by some daemonic power" (17:36). It is the emergence of the compulsion that they fear, as much as the reappearance of a particular fear or desire. It may seem like a quibble to dwell on this difference: surely the awareness of the process of repetition is inseparable from the awareness of something being repeated, for there can be no such thing as sheer repetition. Of course: repetition becomes "visible" when it is colored by something being repeated, which itself functions like vivid or heightened language, lending a kind of rhetorical consistency to what is otherwise quite literally unspeakable. Whatever it is that is repeated—an obsessive ritual, perhaps, or a bit of acting-out in relation to one's analyst—will, then, feel most compellingly uncanny when it is seen as *merely* coloring, that is, when it comes to seem most gratuitously rhetorical. So much for "people unfamiliar with analysis," or for patients recognizing the uncanny effects generated by the transference. But what of the investigator "obliged to operate with the scientific terms, that is to say with the figurative language, peculiar to depth psychology"? Mightn't he, too, experience effects of the uncanny at those moments when the figurativeness of his figurative language is brought home to him in some connection with the repetition compulsion? That is a question we shall return to after considering Freud's reading of "The Sandman."

II

I was most strongly compelled to tell you about Nathanael's disastrous life.

—Narrator of "The Sandman"

Freud offers, in fact, two readings of the story: the first is of its manifest surface, given in the form of a rapid, selective paraphrase of the plot, moving sequentially from the childhood recollections of the hero, Nathanael, on through his attacks of madness to his eventual suicide. The nursery tale of the Sandman who tears out children's eyes, the terror Nathanael experiences when the lawyer Coppelius threatens his own eyes, the death of Nathanael's father— these early experiences, and their subsequent reprise in slightly altered forms, with Coppola the optician standing in for Coppelius—these are the elements that Freud strings together with a minimum of interpretive comment, in the interest of showing that what is uncanny about the story is, as he puts it, "directly attached to the figure of the Sandman, that is, to the idea of being robbed of one's eyes." E. Jentsch, the psychologist whose 1906 article may have drawn Freud's attention to "The Sandman," had located the source of the uncanny in effects of intellectual uncertainty—doubts whether apparently inanimate beings are really alive, for example— but Freud is insistent in rejecting this notion. He grants that a kind of uncertainty is created in the reader in the opening pages of the story, uncertainty whether he is taken into a real world or a fantastic one of Hoffmann's own creation, but he argues that by the end of the story those doubts have been removed, and one is convinced "that Coppola the optician really is the lawyer Coppelius and thus also the Sandman." In other words, Nathanael's sense that he is "the horrible plaything of dark powers" is, within the fiction of the story, correct. "We are not supposed to be looking on at the products of a madman's imagination," Freud comments sardonically, "behind which we, with the superiority of rational minds, are able to detect the sober truth" (17:230).

And yet Freud's second account of the story, offered in a long and stunningly condensed footnote (17:232–33), is precisely that: the sober truth detected behind the products of a madman's imagination, the latent substructure, or what Freud calls the "original arrangement" of the elements of the story. Here, instead of a line of narrative—the unfolding in time of Nathanael's fate—what Freud presents is a series of repeated structures arranged so as to display the forces within Nathanael's mind that generated them. The child's ambivalence toward his father splits that character into two figures, a loving father who is killed off and the threatening Coppelius who can be blamed for this violence, and this pairing is reproduced later in the characters of Spalanzani (the mechanician who is called the father of the doll Olympia) and Coppola (who destroys the doll). Linked to this is a series of triangular relationships, in which the Sandman blocks Nathanael's attempts at love, first in the form of Coppelius coming between Nathanael and his fiancée Klara, then in the form of Coppola taking Olympia away from Nathanael, finally once again as Coppelius, driving Nathanael to suicide just as he is about to marry Klara. The structures are accounted for dynamically, and the story is taken as illustrating, in Freud's words, "the psychological truth of the situation in which the young man, fixed upon his father by his castration-complex, is incapable of loving a woman." The footnote concludes with a glancing remark about Hoffmann's childhood, but it is clear that Freud is not interested in biographical speculation: indeed, his point is that the castration complex is not peculiar to Hoffmann but is universal, and because of this universality its veiled presence in the story is capable of creating the effect of the uncanny, of something that ought to have remained secret and yet comes to light.

Someone suspicious of psychoanalysis might find these two accounts contradictory, and argue that Freud cannot have it both ways—either the story is about Nathanael's being driven to suicide by an evil external power, the Sandman, or it is about the progressive deterioration of someone "fixated upon his father by his castration-complex"—but Freud would have no difficulty answering this objection. The two accounts, he would say, are linked to each other as latent to manifest, the castration complex generates the fiction of the Sandman; the reader, even when he is most convinced of the reality of the Sandman, indeed especially when he is most convinced, senses as uncanny the imminent return of the repressed.

But a more interesting and, I think, more serious objection can be raised to Freud's reading of Hoffmann, and that is that Freud has overstabilized his first account of the story, that there is, indeed, more cause for doubt and uncertainty as one moves through "The Sandman" than Freud allows. Looking back over his paraphrasing of the story we can see one way in which this overstabilization has been accomplished. Freud retells the story, occasionally quoting from the text, but what is remarkable is that everything he includes within quotation marks has already appeared within quotation marks in "The Sandman": that is, he quotes nothing but dialogue, things already said by Nathanael or by some other character; the words of the narrator have completely disappeared, replaced by Freud's own, and we have the illusion of watching Nathanael's actions through a medium considerably more transparent than Hoffmann's text. For Hoffmann's narrative is anything but unobtrusive: it is, rather, vivid, shifty, and extravagant, full of assonance, verbal repetitions, literary allusions, and startling changes in the pace, the mood, and the quasi-musical dynamics of its unfolding. What is more, this narrative exuberance is, at certain moments, rendered thematically important within the story in ways that make Freud's decision to set it aside seem more puzzling. For it may be that what is unsettling, if not uncanny, about "The Sandman" is as much a function of its surface as of the depths it conceals.

Consider one such moment where narrative technique and thematic concerns are intertwined, a moment about which Freud has nothing to say. "The Sandman" opens as if it were going to be an epistolary novel: without introduction or interspersed commentary, we are offered the three letters headed simply "Nathanael to Lothar," "Klara to Nathanael," "Nathanael to Lothar."[7] It is in the first of these that Nathanael describes his "dark forebodings of . . . impending doom," then interrupts himself to exclaim: "Oh, my dearest Lothar, how can I begin to make you realize, even vaguely, that what happened a few days ago really could have so fatal and disruptive an effect on my life? If you were here you could see for yourself; but now you will certainly think I am a crazy man who sees ghosts . . ." (p. 137). The letter then goes on at length, describing his childhood, his terror of the Sandman, the death of his father, and his certainty at having recognized in Coppola his father's murderer, Coppelius. Two shorter letters are exchanged, then there is a slight spacing of the printed text, and a narrator emerges:

> Gentle reader, nothing can be imagined that is stranger and more extraordinary than the fate which befell my poor friend, the young student Nathanael, which I have undertaken to relate to you. Have you, gentle reader, ever experienced anything that totally possessed your heart, your thoughts and your senses to the exclusion of all else? Everything seethed and roiled within you; heated blood surged through your veins and inflamed your cheeks. Your gaze was peculiar, as if seeking forms in empty space invisible to other eyes, and speech dissolved into gloomy sighs. Then your friends asked you "What is it, dear friend? What is the matter?" And wishing to describe the picture in your mind with all its vivid colors, the light and the shade, you struggle vainly to find words. But it seemed to you that you had to gather together all that had occurred—the wonderful, the magnificent, the heinous, the joyous, the ghastly—and express it in the very first word so that it would strike like lightning. Yet every word, everything within the realm of speech, seemed colorless, frigid, dead. [p. 148]

Somewhere along the way, the gentle reader is likely to realize that the torment he is being asked to imagine is not that of Nathanael, though it sounds so much like it, but rather that of the narrator faced with the problem of retelling Nathanael's story. Or, more specifically, faced with that classic problem of the Romantic writer: how to begin. On the next page the narrator mentions some possible opening lines he had tried and rejected, then adds: "There were no words I could find which were appropriate to describe, even in the most feeble way, the brilliant colors of my inner vision. I resolved not to begin at all. So, gentle reader, do accept the three letters, which my friend Lothar has been kind enough to communicate, as the outline of the picture to which I will endeavor to add ever more color as I continue the story" (p. 149).

The point is not that a narrative persona is being elaborated with a character or "point of view" of his own—that would not be very interesting if it were the case, and it is not the case here; nor is it simply that Hoffmann is a supple and entertaining virtuoso of narrative. Rather, his virtuosity is productive of certain very specific and interesting effects, two of which I would like to examine in more detail.

To begin with, consider the structure of the story: Hoffmann's feint in the direction of epistolary fiction confers an odd status on those three opening letters. Like any supposedly documentary evidence embedded in a narrative, a greater degree of authenticity seems to be claimed for them, and the reader is inclined to go along with the illusion and accept them as underwriting the narrator's account. That would be so wherever the letters were placed; as it is, though, because the letters precede the appearance of the narrator, what he says of them has the effect of requiring the reader to make a funny retroactive adjustment, granting them a kind of documentary reality just as he is most strongly reminded both of their fictitiousness and, more important, of how badly the narrator seems to need them to initiate and impel his own writing. The effect is playful but nonetheless complex: in fact, its particular structural complexity—a temporal lag which produces, retroactively, a situation in which a text cannot be characterized as unequivocally "real" or unequivocally "fictitious"—is remarkably close to that of Freud's own notion of the workings of what he termed *Nachträglichkeit* ("deferred action") in conferring meaning and pathogenic power on infantile experiences and fantasies.[8] Nor is it simply the temporal structure of the opening pages of "The Sandman" that seems Freudian *avant la lettre*. The content of Nathanael's first letter—his account of the quasi-castration at the hands of Coppelius and of the subsequent trauma of his father's death—is precisely the sort of childhood material with which Freud's concept of *Nachträglichkeit* was concerned.

But here an important difference is worth remarking. Freud looks to Nathanael's story—as it is presented in his letters—for the signs of his having revised an early traumatic experience, recasting it in the form of a primal scene and drawing it out into an explanatory narrative. The differences he discerns are between a hypothetical early version—some experience (real or fantasmatic) taken in by the child but numbly unassimilated at the time and hence unspeakable—and its subsequent expression in a reassuring, if lurid, form. The forces at play are a complex of Nathanael's wishes (for instance, his "death-wish against the father") that are repressed only to resurface, transformed and acceptably disguised in Nathanael's prose (for example, Coppelius' murder of the father). But while Hoffmann's story could offer Freud material for just such an account of the workings of *Nachträglichkeit,* it also adds an instance of its own of a similar revisionary process, one that is not so easily aligned with Freud's intrapsychic model. When the narrator retroactively produces Nathanael's letters, it is *his* ambivalent desire, not Nathanael's, that is being momentarily displayed: and, I should add, only momentarily, for a reader's interest in the narrator is allowed to fade rapidly; the rest of the story is recounted with practically no traces of his comically anguished self-consciousness. But for the length of the several paragraphs in which the narrator's desire to write occupies our attention, we are obliged to consider a compulsion that has been slightly dislocated, for it seems to be neither exactly exterior and demonic (in the sense that Nathanael imagines himself to be "the horrible plaything of dark powers") nor exactly inner and psychological (in the sense that Klara intends when she reassures Nathanael that "if there is a dark power . . . . it must form inside us, form part of us, must be identical with ourselves"), but something else again.

This is not the only point in "The Sandman" where one is teased with the likeness between the unfolding of Nathanael's fate and the elaboration of a narrative, between the forces driving Nathanael and whatever is impelling the narrator. A similar effect is created by Hoffmann's choice and manipulation of diction. The story consistently presents the pathos (and, almost as often, the comedy) of the psychological/demonic in language that draws on the vocabulary and topics of Romantic aesthetics. It is as if Hoffmann had begun with the commonplace equation of poets, lovers, and madmen, and then clustered together fragmentary versions of that analogy so that the semantic overlapping and sheer accumulation of instances would dazzle his readers, as Nathanael is dazzled by Coppola's display of eyeglasses: "Myriad eyes peered and blinked and stared up at Nathanael, who could not look away from the table, while Coppola continued putting down more and more eyeglasses; and flaming glances criss-crossed each other ever more wildly and shot their blood-red rays into Nathanael's breast" (p. 156).

If we are curious about the effect of such effects, there is no better place to start than with that image of the blood-red rays that shoot into Nathanael's breast: it turns out to be an element in a long series that includes the glowing grains of coal that Coppelius threatens to sprinkle on Nathanael's eyes, the "rays of the mysterious" that can't find their way into Klara's cold heart, that "very first word" that the narrator hoped would "strike like lightning," the music that flows into Klara's admirers when they look at her, penetrating them "to the very soul," Olympia's voice as she sings, that scorches Nathanael to *his* very soul, the bloody eyes that Spalanzani flings at Nathanael's breast, and so on. And this series itself is linked to another, one based on a combination of two aesthetic motifs—the conventional analogy between poetry and painting, and the linking of communication and perception to inscribing or imprinting: to convey in warm and penetrating language is to find words that color in the outlines. That was the narrator's hope in the passage I quoted above: the three authentic letters will serve as the "outline of the picture" to which he will "add ever more color" as the story goes on; it is linked to the mock-allegorical description of Klara in terms of paintings by Battoni and Ruisdael; to the fading of the colors in Nathanael's mental image of Coppelius; to Nathanael's contradictory insistence, earlier in the story, that the image of Coppelius was permanently imprinted on his memory; as well as to a similar play between the vividness and permanence of Nathanael's image of Klara and its subsequent fading when he falls in love with Olympia.

The images and allusions that go to make up these series occur often enough and in sufficiently different tonalities—lyrical, melo-dramatic, ironic, and more—so that their most immediate effect is to create the sense of excess I mentioned, felt sometimes as fatefully enigmatic and burdensome, sometimes as the token of the story-teller's exuberant virtuosity. But this appearance of compulsive or haphazard plurality is slightly misleading, for the series is organized in other ways as well, so as to produce a particular configuration of the themes of power, duration, and what could be called the desire for representation. Briefly we could say that the interaction of any pair of characters in "The Sandman" is figured less as an exchange of meaningful signs (conversation, gestures, letters, and so on) than as a passage of energy between them, sometimes benign, sometimes baneful (warm glances, penetrating words, scorching missiles) and that the effectiveness of such "communication" ought to be measurable by its power to leave a lasting mark. If we take this as a characteristically Gothic rendering of experience, we can see that Hoffmann has complicated this model in at least four respects. (1) He offers conflicting accounts of the source of energy that circulates throughout the story, impelling characters into action or expression: is it a creation of the self, or does it come beaming in from some exterior point? Is the tale psychological or demonic? (2) He insists now on the lasting colors or inscriptions left by these exchanges of energy, now on the odd impermanence of those same marks. (3) He blurs the boundaries between the fields where such marking goes on, the fields of action and expression, of primary event and subsequent representation. And (4) he links the wish to make a mark, the wish for the power to produce durable representations, to the uncertainties generated by (1), (2), and (3). For example, the fading of "the ugly image of Coppelius" in Nathanael's imagination leads him "to make his gloomy presentiment that Coppelius would destroy his happiness the subject of a poem." As a result of Hoffmann's manipulations a reader is made to feel, confusedly, that Nathanael's life, his writings, the narrator's story-telling, Hoffmann's writing and the reader's own fascinated acquiescence in it, are all impelled by the same energy, and impelled precisely, to represent that energy, to color its barely discerned outlines, to oblige it, if possible, to leave an unfading mark. Nathanael's letters, of course, qualify as such an attempt on his part, but the poem I have just alluded to is a still more condensed instance of this desire for representation. It is an episode which is best approached once again by way of Freud's reading of the story.

At the story's end, when Nathanael, in a frenzy, is about to leap from a tower to his death, he is heard shrieking, "Ring of fire! Whirl about!" This is one of the passages Freud quotes, adding that these are "words whose origin we know" (17:229). He is alluding to his own retelling of an earlier episode: "Nathanael succumbs to a fresh attack of madness, and in his delirium his recollection of his father's death is mingled with this new experience. He cries, 'Faster—faster—faster—rings of fire—rings of fire—Whirl about— rings of fire—round and round! . . .'" That is, Freud is tracing the origins of these words from the suicide scene back through the earlier moment of Nathanael's madness to the initiating childhood trauma. But, oddly enough, if we look back to those early scenes for the "ring of fire" (the expression translates the word *Feuerkreis* —an unusual one in German) we find none. There is certainly fire, and a sort of semicircular hearth where Nathanael is tormented, but no *Feuerkreis*. The origin of the word turns out to be elsewhere, in a passage Freud ignores, the poem Nathanael composes and reads to Klara:

> Finally it occurred to him to make his gloomy presentiment that Coppelius would destroy his happiness the subject of a poem. He portrayed himself and Klara as united in true love but plagued by some dark hand that occasionally intruded into their lives, snatching away incipient joy. Finally, as they stood at the altar, the sinister Coppelius appeared and touched Klara's lovely eyes, which sprang into Nathanael's own breast, burning and scorching like bleeding sparks. Then Coppelius grabbed him and flung him into a blazing circle of fire which spun around with the speed of a whirlwind and, with a rush, carried him away. The awesome noise was like a hurricane furiously whipping up the waves so that they rose up like white-headed black giants in a raging inferno. But through this savage tumult he could hear Klara's voice:"Can't you see me, dear one? Coppelius has deceived you. That which burned in your breast was not my eyes. Those were fiery drops of your own heart's blood. Look at me. I have still got my own eyes." Nathanael thought: "It is Klara: I am hers forever." Then, it was as though this thought had grasped the fiery circle and forced it to stop turning, while the raging noise died away in the black abyss. Nathanael looked into Klara's eyes; but it was death that, with Klara's eyes, looked upon him kindly. While Nathanael was composing his poem he was very calm and serene; he reworked and polished every line and, since he had fettered himself with meter, he did not pause until everything in the poem was perfect and

euphonious. But when it was finally completed and he read the poem aloud to himself, he was stricken with fear and a wild horror and he cried out "Whose horrible voice is this?" Soon, however, he once more came to understand that it was really nothing more than a very successful poem. [pp. 152–53]

There is no term in English for what French critics call a *mise en abyme*—a casting into the abyss—but the effect itself is familiar enough: an illusion of infinite regress can be created by a writer or painter by incorporating within his own work a work that duplicates in miniature the larger structure, setting up an apparently unending metonymic series. This *mise en abyme* simulates wildly uncontrollable repetition, and it is just that, I believe, that is imaged here in the whirling *Feuerkreis,* carrying Nathanael into the black abyss. Earlier in the story, the narrator had dreamed of creating images whose coloring was so deep and intense that "the multifarious crowd of living shapes" would sweep his audience away until they saw themselves in the midst of the scene that had issued from his soul. The *Feuerkreis* in Nathanael's poem is the demonic complement to the narrator's literary ambitions—and not only the narrator's: the unobtrusive fluidity with which Hoffmann's prose sweeps the reader into the scene (although not into the text) of Nathanael's poem ("He portrayed himself . . .") and then out again ("Nathanael looked into Klara's eyes; but it was death that, with Klara's eyes, looked upon him kindly. While Nathanael was composing his poem . . .") sets up an indeterminate play between Coppelius' victim and someone expressing a grandiose wish for rhetorical power, for a power that would capture and represent the energies figured in the *Feuerkreis* itself.[9]

The poem, then—more accurately, the prose that stands in for the poem—demands to be read in two quite different ways. One, which I have referred to as the psychological/demonic, is entirely compatible with Freud's reading of the story as a whole, and in this respect his choosing to ignore the poem is unimportant: it could be easily enough assimilated to his description of both the manifest and the latent structure of the story. The Oedipal anxiety associated with Coppelius, the allusions to bleeding eyes, the final image of Klara as death—Freud could explain all these elements and string the episode onto the narrative thread he constructs leading from Nathanael's childhood to his suicide. In another reading, however, a reading I shall label—somewhat willfully—the literary, the poem resists any attempts to situate it in the temporal structures implicit in either of Freud's accounts (that is, in either the fantastic sequential narrative of Nathanael's being driven to his death by the Sandman, or in its psychoanalytic reconstruction as the story of Nathanael's progressive insanity). In this literary reading, Nathanael's writings about his fate—his letters, his poem—are linked to the fading of the image of Coppelius, to the narrator's impulsive wish to tell Nathanael's story and, beyond this, to Hoffmann's own work on "The Sandman." But these instances cannot be organized chronologically or in any genetic fashion— only in a banal metaphor can we speak of Hoffmann as Nathanael's "father" (though we can properly, in Freud's scheme, speak of Coppelius as a figure of the father), and just as the question of Oedipal priority no longer applies, so the possibility of seeing in Nathanael's writing about himself an example of narcissistic regression (a diagnosis applicable, within Freud's framework, to his falling in love with Olympia) is equally irrelevant. My point is not that Freud's reading should yield to this other scheme, but rather that a sign of the story's power—what makes it an instance of Romantic irony at its most unsettling or, if you like, of the uncanny—is its availability to both these schemes, its shifting between the registers of the psychological/demonic and the literary, thereby dramatizing the differences as well as the complicities between the two.[10] When Freud turns aside from these more literary aspects of the story he is making a legitimate interpretive move, but it has the effect of domesticating the story precisely by emphasizing its dark, demonic side.

III

The professor of poetry and rhetoric took a pinch of snuff, snapped the lid shut, cleared his throat, and solemnly declared: "Most honorable ladies and gentlemen, do you not see the point of it all? It is all an allegory, an extended metaphor."

113

But many honorable gentlemen were not reassured by this. The story of
the automaton had very deeply impressed them, and a horrible distrust of
human figures in general arose.

—Narrator of "The Sandman"

The claims I have been making for Hoffmann's well-known lev-
ity and extravagance may seem beside the point, and I can imagine
someone objecting to my characterizing those aspects of the
story—its rhetorical range, its shifting narrative modes and frame-
works—as "unsettling." They may indeed produce a sort of pleasurable dizziness, like a roller-coaster ride, but surely their effects
are not of the same order of emotional seriousness as what Freud's
analysis disclosed? So the objection might run: Hoffmann's bizarre
playfulness would seem considerably less important than "the
theme of the Sandman who tears out children's eyes," a theme,
as Freud pointed out, that draws its intensity from the "peculiarly violent and obscure emotion" excited by the "threat of being
castrated." Given that intensity, given the concealed power of
that threat, does the counteremphasis I have been placing on "The
Sandman" as literature represent a serious qualification of Freud's
critique?

I would like to meet that objection, and take up the question of
emotional seriousness, in a roundabout way, by first setting another narrative down in juxtaposition with "The Sandman" and
with Freud's retelling of it. What I shall offer is a summary of a
book by Paul Roazen, published several years ago, called *Brother
Animal: The Story of Freud and Tausk*,[11] an account of Freud's relationship with one of his followers. Roazen's book has provoked a
good deal of criticism, much of it justifiable: his analysis of his
material is sometimes naïve, and his writing is often thin and overexcited (he is given to saying things like "These three brilliant
people were playing with human dynamite"). But the book's documentation seems to have been done carefully, and it is possible to
verify the accuracy of much of his material in other collections of
letters and journals.[12] Roazen's story is of interest here for two
reasons: first, its dénouement takes place during the early months
of 1919, just before Freud set to work on *Beyond the Pleasure Princi-*

114

ple and "The Uncanny," and, second, because, although Roazen never alludes to Hoffmann's story, his own tale comes out sounding remarkably like it, with Tausk playing the part of Nathanael and Freud in the role of the Sandman. The story goes like this:

In 1912, Lou Andreas-Salomé, the friend of Nietzsche and of Rilke, came to Vienna to learn about psychoanalysis. Freud seems to have welcomed her into his circle, which by then included Victor Tausk, whom she was to characterize as both the most loyal and the most intellectually impressive of Freud's disciples. She was invited to attend what had become the traditional Wednesday meetings of the Psychoanalytic Society and to sit in on Freud's and Tausk's courses of lectures. The journal she kept that year—partly gossip, partly recorded discussions, public and private, about psychoanalytic theory—has been published, along with her correspondence with Freud. From this material Roazen has been able to postulate, convincingly I think, a triangular relationship among Freud, Tausk, and Lou Salomé. Her journals record long conversations with Tausk, and their editor takes it as common knowledge that she became his mistress for some months; they also record talks with Freud about what the two of them came to refer to as "the Tausk-problem," that is, about Tausk's complicated feelings of rivalry with Freud and Freud's reciprocal uneasiness. Toward the end of the following summer there is a long journal entry analyzing Tausk's character, seeing him as repetitively placing himself in the role of the thwarted son vis-à-vis Freud, and, "as if by thought-trans-ference . . . always busy with the same thing as Freud, never taking one step aside to make room for himself" (pp. 166–67).

Roazen's next focal point is the winter of 1918–19, when Tausk, after serving in the army and managing, nevertheless, to write a number of psychoanalytic papers, had returned to Vienna. He asked Freud to take him on as a patient but Freud refused; instead Tausk entered analysis with a younger and less distinguished col-league, Helene Deutsch, who was already, as it happened, several months into her own training analysis with Freud. Roazen's recent interviews with Deutsch convinced him that Freud's motives for refusing Tausk were bound up with fears of plagiarism: Freud spoke of Tausk's making an "uncanny" impression on him, of the impossible complications that would result if Tausk became his patient, for he (Tausk) would be likely to imagine that ideas he had picked up in his hours with Freud were actually his own, and so on. Roazen is rather incautiously willing to attribute motives, but, whatever Freud's motives, Roazen is right to see this newly constituted pattern—of Tausk spending five hours a week with Deutsch while Deutsch was engaged in a similarly intensive analysis with Freud—as a repetition of the earlier triangle, with Deutsch this time substituted for Lou Andreas-Salomé.

This arrangement lasted for about three months; then (again according to Deutsch) the analytic hours began to interpenetrate— Tausk would talk to her mostly about Freud and she, in turn, found herself drawn into talking more and more about Tausk to Freud. Freud finally (in March 1919) moved to break out of the triangle, insisting that Deutsch choose between continuing as his patient or continuing as Tausk's analyst. Roazen interprets this as coercive, no choice at all, given what Freud knew to be Deutsch's investment in her work with him. However that may have been, Tausk's analysis was terminated immediately. Three months later, on the eve of his marriage, he killed himself, leaving a note for Freud full of expressions of gratitude and respect.

Roazen's story may not be as well told as Hoffmann's, but it exercises some of the same lurid fascination and holds out some of the same teasingly uncertain possibilities for interpretation, all the more so when one considers the number of ways the story is intertwined chronologically and thematically with what we know to have been Freud's theoretical concerns in 1919. Roazen speculates on the coincidence of Tausk's suicide (in July) and Freud's "simultaneous . . . explicit postulation of an instinct of primitive destructiveness." As he points out, the letter in which Freud reports Tausk's death to Lou Salomé is also the letter in which he mentions the "theme of death" and writes of having "stumbled on a remarkable notion based on my theory of the instincts"—"the very same letter," as Roazen characteristically writes; and if we would dissociate ourselves from that particular tone, it is less easy to deny the feeling of being intrigued that underlies it. "Could Tausk have been acting out Freud's newest, or even just barely burgeoning, idea?"

Roazen asks. "Or perhaps the notion of a death instinct represented another way for Freud to deny any responsibility for Tausk's suicide?" (p. 143). Well, we know the notion of a death instinct represents considerably more than that in the economy of Freud's thought, and we may find it easier, at this point, to pull free: there is nothing like a reductive interpretation to break the spell of a fascinating anecdote. But let me invoke that spell once more, this time with another series of apparent coincidences, which I think can lead to some more interesting conclusions.

Freud's removing himself from a triangular relation with Tausk and Deutsch (for whatever reasons, with whatever motives) coincides with his beginning work on the first draft of *Beyond the Pleasure Principle,* that is, on the text in which he first formulates a puzzling theory of repetition. In the interval between the conception of that theory and its working-out in terms of the death instinct, he turns back to a manuscript on the uncanny and rewrites it, proposing "the discovery that whatever reminds us of this inner repetition-compulsion is perceived as uncanny," and delineating, as an instance of the activity of that compulsion, a sequence of triangular relations in "The Sandman"—*Coppelius/Nathanael/Klara* followed by its parodic repetition *Coppola/Nathanael/Olympia.* Here again, one may begin to feel the pull of the interpreter's temptation: can we superimpose Roazen's sequence of triangles *(Freud/ Tausk/Salomé, Freud/Tausk/Deutsch)* on Freud's? And if we think we can—or wish we could—what then? Can we make a story out of it? Might we not feel "most strongly compelled" to do so, to arrange these elements in temporal and causal sequences? For example, could we say that the theory of repetition Freud worked out in March 1919 followed close upon—was a consequence of—his realization that he was once again caught in a certain relationship to Tausk? Could we add that Freud was bound to perceive that relation as uncanny—not quite literary, but no longer quite real, either, the workings of the compulsion glimpsed "through" an awareness of something-being-repeated? Could we go on to suggest that it was this experience of a repetitive triangular relationship that underwrites his analysis of "The Sandman" in May? That is, that the glimpse of his relationship to Tausk has the same "documentary" status vis-à-vis Freud's retelling of "The Sandman" that Nathanael's letters have for Hoffmann's narrator, that it serves as both a source of energy and a quasi-fictional pretext for writing? Suppose this were the story one put together. Mightn't one then, like Nathanael crying out "Whose voice is this?" after he had finished his poem, still feel impelled to ask: *Whose story is this?* Is it one's own? Is it Roazen's? Is it Hoffmann's? Is it *The Story of Freud and Tausk* "as told to" Paul Roazen, chiefly by Helene Deutsch?

To the degree that such questions still solicit us and still resist solution, we are kept in a state somewhere between "emotional seriousness" and literary forepleasure, conscious of vacillating between literature and "nonfiction," our sense of repetition-at-work colored in with the lurid shades of aggression, madness, and violent death. At such moments we can say we are experiencing the uncanny; we might just as well say we are puzzled by a question of literary priority.

IV

I am not fond of reading.

—Freud to Lou Andreas-Salomé

I invented psychoanalysis because it had no literature.

—Freud to Helene Deutsch

The Anxiety of Influence: when Roazen describes the tensions between Freud and Tausk as generated by fears of plagiarism, he takes his place among an increasing number of American critics who put Freud's Oedipal model to work accounting for the relations among writers. There is evidence enough in Freud's own texts to suggest that he was not immune to such anxieties. At the beginning of "The Uncanny," for example, he apologetically introduces what he calls "this present modest contribution of mine," confessing that he could not—because of the restrictions imposed on him by the war—make "a very thorough examination of the bibliography, especially the foreign literature" (17:219–29) so that, he goes on, his "paper is presented to the reader without any claim of priority." *Beyond the Pleasure Principle*, too, opens with a firm announcement that "priority and originality are not among the aims that psycho-analysis sets itself" (18:7), but some sixty pages later we come across a qualm about originality expressed at an intriguing point in the argument, and in an odd verbal formula. Freud is about to move from his discussion of the compulsion to repeat to a concept he hopes will help explain its relation to the rest of his theory, the concept of the death instinct, and he begins his paragraph with a question: "But how is the predicate of being instinctual related to the compulsion to repeat?" He then produces, italicized for emphasis, a preliminary statement: "*It seems that an instinct is an urge inherent in organic life to restore an earlier state of things*," a sentence to which he appends the following footnote: "I have no doubt that similar notions as to the nature of the 'instincts' have already been put forward repeatedly" (18:36). It is the word "repeatedly" that is striking; here the twinge about priority seems in some relation to Freud's subject matter: it is as if, at the very moment of grounding the repetition compulsion in a theory he hoped would have biological validity, he was drawn to gesture once more to the ungroundable nature of repetition.[12]

A similar instance can be found in the case history of the "Wolf Man," where Freud again is engaged with questions of origins and their subsequent rehearsals. This time what is at stake is the degree of reality to be attributed to the primal scene and the limit of the effects of *Nachträglichkeit* in constituting, retroactively, that scene's importance and meaning. Freud had revised his first draft of the case so as to counter the rival claims of Jung and Adler, and, after arguing his own reconsidered position carefully and at length, he adds this testy footnote:

> I admit that this is the most ticklish question in the whole domain of psychoanalysis. I did not require the contributions of Adler and Jung to induce me to consider the matter with a critical eye, and to bear in mind the possibility that what analysis puts forward as being forgotten experiences of childhood (and of improbably early childhood) may on the contrary be based upon phantasies brought about upon occasions occurring late in life . . . . On the contrary,

no doubt has troubled me more; no other uncertainty has been more decisive in holding me back from publishing my conclusions. I was the first—a point to which none of my opponents have referred—to recognize the part played by phantasies in symptom formation and also the phantasying-back of late impressions into childhood and their sexualization after the event. (see *Traumdeutung*, First Edition, 1900 . . . and "Notes upon a Case of Obsessional Neurosis," 1908) [17:103]

Whatever anxiety Freud may be imagined to have felt about his own originality, then, may not be exactly illusory, but displaced. These passages suggest that more fundamental "doubts" and "uncertainties"—doubts about the grasp any figurative language has on first principles, especially when the principles include a principle of repetition—may be at work generating the anxiety that is then acted out in the register of literary priority. The specificity of that range of wishes and fears—the wish to be original, the fear of plagiarizing or of being plagiarized—would act to structure and render more manageable, in however melodramatic a fashion, the more indeterminate affect associated with repetition, marking or coloring it, conferring "visibility" on the forces of repetition and at the same time disguising the activity of those forces from the subject himself.

But here, I think, I should turn back to the doubts I mentioned earlier, doubts about the appropriateness of the compound analogy I proposed between that-which-is-repeated, coloring matter, and figurative language. All three, I suggested, could be thought of as means of representing processes and energies that might otherwise go unnoticed. But this model seems unsatisfactory and wishful in at least two ways. First, it depends upon the notion of a real preexistent force (call it sheer repetition, the death instinct, or whatever) that is merely rendered more *discernible* by that-which-is-repeated, or by the lurid colors of the erotic, or by some helpful figure of speech; and, it suggests that the workings of figurative language (like acting-out or coloring-in) do indeed have the effect of rendering that force "visible." But we know that the relation between figurative language and what it figures cannot be adequately grasped in metaphors of vision; and we might well doubt that the forces of repetition can be isolated—even ideally—from that-which-is-repeated. The wishfulness inherent in the model is not simply in its isolating the *forces* of repetition from their representations, but in its seeking to isolate the *question* of repetition from the question of figurative language itself. But suppose, as Gilles Deleuze has suggested,[14] that implicit in Freud's theory of repetition is the discovery that these two questions are impossible to disentangle, that in trying to come to terms with the repetition compulsion one discovers that the irreducible figurativeness of one's language is indistinguishable from the ungrounded and apparently inexplicable notion of the compulsion itself. At such moments the wish to put aside the question of figurative language might assert itself as a counterforce to one's most powerful apprehension of the compulsion to repeat, and it might take the form it does in Freud's reading of "The Sandman," the form of a wish to find "no literature" there.

7.
DORA'S SECRETS, FREUD'S TECHNIQUES

IMAGINE AN older man intrigued by the following story: a young girl is drawn—perhaps in all innocence,
perhaps in frightened or even fascinated complicity—into an adult,
adulterous sexual tangle involving her father and an Other Woman,
a woman she had come to trust. How would this play itself out?
How would the daughter's observations and principles make themselves felt? How would she bear the burden of her knowledge?
What would that knowledge do to her? Add to this set of questions
another set, of equal interest to the older man: How can this story
be told? Who can tell it? Can the daughter tell it unaided? Or must
her account be supplemented and revised by a more informed, a
more articulate, adult consciousness? And if it is so supplemented,
how can the adult be sure he is getting the story straight, setting it
down in unadulterated form? That is, how can he be sure that his
telling of the story isn't itself a further violation of the young girl's
integrity?

I have been paraphrasing bits of Henry James's preface to *What
Maisie Knew,* but paraphrasing rather selectively, blurring the considerable differences between Maisie's story and Dora's, so as to
dwell on the ways the two stories, and the concerns of their authors, overlap. James and Freud alike anticipate being reproached
for the nature of the stories they have to tell and for the manner of
the telling. And both meet these imagined reproaches in ways that

suggest that the two faults might be one, that they run the risk of being accused of a perverse and distasteful confusion, of not striking the right balance between the child's world and the adult's. There is, to begin with, the possibility that each is gratuitously dragging his heroine into more sordid knowledge than girls of her age need to come to terms with. Here is James:

> Of course . . . I was punctually to have had read to me the lesson that the "mixing-up" of a child with anything unpleasant confessed itself an aggravation of the unpleasantness, and that nothing could well be more disgusting than to attribute to Maisie so intimate an "acquaintance" with the gross immoralities surrounding her.[1]

and Freud, answering a similar charge:

> There is never any danger of corrupting an inexperienced girl. For where there is no knowledge of sexual processes even in the unconscious, no hysterical symptoms will arise; and where hysteria is found there can no longer be any question of "innocence of mind" in the sense in which parents and educators use the phrase.[2]

Furthermore, there is the possibility that both authors are (in dangerous and, it is hinted, somehow self-serving ways) imposing not experience but language on the less sophisticated consciousness of the child. Freud meets this charge with a familiar distinction: "With the exercise of a little caution all that is done is to translate into conscious ideas what was already known in the unconscious" (p. 66). James too imagines himself chiefly as his heroine's interpreter and, like Freud, assumes that there is some fund of knowledge there not immediately accessible but peculiarly worth the effort of translation:

> Small children have many more perceptions than they have terms to translate them; their vision is at any moment much richer, their apprehension even constantly stronger, than their prompt, their at all producible vocabulary. Amusing therefore as it might at the first blush have seemed to restrict myself in this case to the experience, it became at once plain that such an attempt would fail. Maisie's terms accordingly play their part—since her simpler con-

clusions quite depend on them; but our own commentary constantly attends and amplifies. This it is that on occasion, doubtless, seems to represent us as going so "behind" the facts of her spectacle as to exaggerate the activity of her relation to them. The difference here is but of a shade: it is her relation, her activity of spirit, that determines all our own concern—we simply take advantage of those things better than she herself. Only, even though it is her interest that mainly makes matters interesting for us, we inevitably note this in figures that are not yet at her command and that are nevertheless required whenever those aspects about her and those parts of her experience that she understands darken off into others that she rather tormentedly misses. [Preface, p. 146]

Just here our analogy may begin to show signs of strain, however. Freud is writing about translating "what was already known in the unconscious" of a young patient whose mind was by no means an open book; James, on the other hand, is Maisie's creator: how can he pretend that anything impedes his knowing the contents of her mind? We may think we know what he means: Maisie may be a fiction, but children are real, and relatively opaque to adult inspection. Some distance is inevitable, some interpretative effort required. But as James goes on to write of Maisie, in sentences which exhibit that odd dexterity that allows a novelist to speak of his characters almost in the same breath as both products of his imagination and autonomous beings, we sense that James's interest in Maisie is not simply that of a mimetic artist challenging himself to produce a tour de force of accuracy. The note of admiration we catch in the preface suggests that whatever it is that Maisie knew, James envies that knowledge and sets a peculiarly high value on it. His own language darkens with hints of mourning, then glows in intense pastoral identification, when he speaks of her:

> Successfully to resist (to resist, that is, the strain of observation and the assault of experience) what would that be, on the part of so young a person, but to remain fresh, and still fresh, and to have even a freshness to communicate?—the case being with Maisie to the end that she treats her friends to the rich little spectacle of objects embalmed in her wonder. She wonders, in other words, to the end, to the death—the death of her childhood, properly speaking. . . . She is not only the extraordinary "ironic centre" I have

already noted; she has the wonderful importance of shedding a light far beyond any reach of her comprehension; of lending to poorer persons and things, by the mere fact of their being involved with her and by the special scale she creates for them, a precious element of dignity. I lose myself, truly, in appreciation of my theme on noting what she does by her "freshness" for appearances in themselves vulgar and empty enough. They become, as she deals with them, the stuff of poetry and tragedy and art; she has simply to wonder, as I say, about them, and they begin to have meanings, aspects, solidities, connexions—connexions with the "universal!"—that they could scarce have hoped for. [Preface, p. 147]

Maisie's "wonder"—and this seems to be its value for James—both illuminates and embalms; she, in turn, remains fresh and yet wonders "to the end, to the death—the death of her childhood." Although the novel concludes with Maisie alive, having weathered "the assault of experience," this strong but fleeting touch of pathos nevertheless suggests a thematics of sacrifice and compensation. The figurative death Maisie is said to endure is made to seem the price paid for the remarkable transforming effects of her wonder, her embalming of what is inherently "vulgar and empty enough" into "the stuff of poetry," that is, into the matter of the novel. *What Maisie Knew*, James seems to be claiming, could not have been written if he hadn't had access to what Maisie in fact knew, and it is she who—at some large but indeterminate cost to herself—somehow made that possible. "I lose myself, truly, in appreciation of my theme on noting what she does by her freshness . . .": the shifting personal pronouns trace the distribution of fond investment here—it is simultaneously beamed at "myself," at "my theme," and at "her." Nor is it clear where one of these agents or sources of value and power leaves off and another begins: James is writing out of a strong identification with a composite idea/theme/character/surrogate/muse. When he speaks of the death of Maisie's childhood, we can take that phrase as gesturing toward her growing up (and out of the world of this particular story) but also as figuring the collapse of that charged distance and equivocal commerce between James and his surrogate that attends the completion of the novel.

We are accustomed to these modes of imaginative identifica-

tion—and to the confusions they give rise to—in considering the
genesis of works of fiction. When we turn to the relation of a
psychoanalyst to his patient, or of the author of a case history to its
central character, we are more prepared to believe that the forms of
phantasmic confusion we are likely to encounter are classifiable as
transferential or countertransferential effects. And indeed much of
the reconsideration of Freud's dealing with Dora—as her therapist
and as the teller of her story—has tended to appraise his work in
these terms. If Freud, as he himself acknowledged, failed to heal
Dora, or if his account of her, what Philip Rieff refers to as his
"brilliant yet barbaric"[3] account of her, failed to get at the truth of
her case, it is usually held to be because he didn't notice, or didn't
give sufficient weight to, the ways in which Dora was burdening
him with feelings about her father, or Herr K., or the governess, or
Frau K.; or he was insufficiently alert to his own erotic or paternal
or eroticopaternal feelings about Dora; or—to extend this allusion
to the countertransference into a sociological dimension—that
Freud's attitudes toward young, unmarried, unhappy women
shared the blindness and exploitative bent of the prevailing patriarchal culture. Each of these accusations can be made to stick; I
shall be taking them for granted and pursuing another line of questioning. Suppose what went wrong between Freud and Dora was
not just a matter of unrecognized transferences (and countertransferences) but also of an unrecognized—or refused—identification? Suppose what Freud missed, or did not wish to see, was not
that he was drawn to (or repelled by) Dora, but that he "was" Dora,
or rather that the question of who was who was more radically
confusing than even nuanced accounts of unacknowledged transferences and countertransferences suggest? Is it possible that one of
the sources of energy and of distortion in the "Fragment of an
Analysis" is to be located here, in the confusion of tongues between
an author and his young surrogate, and that we can find in Freud's
text some of the extravagant tones as well as some of the gestures of
sacrifice and self-location that inform James's writing about Maisie?
We can find them, I believe, but with this telling difference: that the
kind of fancied identification that can be happily, even amusedly
acknowledged by James will represent something more of a threat

to Freud. The "Fragment of an Analysis" exhibits the grounds for such a confusion and the means by which Freud fended it off.

I

A first point of resemblance: neither Dora nor Freud tells all. In Dora's case it would seem to be because she simply can't: how could she either reveal or intentionally conceal secrets she doesn't know she has? As for Freud, he would seem to be consciously, but not willfully, choosing what he will communicate to his readers:

> There is another kind of incompleteness which I myself have intentionally introduced. I have as a rule not reproduced the process of interpretation to which the patient's associations and communications had to be subjected, but only the results of that process. Apart from the dreams, therefore, the technique of the analytic work has been revealed in only a very few places. My object in this case history was to demonstrate the intimate structure of a neurotic disorder and the determination of its symptoms; and it would have led to nothing but hopeless confusion if I had tried to complete the other task at the same time. [p. 27]

This decision not to say much about "the technique of the analytic work," or what he calls elsewhere in the text—and repeatedly, until the word "technique" and its cognates come to seem particularly salient—"psychoanalytic technique," "the technical rules," "the technical work," etc., hardly qualifies as a concealment, once the reasons for such prudence have been so sensibly set forth. Yet as the case history goes on, Freud renews his reminders of what it is he won't talk about, and often in contexts that lend them a puzzling resonance. Here, for example, he is discussing the relation between unconscious sexual fantasies and the production of hysterical symptoms:

> An opportunity very soon occurred for interpreting Dora's nervous cough in this way by means of an imagined sexual situation. She had once again been insisting that Frau K. only loved her father because he was "*ein vermögender Mann*" ["*a man of means*"].

Certain details of the way in which she expressed herself (which I pass over here, like most other purely technical parts of the analysis) led me to see that behind this phrase its opposite lay concealed, namely, that her father was "*ein unvermögender Mann*" ["*a man without means*"]. This could only be meant in a sexual sense—that her father, as a man, was without means, was impotent. Dora confirmed this interpretation from her conscious knowledge: whereupon I pointed out the contradiction she was involved in if on the one hand she continued to insist that her father's relation with Frau K. was a common love-affair, and on the other hand maintained that her father was impotent, or in other words incapable of carrying on an affair of such a kind. Her answer showed that she had no need to admit the contradiction. She knew very well, she said, that there was more than one way of obtaining sexual gratification. (The source of this piece of knowledge, however, was once more untraceable.) I questioned her further, whether she referred to the use of organs other than the genitals for the purpose of sexual intercourse, and she replied in the affirmative. [p. 64]

It is the question of knowledge that makes possible comparisons between doctor and patient here. For the relation between them isn't as asymmetrical as it might be if Dora were suffering from some organic disease. If that were the case, Freud's techniques would be diagnostic procedures of one sort or another, and would in no way resemble Dora's as yet unknown and hence "secret" condition. But Dora's condition is, in fact, her way of living *her* knowledge; a number of secrets lie behind her symptoms, some easier for Freud to get at than others, but all turning on what Dora knew. There is what she can confirm "from her conscious knowledge"—her awareness of male impotence, her knowing "very well" that there are various paths to sexual gratification—as well as secrets more elusive, the "source" of what she knew, for example. Or the relation between what she knows and what she suffers, the complicated set of mediations, phantasmic and physiological, which Freud characterizes as "the intimate structure of a neurotic disorder" (p. 27) or "the finer structure of a neurosis" (p. 26) or "the internal structure of her hysteria" (p. 134). It is in the course of pursuing these connections and uncovering that intimate structure that a further point of resemblance between Freud and his patient

128

becomes noticeable. To pick up where the previous quotation left off:

> she replied in the affirmative. I could then go on to say that in that case she must be thinking of precisely those parts of the body which in her case were in a state of irritation—the throat and the oral cavity. To be sure, she would not hear of going so far as this in recognizing her own thoughts; and indeed, if the occurrence of the symptom was to be made possible at all, it was essential that she should not be completely clear on the subject. But the conclusion was inevitable that with her spasmodic cough, which, as is usual, was referred for its exciting cause to a tickling in her throat, she pictured to herself a scene of sexual gratification *per os* between the two people whose love-affair occupied her mind so incessantly. A very short time after she had tacitly accepted this explanation her cough vanished—which fitted in very well with my view . . . . [p. 65].

Dora's lack of clarity on the relation between her cough and her father's affair is captured in the slight abstraction of the language in which the sexual scenario is presented: "she pictured to herself a scene of sexual gratification *per os.*" As in the fantasy Freud called "A Child Is Being Beaten," in which the fantast can occupy any of three positions—that of the child, that of the person punishing him, or that of an excited onlooker—it isn't clear from this sentence who is gratifying whom, *per* whose *os* the pleasure is being procured, or with whom Dora is identifying. But it isn't clear, either, just who isn't being clear, Dora or Freud. Freud certainly intends to be clear: he will go on to refer to the sexual act as one in which a woman is "sucking on the male organ" (p. 68); he seems convinced that what Dora knows about is *fellatio*. But that isn't immediately obvious: in Jacques Lacan's commentary on the case he remarks, very much in passing, in the course of correcting Freud on Dora's relation to Frau K. and to femininity in general, that, of course, "everyone knows that *cunnilingus* is the artifice most commonly adopted by men of means whose forces are beginning to abandon them."[4] It is hard to guess what Freud would have made of this note of high Parisian *savoir vivre;* whatever everyone else knew, he seems to have taken for granted the more phallic—and phallocentric—option.

But if this is, as Freud's feminist critics have pointed out, a stereotypical prejudice, it is also compact with some other factors in Freud's thinking which engage questions of oral intercourse in the other sense of that term. He next turns, in what appears to be a slight digression but is nonetheless thematically continuous with the previous discussion, to anticipate the "astonishment and horror" a hypothetical "medical reader" may feel on learning that Freud dares "talk about such delicate and unpleasant subjects to a young girl" or that there is a possibility that an "inexperienced girl could know about practices of such a kind and could occupy her imagination with them" (p. 65). There are those, he goes on, "who are scandalized by a therapeutic method in which conversations of this sort occur, and who appear to envy either me or my patients the titillation which, according to their notions, such a method must afford." Earlier, he had anticipated the same objection—specifically that psychoanalytic conversation is "a good means of exciting or gratifying sexual desires" (p. 23), and he had defended himself, as he does here, by insisting that his practice is no more gratifying in this respect than that of a gynecologist. What is thrust aside is the possibility of the doctor's deriving pleasure from these oral exchanges: it is the gynecologist's willed professional anesthesia that is being invoked here:

> The best way of speaking about such things is to be dry and direct; and that is at the same time the method furthest removed from the prurience with which the same subjects are handled in "society," and to which girls and women alike are so thoroughly accustomed. I call bodily organs and processes by their technical names, and I tell these to the patient if they—the names, I mean—happen to be unknown to her. [p. 65]

"Technical" here means, among other things, "unexciting": and if this explanation of Freud's is both honest and convincing, it also has the (unintended) result of aligning his own refusal-of-pleasure with the "internal structure" he has just been describing at work in Dora, the repressive mechanism whereby a distinctly uncomfortable system had been substituted for a possibly pleasurable fantasy. Dora refuses to "know" that when she coughs she is picturing to herself a scene of oral gratification; and Freud has every reason to deny that his own conversations with girls like Dora are titillating. What she secretly represses he subdues through a consciously elaborated professional technique.[5]

II

A psychoanalyst can resemble his patient in eschewing sexual pleasure; on her side, a patient can resemble her psychoanalyst in the intensity with which she pursues secret knowledge—or so, at least, the language of Freud's text would suggest. One of the threads that binds him to Dora reappears with increasing visibility as his narrative goes on: it is the problem (or "puzzle," or "riddle," as he calls it) of *where* she learned what she knew. Still more specifically, whether she learned it "orally" or from a book. Moreover, this question is soon linked to another one, that of Dora's relations with women, what Freud calls her "gynaecophilic" (pp. 81, 142) currents of feeling. For Freud's defense of his own procedures as dry and gynecological is paralleled by his evocation of the slightly unusual term "gynaecophilic" to describe Dora's homoerotic tendencies: it is as if Freud had a strong interest in clearly marking off the separation of the two realms, in keeping *logos* uncontaminated by *philia*—that is, in defusing the erotic content of acts of knowledge. But for the moment, let us follow the way these two strands—one concerned with the sources of Dora's knowledge of sexual matters, the other with the quality of her gynecophilia—become entangled in Freud's account.

There is, first of all, the governess, "an unmarried woman, no longer young, who was well-read and of advanced views" and of whom Freud remarks in a footnote: "For some time I looked upon this woman as the source of all Dora's secret knowledge, and perhaps I was not entirely wrong in this" (p. 52). Perhaps not entirely wrong, but not, to his own satisfaction, entirely correct either. For, in addition to this person "with whom Dora had at first enjoyed the closest interchange of thought" (p. 78), there are others whose effects must be calculated: the "younger of her two cousins" with whom she "had shared all sorts of secrets" (p. 78), and, of course, Frau K., with whom she "had lived for years on a footing of the closest intimacy. . . . There was nothing they had not talked about" (p. 79). As Freud pursues these matters to more or less of a resolution, it may seem that the question of where Dora learned about sex was merely instrumental—a way of getting at more important material about whom Dora loved. Freud reasons that Dora wouldn't have been so vague—so positively amnesiac—about the sources of her knowledge if she weren't trying to protect someone; hence he worries the question of sources so as to press toward a discovery about "object-relations." The process is summarized in his final footnote, which begins, "The longer the interval of time that separates me from the end of this analysis, the more probable it seems to me that the fault in my technique lay in this omission: I failed to discover in time and to inform the patient that her homosexual (gynaecophilic) love for Frau K. was the strongest unconscious current in her mental life. I ought to have guessed that the main source of her knowledge in sexual matters could have been no one but Frau K. . . ." (p. 142). But this note, with its slightly redundant allusion to "gynaecophilia," rehearses interpretations Freud had set down sixty pages earlier, just before he turned to analyse Dora's two dreams. There too he had located Frau K. as both the source of Dora's knowledge and the reason for her forgetfulness, and there too he had concluded that "masculine, or more properly speaking gynaecophilic currents of feelings are to be regarded as typical of the unconscious erotic life of hysterical girls" (p. 81). What has transpired in the intervening sixty pages? To begin with, the close analysis of the two dreams—that is, the demonstration of the particular feature of psychoanalytic technique that had prompted the publication of the case history in the first place. But also, in the course of that demonstration, and always in relation to specific associations—sometimes Dora's, sometimes his own—Freud has continued teasing the material of oral as opposed to written sources, teasing it in ways that seem no longer appropriate, once he had formulated his conclusions about Frau K. on pp. 80–81, and which, moreover, are presented in a condensed, repetitive, and confusing fashion in these later pages. One is led to suspect that, as

Freud would say, "other trains of thought" are operative in fixing his attention on this subject, and it is to them I wish to turn now.

III

Steven Marcus has drawn attention to some passages of bizarre writing in the "Fragment of an Analysis," passages expressing what he calls "fantasies of omniscience . . . where the demon of interpretation is riding [Freud]."[6] They occur as Freud is zeroing in on what he takes to be one of Dora's most closely guarded secrets, her childhood masturbation, and in the immediate context of his confronting her with the meaning of a particular "symptomatic act," her fingering the small reticule she wore at her belt. It is worth following Freud's text closely at this point, attending to both the passages Marcus cites and the page of writing which separates them. Marcus's Exhibit A is this paragraph of fierce boasting, or gloating:

> There is a great deal of symbolism of this kind in life, but as a rule we pass it by without heeding it. When I set myself the task of bringing to light what human beings keep hidden within them, not by the compelling power of hypnosis, but by observing what they say and what they show, I thought the task was a harder one than it really is. He that has eyes to see and ears to hear may convince himself that no mortal can keep a secret. If his lips are silent, he chatters with his finger-tips; betrayal oozes out of him at every pore. And thus the task of making conscious the most hidden recesses of the mind is one which it is quite possible to accomplish. [p. 96]

Though the vehemence of Freud's tone here is certainly produced by the excitement of his work with Dora, the claims he is making are hyperbolically generalized: "no mortal can keep a secret." In the next paragraph he focuses back on Dora again, and on the details of one particular analytic session: he notices Dora concealing a letter as she enters the room—a letter of no special significance, as it turns out—and concludes that she is signaling, ambivalently, her wish to

133

hold onto her secret. He knows, by now, what that secret is, and because he knows it he can offer to explain to her "her antipathy to every new physician." She is afraid, he tells her, that she will be found out, then immediately contemptuous of the doctors "whose perspicacity she had evidently overestimated before." The situation is defined in adversarial terms: Freud sees himself as one more in a line of "new physicians" but he is determined to be the one who vindicates the profession by successfully extracting Dora's secret. The next sentences celebrate that discovery with a paean of intellectual glee:

> The reproaches against her father for having made her ill, together with the self-reproach underlying them, the leucorrhea, the playing with the reticule, the bed-wetting after her sixth year, the secret which she would not allow the physician to tear from her—the circumstantial evidence of her having masturbated in childhood now seems to me complete and without a flaw. [p. 97]

That listing conveys the triumphant scene of wrapping up the package of evidence "complete and without a flaw" (in German, *lückenlos*): this is a moment of exuberant intellectual narcissism, of investment in the beautiful totality of one's imaginative product. As such, it is the equivalent of Henry James's fond exclamation about what he had managed to do with Maisie—or with Maisie's help: "I lose myself, truly, in appreciation of my theme. . . ." But again, with a difference: for if James's excitement has a Pygmalion quality to it—he has fallen in love with his creation, his theme and helpmate—Freud's overflowing fondness can hardly be said to include Dora: if anything, she is diminished by it, thoroughly seen through. Indeed, Freud's ecstasy here might seem totally self-involved, with no other object than his own interpretative achievement, if it weren't for the sentences which follow, sentences Marcus cites as astonishing instances of "the positive presence of demented and delusional science," a gesture of manic documentation and collegial acknowledgment:

> In the present case I had begun to suspect the masturbation when she had told me of her cousin's gastric pains, and had then identified herself with her by complaining for days together of similar

134

painful sensations. It is well known that gastric pains occur especially often in those who masturbate. According to a personal
communication made to me by W. Fliess, it is precisely gastralgias
of this character which can be interrupted by an application of
cocaine to the "gastric spot" discovered by him in the nose, and
which can be cured by the cauterization of the same spot. [p. 97]

We might wish to ask whether that "personal communication" was
made orally or in writing: Marcus reminds us of the powerful
transferential elements at work in Freud's relation to Fliess, and
suggests that "the case of Dora may also be regarded as part of the
process by which Freud began to move toward a resolution of that
relation," a relation Freud himself could later characterize as
charged with homoerotic feeling. For our purposes what is particularly interesting is the sequence of gestures these paragraphs of
Freud's reproduce: the antagonistic, contemptuous pinning down
of Dora's secret (significantly, here, it is the secret of self-affection),
followed by a giddy celebration of that achievement ("Complete
and without a flaw!"), then *that* inherently unstable moment followed by the hyperbolic ("it is *precisely* gastralgias of this type")
and somewhat beside-the-point invocation of a colleague's exper-
tise, with the homoerotic component that such collegial gestures
usually involve here considerably amplified. It is likely that the
intensity of Freud's appeal to Fliess is proportionate to the vigor
with which he is differentiating himself from Dora, his own mode
of knowing from hers; and, by a predictable irony, that intensity
leads Freud into a momentary confusion of persons—of himself
with his colleague—that resembles the uncertain combination of
erotic intimacy and exchanged knowledge that Freud detects in
Dora's gynecophilic friendships.

For when Freud takes up the question of how much of Dora's
knowledge came to her "orally," although he may be primarily
tracking down the erotic relations in which she had unconsciously
overinvested, following the trail that leads to Frau K., he is also
investigating a mode of intercourse that, as we have seen, resembles
the oral exchanges of psychoanalytic conversation. We have remarked on the care Freud takes to defend the innocence of those
exchanges, to insist that, despite their intimate subject matter, they

bring him no "gratification." But we may now suspect that there is
yet a further danger that he must defend against, the possibility not
of sexual misconduct between analyst and patient but of a thoroughgoing epistemological promiscuity, in which the lines would
blur between what Freud knew and what Dora knew and, conse-
quently, in which the status of Freud's knowledge, and of his
professional discourse, would be impugned. In the text of the
"Fragment of an Analysis," that danger is figured as the possibility
of oral sexual intercourse between two women, the scenario—sensual and discursive at once—that Luce Irigaray was subsequently to
call "quand nos lèvres se parlent," "when our lips—the lips of the
mouth, the lips of the vagina—speak to each other, speak to themselves, speak among themselves."[7] We can watch Freud at work
parrying this threat at one point in his interpretation of Dora's
second dream, and doing so by insisting once more on the importance of distinguishing oral from written sources of knowledge.
The fragment of the dream being considered is "I then saw a thick
wood before me which I went into . . .":

> But she had seen precisely the same thick wood the day before, in a
> picture at the Secessionist exhibition. In the background of the
> picture there were *nymphs*.
>
> At this point a certain suspicion of mine became a certainty. The
> use of "*Bahnhof*" ["*station*"; *literally, "railway-court"*] and "*Friedhof*"
> ["*cemetery*"; *literally, "peace-court"*] to represent the female genitals
> was striking enough in itself, but it also served to direct my
> awakened curiosity to the similarly formed "*Vorhof*" ["*vestibulum*";
> *literally, "fore-court"*]—an anatomical term for a particular region of
> the female genitals. This might have been no more than a mislead-
> ing joke. But now, with the addition of "nymphs" visible in the
> background of a "thick wood," no further doubts could be enter-
> tained. Here was a symbolic geography of sex! "Nymphae," as is
> known to physicians though not to laymen (and even by the for-
> mer the term is not very commonly used), the name given to the
> labia minora, which lie in the background of the "thick wood" of
> the pubic hair. But any one who has employed such technical
> names as "vestibulum" and "nymphae" must have derived his
> knowledge from books, and not from popular ones either, but
> from anatomical text-books or from an encyclopedia—the com-
> mon refuge of youth when it is devoured by curiosity. If this

interpretation were correct, therefore, there lay concealed beneath the first situation in the dream a phantasy of defloration, the phantasy of a man seeking to force an entrance into the female genitals. [pp. 119–20]

What is puzzling here is the line of reasoning developed in the last three sentences. Dora's knowing what "nymphae" means may indeed show that she has more than a layman's acquaintance with such "technical" terms; and that, in turn, may betray her reading of encyclopedias; but why should this lead Freud to glimpse a fantasy of defloration, or serve as supplementary evidence for the existence of such a fantasy? What does the "therefore" of the last sentence point to? "Anyone who employed such technical names . . . must have derived *his* knowledge from books": is the shift back to the universal masculine pronoun a way of suggesting that such reading habits, though indulged in by women, are essentially masculine, and hence coordinate with male fantasies of defloration? That would seem to be the logic of this passage; if so, the suggestion that Dora's imagining of the female genitals is bound to be from a man's point of view is of a piece with Freud's persistence in characterizing Dora's love for Frau K. as "masculine." I don't think this is a sign that Freud was squeamish about lesbian love; rather that he was anxious to preserve certain clarities in his thinking about the transfer of psychoanalytic knowledge. It required a vigilant effort, it would seem, to draw the line between the operations in the hysteric which produce the text of her illness, and those in the analyst which seek to interpret and dissolve that text, between the production of secrets and the deployment of techniques.

IV

Consider the standard account of the relation between hysterical symptoms, secrets, and sexuality: an infantile practice, most often masturbatory, is repressed throughout the latency period, then reappears in puberty, converted into a symptom. What Dora knows, what is written in her physical symptoms, she knows only unconsciously and after the fact, *nachträglich,* and if she is to come to know it consciously, she needs the help of an interlocutor. But what of Freud's knowledge? How did he come by it, and what was the rhythm of its acquisition? Some pages from the beginning of *The History of the Psychoanalytic Movement* offer an intriguing answer. The pages are unusual in a number of respects: unlike the rest of the book, they are not just historical but anecdotal. The narrative powers one sees at work in the "Fragment of an Analysis" are here displayed in miniature, elaborating three brief stories, each with its punchline, that could have appeared in Freud's study of *Witz*. Indeed, they convey the verve—undiminished with repetition—of the inveterate teller of jokes: they sound like stories Freud told again and again and again, bits of autobiographical mythmaking. Their subject: the origins of the "new and original idea" that the neuroses had a sexual etiology, or How I Stumbled on Psychoanalysis. Their fascination lies in the image of himself Freud chooses to present: here he is neither Conquistador nor Impassive Scientist, but Impressionable Junior Colleague. In that role, he finds himself participating in a drama whose temporal structure is that of the belated surfacing of unconsciously acquired knowledge. Here is how Freud introduces the stories:

> There was some consolation for the bad reception accorded to my contention of a sexual aetiology in the neuroses even by my most intimate circle of friends—for a vacuum rapidly formed itself about my person—in the thought that I was taking up the fight for a new and original idea. But, one day, certain memories gathered in my mind which disturbed this pleasing notion, but which gave me in exchange a valuable insight into the processes of human creative activity and the nature of human knowledge. The idea for which I was being made responsible had by no means originated with me. It had been imparted to me by three people whose opinion had commanded my deepest respect—by Breuer himself, by Charcot, and by Chrobak, the gynaecologist at the University, perhaps the most eminent of all our Vienna physicians. These three men had all communicated to me a piece of knowledge which, strictly speaking, they themselves did not possess. Two of them later denied having done so when I reminded them of the fact; the third (the great Charcot) would probably have done the

same if it had been granted me to see him again. But these three identical opinions, which I had heard without understanding, had lain dormant in my mind for years, until one day they awoke in the form of an apparently original discovery.[8]

"These three men had all communicated to me a piece of knowledge which, strictly speaking, they themselves did not possess": questions of possession are important here, of the possibility of possessing knowledge, of "having" an idea, and of the degree of honor, or infamy, that goes with such possessing. Freud, who has experienced what it feels like to be "made responsible" for a disagreeable idea, might wish to share the onus, if not the honor. But he is still more interested in dramatizing the "valuable insight" for which he has—involuntarily, to be sure—exchanged his claim to originality, an insight he finds at once exhilarating, profoundly serviceable, and not a little dismaying: like those jokes he calls "sceptical jokes" it is an insight that might seem to undermine "not a person or an institution but the certainty of our knowledge itself, one of our speculative possessions."[9] Here is his account of the first sowing of the seed:

> One day, when I was a young house-physician, I was walking across the town with Breuer, when a man came up who evidently wanted to speak to him urgently. I fell behind. As soon as Breuer was free, he told me in his friendly, instructive way that this man was the husband of a patient of his and had brought him some news of her. The wife, he added, was behaving in such a peculiar way in society that she had been brought to him for treatment as a nervous case. He concluded: "These things are always *secrets d'alcôve!*" I asked him in astonishment what he meant, and he answered by explaining the word *alcôve* ("marriage-bed") to me, for he failed to realize how extraordinary the *matter* of his statement seemed to me. [p. 48]

The distribution of roles that will prevail in all three stories is set here: Breuer is the master, friendly and instructive, an older man whose worldliness allows him to sprinkle his speech with bits of French innuendo; Freud is the "young house-physician," deferential, grateful for Breuer's attention, still capable of the "astonishment" of the sexually naive, a country boy, *ein Mann vom Lande,* in Kafka's phrase. There is a hint that his astonishment might be, finally, more valuable than the more sophisticated obtuseness that keeps Breuer from realizing how extraordinary what he is saying might seem to his colleague. But this is just a hint: the emphasis is on the contretemps. The value of Freud's "freshness," his Maisie-like capacity to "wonder" until "appearances in themselves vulgar and empty enough . . . begin to have meanings, aspects, solidities, connexions," remains to be brought out more dramatically in the next anecdote:

> Some years later, at one of Charcot's evening receptions, I happened to be standing near the great teacher at a moment when he appeared to be telling Brouardel a very interesting story about something that had happened during the day's work. I hardly heard the beginning, but gradually my attention was seized by what he was talking of: a young married couple from a distant country in the East—the woman a severe sufferer, the man either impotent or exceedingly awkward. "Tâchez donc," I heard Charcot repeating, "je vous assure, vous y arriverez." Brouardel, who spoke less loudly, must have expressed his astonishment that symptoms like the wife's could have been produced by such circumstances. For Charcot suddenly broke out with great animation: "Mais, dans des cas pareils c'est toujours *la chose génitale,* toujours . . . toujours . . . toujours"; and he crossed his arms over his stomach, hugging himself and jumping up and down in his own characteristically lively way. I know that for a moment I was almost paralyzed with amazement and said to myself: "Well, but if he knows that, why does he never say so?" But the impression was soon forgotten; brain anatomy and the experimental induction of hysterical paralyses absorbed all my interest. [p. 48]

This skit is more complicated: now it is Brouardel who is in the position of the astonished Junior Colleague and Freud, younger still, is off to one side, overhearing fragments of a conversation whose effect on him is still more forceful. Two impressions remain vivid over the years: that of the master "hugging himself and jumping up and down" with the delight of knowing what he knows, a moment analogous to Freud's own exhilaration when he was to exclaim "complete and without a flaw!" twenty years later, and the sense of being "almost paralysed with amazement" by what he had just heard. If that shock is registered unconsciously, it is nevertheless soon forgotten, replaced, among other things, Freud tells us, by considerations of "hysterical paralyses." We should linger on these two allusions to paralysis, so gratuitously juxtaposed. They would seem to be linked: Freud's distinctly marginal relation to this scene of professional knowingness, almost out of earshot, listening to two men talking—in French, of course—about suggestive matters, *secrets d'alcôve,* locates him close to the position of the woman in his analysis of obscene jokes (pp. 97–101), just as his being paralyzed with amazement aligns him with the (mostly female) victims of hysterical paralysis. In his innocence, in his capacity to receive impressions, he is feminized. Or so he keeps insisting:

> A year later, I had begun my medical career in Vienna as a lecturer in nervous diseases, and in everything related to the aetiology of the neuroses I was still as ignorant and innocent as one could expect of a promising student trained at a university. One day I had a friendly message from Chrobak, asking me to take a woman patient of his to whom he could not give enough time, owing to his new appointment as a University teacher. I arrived at the patient's house before he did and found that she was suffering from attacks of meaningless anxiety, and could only be soothed by the most precise information about where her doctor was at every moment of the day. When Chrobak arrived he took me aside and told me that the patient's anxiety was due to the fact that although she had been married for eighteen years she was still *virgo intacta.* The husband was absolutely impotent. In such cases, he said, there was nothing for a medical man to do but to shield this domestic misfortune with his own reputation, and put up with it if people shrugged their shoulders and said of him: "He's no good if he can't cure her after so many years." The sole prescription for such a malady, he added, is familiar enough to us, but we cannot order it. It runs:
>
> $$R_x \text{ Penis normalis}$$
> $$\text{dosim}$$
> $$\text{repetatur!}$$
>
> I had never heard of such a prescription, and felt inclined to shake my head at my kind friend's cynicism. [pp. 48–49]

"I had never heard of such a prescription": the note of the ingenue is caught in that phrase, but Freud's rueful shake of the head is not quite a gesture of astonishment or amazed paralysis. It is his more settled acknowledgment of a cast of mind he finds cynical, one that has gynecologists aligning themselves with impotent husbands, willing to risk their reputations "to shield this domestic misfortune," though unwilling—or simply unable—to include the wife's "misfortune" as part of the calculation. Freud is not taking a strong polemical stance against these commonplace sexual and medical arrangements, but he is glancing at the structures of complicity, between doctors and husbands, that keep the sexual etiology of the neuroses a well-kept, smoking-room secret. His own position is no longer that of the impressionable hysteric, taking in knowledge she will not know she has, but it is still outside the circle of collegiality. Freud presents himself as susceptible to the lures of that primarily male world, flattered, for instance, by Chrobak's friendship and patronage, but with more serious intellectual ambitions; his imagery shifts to more masculine resonances:

> I have not of course disclosed the illustrious parentage of this scandalous idea in order to saddle other people with the responsibility for it. I am well aware that it is one thing to give utterance to an idea once or twice in the form of a passing *aperçu*, and quite another to mean it seriously—to take it literally and pursue it in the face of every contradictory detail, and to win it a place among accepted truths. It is the difference between a casual flirtation and a legal marriage with all its duties and difficulties. "*Épouser les idées de . . .*" is no uncommon figure of speech, at any rate in French. [p. 49]

At this point, Freud is back in the world of men, of Oedipal rivalry, to be precise. Breuer, Charcot, and Chrobak have their flirtations with the sexual etiology of the neuroses, but Freud has made an honest woman of her, by his persistence, his intellectual mastery, the stolid virility of his pursuit. But the "idea" that he has wed was—and that is the point of these stories—acquired in a structure of *Nachträglickheit,* analogous to the hysteric's acquisition of her often paralyzing secrets. Freud both needs to acknowledge the strangeness of this procedure—it is his claim, after all, to be taken more seriously than Breuer, Charcot or Chrobak—and he needs to domesticate that structure, to bring it into the light of conscious reflection, to deploy it as technique.

We have been locating the same ambivalence in Freud's dealings with Dora. For the session-by-session acquisition of knowledge about his patients, in the interplay of their (oral) free associations and his own free-floating attention and (oral) interventions, is governed by the same rhythms of unconscious, latent acquisition, of overhearing, that Freud has dramatized in these stories about his original discovery. Just as in those anecdotes he seems to be running the risk of feminization, so in the "Fragment of an Analysis" he would seem, at points, to be fending off whatever reminds him of the possibility that such oral intercourse is regressive, epistemologically unstable. He isn't speaking lightly when he says, toward the end of his case history, that it would have been "quite impracticable . . . to deal simultaneously with the technique of analysis and with the internal structure of a case of hysteria" (p. 134). The matter of Dora and the matter of the techniques that are brought into touch with her symptoms and words are quite literally out-of-phase in Freud's thinking; they have to be, he believes, if he is to claim scientific status for those techniques and the discoveries that prompted them. The mistakes Freud made in his sessions with Dora and the misconstructions he permitted himself in writing the case up suggest that, among other things, Dora was sacrificed to underwrite that claim.

8.
TWO EXTRAVAGANT TEACHINGS

FOR MANY YEARS, students entering Cornell have been handed a pamphlet, prepared by the English department, entitled "A Writer's Responsibilities." The plural is slightly misleading: the pamphlet addresses itself to only one "responsibility," the student's "responsibility always to demonstrate the extent to which he is master of what he is learning." And, lest this seem too massive, too unbearable a charge, the next sentences go on to specify it somewhat: "He must make clear what is his and what is someone else's. His teacher must know whose words he is reading or listening to." The pamphlet, in other words, is about plagiarism, and it contains the usual mixture of sensible advice (about paraphrasing, quoting, footnoting, etc.) and ill-assured moral exhortation. For our purposes its interest lies in its ill-assurance, in a rhetoric that wavers in its address to student-readers in a predictable and symptomatic fashion. Here, for example, are the pamphlet's opening words:

> Education at its best, whether conducted in seminar, laboratory, or lecture hall, is essentially a dialogue between teacher and pupil in which questions and answers can be explored, arguments can be posed and resolved, data can be sought and evaluated. From the time of Socrates and his disciples to that of the nightly discussion on the corridor, this dialogue has been the mark and delight of the intellectual life.

The allusion of Socrates may not be obligatory, but it is characteristic of this earnest moment in teachers' imaginings of themselves, their students, and what passes between them. Equally characteristic of the complementary cynical moment is the note of tight-lipped institutional fussiness struck on the pamphlet's last page:

The Policy of the English Department
For the first instance of plagiarism or of any other kind of academic dishonesty or irresponsibility, the student will immediately receive a failing grade in the course and be reported to the appropriate department, division or college for whatever further action may be in order.

The lineaments of an American Scene of Instruction are sketched in these passages. The student might be Alcibiades, but then again he might be Al Capone; his teacher is either a master of instructive dialogue or a disciplinarian, and the whole operation can feel like "the intellectual life" one moment, the next like a low budget cops-and-robbers routine. Or so it would appear from language of this sort: I don't think I'm describing higher education in America so much as calling attention to some common teacherly fantasies about it, fantasies largely ignored by serious writers engaging the sociology or the economics of universities, or else alluded to obliquely under some more general rubric, like professorial "conservatism." Yet the fantasies I propose to dwell on seem pervasive, sluggishly unresponsive to changes in the system of higher education, and distributed across generational and political lines. You don't have to be over thirty or a bourgeois humanist, for example, to find yourself beside yourself about a paper you suspect was plagiarized.

I have picked two documents which embody such fantasies, characterizations of the relations between teachers and students that take the form of images or, sometimes, of tendentious implicit narratives. Each seems to have been elaborated by a teacher in response to a perceived threat. I shall be arguing that in each case that threat has been misperceived, that indeed the function of the characterization would seem to be first to misrepresent a threat and then to respond, more or less aggressively, to that misrepresentation. The extravagance of these teachings, then, lies both in the misrepresentation and in the vehemence of the response.

I

The pamphlet "A Writer's Responsibilities" is not wholly the work of the Cornell English department. About half of it is excerpted (with appropriate acknowledgment) from what was, in the 1960s, a popular freshman textbook, Harold C. Martin's *The Logic and Rhetoric of Exposition*.[1] In these pages, entitled "A Definition of Plagiarism," Martin leads his readers through the variety of forms—some bald-faced, some more subtle and devious, some conscious, some inadvertent—of what he calls, in ironic quotation marks, "borrowing," then ends his discussion with these untypically intense sentences:

> Since one of the principal aims of a college education is the development of intellectual honesty, it is obvious that plagiarism is a particularly serious offense and the punishment for it is commensurately severe. What a penalized student suffers can never really be known by anyone but himself; what the student who plagiarizes and "gets away with it" suffers is less public and probably less acute, but the corruptness of his act, the disloyalty and baseness it entails, must inevitably leave an ineradicable mark upon him as well as on the institution of which he is privileged to be a member.

A strange passage, urgent in its wish to stigmatize the crime it knows it can't be sure won't be committed, can't be sure won't go undetected, no matter what one says. Hence the rising rhythms of the last sentence ("the corruptness of his act, the disloyalty and baseness it entails"), the echoing absolutes ("inevitably," "ineradicable"), the huff and puff of its concluding phrase. And what are we to make of "gets away with it" in quotation marks? Does that mean "he only thinks he gets away with it—we know better"? Or is it perhaps mimicking student diction and presenting the difference between the vulnerable institution and its disloyal member as if it were also a difference in verbal refinement: *we* are polysyllabic, *they* are slobs?

More intriguing are the passage's speculations about the consequences of plagiarism, not its explicit consequences but its ideal or imagined ones, some odd combination of interior suffering (which "can never really be known by anyone but" the sufferer) and an ineradicable mark which, if not literally exterior, must at least be conceived as somehow legible, if only to the eye of God. For this is pure fantasy, compensatory to its function and moral-theological in its form. The inevitable, ineradicable mark is a lineal descendant of the mark of Cain, like the Scarlet Letter or the inscription on the body of the criminal in Kafka's penal colony. It is "inevitable" in this brief fiction because it is anything but inevitable in fact: plagiarists do, we all know, get away with it. And they get away with it because it is always possible for profiteers of difference to take advantage of the distance between legitimate authors and the sheets of paper on which their words are registered and distributed. The fantasy, then, is constructed so as to produce the sense of satisfaction that comes with contemplating a punishment so aptly fitted to its crime: the "author" of *this* mark, at least, *will* be inseparable from it; here, for once—so the wish would have it—mark, paper, and author will be fused. For this is, among other things, a fantasy of integration, of the overcoming of difference.

We may still wonder why the passage dwells on the student's "suffering"; is it because a *soupçon* of sadism clings to all such dreams of punishment? Perhaps; but notice that this is at once a dream of punishment and a dream of interpretation: what is at issue is not just suffering but the extent to which it can be known, and by whom. The passage moves from the apparent unknowability of the penalized student's suffering to the wished-for legibility of the ineradicable mark. Private pain is conjured up not to be gloated over but rather because it indicates a region where it may be thought to exist, an interior space about whose contents we outsiders may make some guesses—gravely weighing the pains, deciding that one is "probably less acute" than another—but about which we "can never really know" as much as the sufferer himself.

Here again we can see the teacher's fantasy blending the student and his paper, or rather substituting the student for his paper as an object of interpretation. And, of course, that is what usually goes on in "cases" of plagiarism. Recall the scenario: you have either found yourself caught up in the process or listened as some colleague eagerly recited the details of his own involvement. There is, first, the moment of suspicion, reading along in a student's paper; then the verification of the hunch, the tracking down of the theft, most exhilarating when it involves a search through the library stacks; then the moment of "confrontation" when the accusation is made and it is no longer the student's paper but his face which is read for signs of guilt, moral anguish, contrition, whatever. The most telling account of such a moment comes from George Orwell's recollection of school days in England:

> Another boy, Beacham, whom I have mentioned already, was similarly overwhelmed with shame by the accusation that he "had black rings round his eyes."
> "Have you looked in the glass lately, Beacham?" said Bingo. "Aren't you ashamed to go about with a face like that? Do you think everyone doesn't know what it means when a boy has black rings round his eyes?"
> Once again the load of guilt and fear seemed to settle down upon me. Had *I* got black rings round my eyes? A couple of years later I realized that these were supposed to be a symptom by which masturbators could be detected. But already, without knowing this, I accepted the black rings as a sure sign of depravity. And many times, even before I grasped the supposed meaning, I have gazed anxiously into the glass, looking for the first hint of that dreaded stigma, the confession which the secret sinner writes upon his own face.[2]

Which is more dismaying to the secret sinner: to have sinned or to have written out his confession on his own face? Which is more rewarding to his judge: to have saved a boy from masturbation or to have accurately read the signs of his depravity? These are not rhetorical questions to the extent that neither sinner nor judge can be sure of the answers to them. Indeed, the aim of such fantasies of moral legibility, whether they are elaborated by sinners or judges, is precisely that exciting confusion of ethical and hermeneutical motifs; for fantasies are compromise-formations, they seek to have things both ways. Our text about plagiarism offers just such a

compromise: the ineradicable mark is there to satisfy the interpreter's wish to read stable and undeceptive signs, while the unknowable suffering is there to satisfy the teacher's wish to be
something other than a reader—it serves as an acknowledgment of
an interiority opaque enough to baffle his hermeneutical skills, a
residual *je-ne-sais-quoi* that is there to remind him of (and, spec-
ularly, to confirm him in) his own private humanity.

So much for the terms of the fantasy; what of its motivation? We
might attribute it to justifiable moral indignation, the righteous
contempt of the honest for the dishonest, but that wouldn't quite
account for either the intensity of this rhetoric or its peculiar figuration—or for the strong fascination that student plagiarism generally seems to hold for academics. Here again the passage from
Orwell may be of some help: just as the masturbation of children
can serve to focus the anxieties of their elders about sexuality in
general, so the plagiarizing of students can focus their teachers'
anxieties about writing in general, more particularly about the kind
of "writing" involved in teaching—the inscription of a culture's
heritage on the minds of its young. A teacher's uncertainty about
(to quote the pamphlet again) "whose words he is reading or listening to" begins, in the classroom, with his own words—and this
would be true not merely for those colleagues we think of compla-
cently as less original than ourselves. The recurrent touting of originality—in letters of recommendation, reports of *ad hoc*
committees, etc.—is no doubt a sign of the same uneasiness that
produces the ritual condemnation of student plagiarists when they
are unlucky enough to be caught. The paragraph we have been
considering is an imagined version of such a scapegoating. Its
structure is that of projection. An interior difference—the sense of
self-division implicit in all linguistic activity, sometimes more pronounced, sometimes less so, depending on the social context in
which speech or writing is produced—that difference is exteriorized as the difference between the offended institution and its
delinquent member. And, in one of those nicely economical turns
that characterize powerful fantasies, the delinquent member is himself made to unwillingly represent an emblem of integrity, of the
binding of the self and its signs.

II

What can be made of the gestures by which a teacher places himself somewhere between his subject and his students? I have a very specific gesture in mind—Earl Wasserman, conducting a semi-nar on *The Rape of the Lock,* leaning forward across the table and asking his audience, a group of young men and women, graduate students and junior faculty, in a tone that was at once pugnacious and coy, "How far can I go?" I recall it as a nicely appropriate question, not just because it seemed obscurely in touch with all the erotic aggression and coquetry in Pope's poem, but because it was so much the interpreter's question par excellence, whether you took it straight or rhetorically. If it called for an answer, that answer would bear on the theoretical limits of interpretation—was it a terminable or an interminable activity? If instead the question was rhetorical, it could be heard as a sort of teasing cry for help, like those phone calls police stations receive from time to time: "Stop me before I strike again! I can't help it!", and then the phone goes dead, the Mad Rapist having hung up without giving his name or address. There is something obsessive about interpretation; there is something flirtatious about teaching: both impulses seemed at work in Wasserman's questions in ways that invited one to reflect on the relation between them.

The material of the seminar was later published in a paper called "The Limits of Allusion in *The Rape of the Lock,*"[3] so it was possible to review its argument in detail, and to notice another scene fram-ing Wasserman's interpretive gestures, this one not of instruction but of professional polemic. Though he had mentioned no names at the seminar, and included no footnotes in its published version to anything more recent than *Tristram Shandy,* it was clear that Wasser-man was out to counter what had become, by the 1960s, the current informed reading of *The Rape of the Lock.* It was also clear that a quarrel about how to read the poem was part of a larger argument, that between interpreters associated more or less closely with the New Criticism and those who accused the New Critics of ignoring literary and intellectual history. During the 1930s critics like Emp-son and Leavis and Tillotson had redirected attention to Pope's remarkable verbal control and a series of acute and tactful readings had appeared praising Pope for his acuteness and tact. When these critics turned to *The Rape of the Lock* what they found was a poem which, if not the high point of Pope's art, was at least the epitome of his talents, a poem to which words like tact, balance, or control could be easily applied.

But what exactly was it that Pope was so tactfully balancing? For critics like Tillotson, Brooks, Wimsatt, or Brower, one answer was "his attitudes toward poetry." The particular finesse with which Pope wrote mock heroic couplets could be read as simultaneously parodying the language and apparatus of major epic, invoking epic values to sustain a satiric attack on a decidedly unheroic contemporary scene, and, still further, conferring poignancy and charm on that same scene. More intriguing was the fact that, within the poem itself, that balancing act was doubled by another: the presentation of Pope's heroine, Belinda, who was rendered—and this was the point of Brooks' essay in *The Well-Wrought Urn*—as both a goddess and a "frivolous tease." These two balancings were easily analogized: Belinda became, in the discourse of these critics, a synecdoche for the poem—for, as the phrase went, "the poem itself." Both were objects of fascination, diminutive, perhaps trivial, but highly desirable; like frail china, bound to be handled but requiring of their admirers a lightness of touch mimicking that of their creator. The metaphor of tactful balancing easily slid into one of controlled erotic involvement. Tillotson could say:

> The poem provides a picture, rather than a criticism; or, rather, the poem is so elaborate, shifting, constellated, that the intellect is baffled and demoralized by the emotions. One is left looking at the face of the poem, as at Belinda's.[4]

And Wimsatt could add:

> The sophistication of the poem lies in its being no less affectionate than critical. . . . The critic's difficulty with *The Rape of the Lock* is to find words not too heavy to praise the intricacies of its radiant sense.[5]

Earl Wasserman's arrival on this scene of admiration—of critics admiring Pope who is himself admiring Belinda who is, of course, admiring herself—is something like the arrival of the bull at the china shop. He argues carefully but he is not excessively tactful and, though he admires Pope, he does not admire Belinda, does not think Pope really does either, and is, in general, all for disrupting what he refers to as "the sheltered Petit Trianon world of conventionalized manners that the . . . poem constructs" (p. 427).

Wasserman's strategy is twofold: he attacks the insularity implicit in a New Critical reading of the poem by insisting on the range and importance of Pope's allusions to traditional motifs and *topoi*, and (it is, structurally, the same move) he attacks Belinda as a "narcissistic coquette" (p. 430), or, more accurately, he takes Pope to be himself elaborating and criticizing "the prideful image of Belinda as an independent world and female society as a self-sufficient scheme." (p. 434). I shall trace these lines of attack one at a time, then consider the links between them and suggest how they bear on the relations of poems, teachers, and students.

Wasserman begins by posing the question of what he calls the limits of allusion: granting the steady allusiveness of Pope's verse— to Dryden and Milton and Shakespeare, but more especially to Virgil and Homer and the Bible—how did these allusions function? How far was one entitled to go on interpreting them? If a phrase of Pope's turned out to be a literal translation of a phrase in the *Aeneid,* how much of the context of that fragment of Virgil's poem was drawn along with it into Pope's? As one might guess, the answer to the theoretical question of the limits of allusion is that no theoretical limits can be set at all: Pope's interpreter is entitled, Wasserman argues—and not only entitled but positively encouraged by Pope— to go as far as he can; he is, Wasserman concludes, "actively invited by [the allusions] to exercise, within poetic reason, his own invention by contemplating the relevances of the entire allusive context and its received interpretation" (p. 443). It would seem that some principles of limitation are "implicit in expressions like "within poetic reason" or "received interpretation," but what is principally interesting about them is their vagueness. They gesture in the direction of the reader who would adequately embody them, for the question of how far an interpreter should go is obviously inseparable from the question of the interpreter's own erudition: one needs to know the texts Pope was alluding to in order to spot an allusion in the first place, and one needs to know enough about neoclassical practice to know when to stop interpreting. Both the occasion that initiates an interpretative process and the restraints regulating it are functions of one's learning. And Wasserman makes it clear that while we might—with an effort, perhaps a lifetime's effort—familiarize ourselves with the range of Pope's reading, we could never possess that knowledge with the same degree of easy authenticity as did Pope or his ideal contemporary reader:

> The mind that composed *The Rape of the Lock* was less an English one hearkening back to the classics for witty reference than one applying itself to an English social situation from the viewpoint of a deeply ingrained classicism. Classical literature and its manners, together with Scripture and its exegetical tradition, are not merely Pope's acquired learning, they shaped the character and processes of his thought. Correspondingly, his poems consistently ask for a reader who is equally native to the whole classical-Scriptural world, a Christian Greco-Roman scrutinizing eighteenth-century English culture. [pp. 426–27]

Confronted with a statement of this sort, one might want to say, "Of course Wasserman is being hyperbolical, but you know what he means." Suppose, instead, one were to reverse the weightings of that response and say, "Of course we know what he means, but why should he put it so hyperbolically?" Why this fiction of a transhistorical meeting of minds—the "mind that composed *The Rape of the Lock*" and that of his perfect reader, someone "equally native to the whole classical-Scriptural world?" Is this merely a heuristic fiction, an ideal totalization posited to urge us on to some serious, if only approximating, interpretative activity? Perhaps; but it is also a figure of perfect communication, suitable for framing and display in the classroom, where it might function rather like an allusion to the conversations of Socrates and his disciples.

Now Wasserman also suggests a related figure for what goes on in the classroom, not that of a closed circuit of ideal communication, but rather that of a controlled linearity, a graded series: at the head of the line is "the mind that composed *The Rape of the Lock,*" a mind whose learning is not something acquired but rather "deeply ingrained" or—as he says elsewhere—"deeply embedded." Next in line, in a middleman's position, is the teacher, whose knowledge *is* acquired. Finally there are the students, presumably there to acquire the erudition that their teacher already possesses in part. This is a familiar enough account of academic lineage, and it might be that at moments literary education comes to feel like that. But more often what happens is that—by a trick of the mind, call it a deeply embedded inclination to convert series into binary oppositions—the teacher's position is experienced (by the teacher as well as by his class) not as a middle ground somewhere between his author and his students but as a dramatic occupation, more or less earned, of the position of authority itself. The series becomes a proportion: Wasserman is to his seminar as Pope is to Wasserman. When that happens the teacher-interpreter's mind stands in for "the mind that composed *The Rape of the Lock*" and the distinction between knowledge that is deeply ingrained and knowledge that is merely acquired starts to fade. One sentence of Wasserman's article begins "Disinherited as we are from (Pope's) referential systems . . ." (p. 425): the classroom becomes the place where the teacher-scholar, at least, can appear to reclaim his inheritance.

I offer this not as a description of classroom teaching so much as a readily available possible mystification, a common and reassuring way of bringing the activity of reading into touch with that of teaching. The relation of teacher to student, figured as a descent, a lineage, reinforces the fiction of the perfect play between the mind of the poet and that of the ideal reader. Both figures—that of lineage and that of the closed circuit—depend for their intelligibility on a radical reduction of what is in fact plural (a certain number of students in a class, many of them unresponsive; a still greater number of texts in the tradition, many of them at odds with one another, many of them unread, even by Wasserman, even by Pope)—a reduction of plurals to an imagined interplay of paired elements: poet and tradition, poet and reader, teacher and student. The power such figures exert over readers is in proportion to the reduction they promise to perform.

Turning to Belinda, Wasserman rejects the notion that Pope's attitude toward her was "no less affectionate than critical" and instead proposes another way of dealing with the subtleties of her presentation: he would see Pope superficially praising his heroine but systematically undercutting that praise with ironic allusions to Christian and classical texts. Pope, in this reading, mobilizes his allusions to break the fragile construct Wasserman calls "the beau monde, made of conventional signs, decorative and playful, that substitute for flesh-and-blood reality." And "flesh-and-blood reality," as Wasserman's analysis makes clear, is primarily sexual. Citing the words Belinda's guardian sylph whispers in her ear as the poem begins ("Hear and believe! Thy own importance know, / Nor bound thy narrow views to things below" 1.35–36), Wasserman writes

> As Plutarch wrote in one of the major *loci* of the doctrine, to "know thyself" means to "use one's self for that one thing for which Nature has fitted one"; and exactly what Belinda is most fitted for and what is radical for Pope in the carnal world that Belinda ought to accept is intimated by "Things below", a term we may let Swift explicate for us. [p. 432]

The passage Wasserman takes from Swift is his retelling of the old tale of the philosopher Thales, who, while looking at the stars, found himself "seduced by his *lower parts* into a *Ditch.*" Wasserman remarks:

> No one who had read at least his Juvenal—to say nothing of the Priapeia—would have failed to understand the real meaning of *fossa,* or ditch, any more than he would have failed to understand Pope's "Things below." [p. 432]

And, lest we fail to understand, a footnote delicately spells it out:

> For this sense of *res,* see Martial, XI, 44. In his "Sober Advice from Horace," Pope translated Horace's "magno prognatum deposco consule CUNNUM" as "A Thing descended from the Conqueror." [p. 432 n. 16]

Disinherited though he may be, Wasserman's acquired learning seems to have put him in a position to know "exactly what Belinda is most fitted for": what this girl needs is a good Judeo–Christian Greco–Roman husband.

Wasserman's *paideia* seems to be advancing under a banner with a familiar enough device: "I'll teach you a thing or two" is the motto. But it would be a mistake to assume that the aggressive misogyny here is all the critic's, that he is simply seeing things in an innocuous text. The bawdry and misogyny are there—in Swift most obviously but in Pope as well. Wasserman's assertive proclamation of this element in the poem can be taken as corrective of the rhetoric of delicacy and tact preferred by the New Critics, a readjustment that has the virtue of reminding us that *The Rape of the Lock* is not least of all about a struggle for power. Moreover, Wasserman's own rhetoric—its stridency and its implicit thematic linkings—can give us a better idea of what the elements of that struggle might be. For it is not simply a struggle between men and women, any more than Western misogyny is the simple antagonism of one group of people to another. If we follow Wasserman's polemic we shall see that what he is attacking in Belinda is what he takes to be her imaginary relation to herself, her narcissism, which Wasserman treats as a perverse upsetting of the proper hierarchical relation of "conventional signs" to "flesh-and-blood reality" (p. 429). Tracing the motif of the shearing of the lock back to Appolonius and, along with him, to "Euripides, Herodotus, Callimachus, Valerius Flacchus, Pausanias, and Lucian, among others" (pp. 423–29), Wasserman reminds us of the tradition of offering up a lock of a maiden's hair as a nuptial rite. "What the Baron has raped," he comments, is not Belinda's virginity but . . . the ritualistic sign of it." And Belinda's distress is a function of her commitment to a world of signs, "in which a rouged cheek surpasses a real blush, . . . a card game takes the place of the contest of the sexes, China jars stand for virginity, and a mirror reflection transcends the viewer" (p. 429). Wasserman's misogyny here is hard to distinguish from what seems like a more general semiotic uneasiness: what troubles him about Belinda is not that, being a woman, she is different, but that, being a woman, she has somehow been beguiled by "conventional signs" into a confusing self-alienation. She is both different and self-divided: hence the prurient allusions to flaws, cracks, ditches, etc. It isn't clear from Wasserman's account why this confusion should be limited to Belinda—or to women; we know that some distinguished formalist critics (all male) have been equally beguiled by the delicacy and glitter of Belinda's world of signs. What is clear, however, is that Wasserman would like so to limit it, to focus his uneasiness on *one* form of the relation of signs and reality, the beautiful woman's fascination with her reflected image. Our earlier glance at Orwell might lead us to expect—in this region where semiotic and sexual questions seem to be converging—some further fine tuning of the notion of narcissism in the form of a denunciation of autoerotic behavior, and indeed in Wasserman's account that is one of the forms Belinda's self-sufficiency is made to take: we are told that "she is wedded to and sexually gratified by her own virginity" (p. 430).

But just as we watched Harold Martin simultaneously stigmatize the plagiarist and confer on him a poignantly unknowable interior life, so we can follow a movement in some ways similar in Wasserman's dealings with Belinda. There are depths behind all that surface, it turns out. And the last pages of Wasserman's paper are devoted to the discovery, within those depths, of the heterosexual desire that Belinda cannot consciously acknowledge, a secret passion for the Baron, a wish to marry, to perform what Wasserman describes as "the heroic sacrifice that makes female life meaningful and glorious" (p. 436). Teasing out the signs of that desire involves Wasserman in his most elaborate effort at documenting and interpreting Pope's allusions to the classics, and it produces a strong case for their importance in the poem. At a series of points Wasserman can show that when Belinda is heard complaining about the loss of her lock, her language—or the poet's language about her—echoes passages in Virgil, in Catullus, and in Martial which, read in context, bear a meaning at cross-purposes to Belinda's: "Pope's words and their allusive context contradict each other," Wasserman comments, "and if we take the contradiction as the conflict between Belinda's conscious and subconscious mind, it only confirms Pope's psychoanalysis of her elsewhere." There is after all, as Pope had made explicit earlier in the poem, "an Earthly Lover lurking at her Heart" (pp. 440–41).

But it's worth noting that Pope *had* made that explicit earlier in the poem, just as he had placed in the mouth of one of his characters, Belinda's sensible friend Clarissa, a long speech advising her to marry. Wasserman's tracing of Pope's allusions in order to explore Belinda's unconscious desires discovers nothing that he didn't already know; in fact it is because of what he already knew from the more explicit passages in the poem that he could decide how much of the original context of each allusion was pertinent. Wasserman isn't mistaken about either the presence or the meaning of these allusions, but he has organized his account of them so as to introduce an element of hermeneutic suspense that is absent from the poem. What Pope offers is a variety of forms—explicit statement, hint, coded allusion—in the course of a narrative which unfolds in accordance with its own plotting, Wasserman presents as an *inquest:* he marshals his evidence sequentially, as if preparing for the moment when he can confront Belinda with the unacknowledged signs of her desire: "Perhaps this will refresh your memory!" What comes through in the tone of his article—and was conspicuous in the seminar as I recall it—is the intellectual energy and muted glee of a particularly zealous *juge d'instruction.* It is not unlike the tone of the teacher confronting the plagiarist, nor is it entirely out of touch with the tone of a teacher teasing his seminar: "How far can I go? Tell me when to stop!"

What is sought in each case is an end to an ongoing interpretive process, and what makes the end feel like an end in each case is not that the interpreter runs out of signs to interpret but that he achieves a state of equilibrium with another person. When the teacher gets the plagiarist to admit that he copied something from one book, he doesn't have to return to the stacks to see how many other books his student cribbed: the process comes to an end with the acknowledgment of guilt. When Wasserman can produce enough evidence so that he can say that "despite the conscious social artfulness of her mind, Belinda is flesh and blood," he can put aside his Virgil, his Catullus, his Martial, his Juvenal, his Euripides, his Herodotus, his Callimachus . . . . *ad* (no longer) *infinitum:* his hermeneutical task is done.

The instances I just cited suggest that it may be worth distinguishing two different aspects of this achieved equilibrium. When the tracking down of a plagiarist is over, we can say it is over because we know the rules of such procedures: a more or less explicit code governs criminal investigations and stipulates what counts as a satisfactory conclusion—for example, a confession. But there is also an element of fantasy that frequently enters into the structure of such moments: I suggested as much in discussing Martin's language about the plagiarist, where the concern with unknowable suffering is there, oddly enough, to establish a rapport between the teacher and the guilty student. They meet—so the fantasy would have it—as fellow possessors of distinct but resonantly analogous interior lives. This is even more obvious in the case of Wasserman's tracking down of Belinda's secret desire: it is what allows him to use the phrase "flesh and blood" to describe what he has discovered her to be. She has crossed over from her position under the sign of "conventional signs" to join Wasserman where he has all along imagined himself to stand, in the world of "flesh-and-blood reality." It is as if he had bullied and wooed her into acknowledging that she, just like himself, is heterosexual.

In both Martin's text and Wasserman's it is that establishment of a fancied consubstantiality with the offending party—the student plagiarist, the female narcissist—that allows the gesture of scapegoating to take place. Anxiety about the relation of authors to their words, anxiety about the relation of flesh-and-blood reality to conventional signs—these may be exorcised if they can be laid on the head of a figure not wholly unlike the fantasist. We can see this most clearly when we think of the most benign encounter of the ones we've been considering, the humorous gesture of a scholar to a room full of graduate students, asking "How far can I go?" In that gentle parody of anxiety, the obsessive interpreter becomes the flirtatious teacher, entering into a mildly erotic intersubjective relation, fully within his control (for who around that table, after all, could have told Earl Wasserman how far he could or couldn't go?), an equilibrium that replaces the scholar's prior set of dealings with a long list of texts, each made up of many conventional signs.

Figure 1. *The Contrast* (unattributed), 1792.
Courtesy of Isaac Kramnick.

9.
MEDUSA'S HEAD: MALE
HYSTERIA
UNDER POLITICAL PRESSURE

Alios age incitatos, alios age rabidos

In THE PAGES that follow, I shall be considering some examples of a recurrent turn of mind: the representation of what would seem to be a political threat as if it were a sexual threat. Freud alludes to this at one point in his article on fetishism, where he is momentarily led into a bit of dramatic miming, simulating the terror he imagines the little boy feels when he first discovers his mother has no penis: "No," he writes, "that cannot be true, for if a woman can be castrated then his own penis is in danger; and against that there rebels part of his narcissism which Nature has providentially attached to this particular organ." Freud then adds drily, "In later life grown men may experience similar panic, perhaps when the cry goes up that throne and altar are in danger."[1] Questions of sexual difference, of perception, and of politics are rapidly brought into relation here, and it is that set of relations that I should like to explore. My chief examples are Parisian, taken from accounts of the 1848 Revolution and of the Commune, but in order to suggest that what I'm considering is not something merely febrile and all too French, I shall glance first at an eighteenth-century British instance.

Burke's *Reflections on the Revolution in France* was published in 1790; two years later an antirevolutionary cartoon appeared (figure 1) which, like Classic Comics generally, can be read as an inadvertent parody of the work it condenses and illustrates. The "contrast" is Burke's, and so is the francophobia that gives it its edge. Its images are drawn from the pages of the *Reflections:* the composed scene within "the shadow of the British oak" on the one hand, on the other the noble victim "hanged on the lamppost" and serving as a backdrop, if that's the right term, for one of those figures Burke refers to as "the furies of hell, in the abused shape of the vilest of women."[2] She is, however, not a Fury but a Gorgon—Medusa, in fact—here depicted as a beheader, her own head recognizably snaky yet still firmly attached to her shoulders: Medusa usurping the pose of Cellini's Perseus (figure 7 below), a decapitated male at her feet. Still another way—the print seems to suggest—in which the world has been turned upside down. The question is, why should revolutionary violence be emblematized in this way, as a hideous and fierce but not exactly sexless woman?

I

A related question is prompted by the first of the French texts, a brief one by Victor Hugo which appeared in a posthumously published collection of fragments assembled by his literary executors and entitled, by them, "Things Seen," *Choses vues*.[3] It describes the fighting on the first of the June Days in 1848, and it appears to have been written shortly thereafter. Hugo's relation to the events of 1848 shifted as the year went on, and could be described as an incomplete (and never to be completed) process of radicalization. In February, after the overthrow of Louis-Philippe, he had hoped for a regency and had refused to join Lamartine's provisional government. He was elected to the National Assembly in early June on a conservative ticket, but he was uneasy about government policy even then and had mixed feelings about the closing of the National Workshops—the action by the government that precipitated the fighting in late June. His apartment was invaded by the revolution-

aries on June 24—the day following the day described in this anecdote—and in succeeding weeks one finds him wavering, joining the
conservative majority in a vote of thanks to General Cavaignac for
putting down the rebellion, but voting against the majority when
they wished to prosecute Louis Blanc.[4] Some sense of those equivocal feelings comes out in his account of June 23:

> The June uprising, right from the start, presented strange linea-
> ments. It displayed suddenly, to a horrified society, monstrous and
> unknown forms.
>   The first barricade was set up by Friday morning the 23rd, at the
> Porte St. Denis: it was attacked the same day. The National Guard
> conducted itself resolutely. They were battalions of the 1st and 2nd
> Legions. When the attackers, who arrived by the Boulevard, came
> within range, a formidable volley was loosed from the barricade
> and it strewed the roadway with guardsmen. The National Guard,
> more irritated than intimidated, charged the barricade at a run.
>   At that moment a woman appeared on the crest of the barricade,
> a young woman, beautiful, dishevelled, terrifying. This woman,
> who was a public whore, pulled her dress up to the waist and cried
> to the guardsmen, in that dreadful brothel language that one is
> always obliged to translate: "Cowards! Fire, if you dare, at the
> belly of a woman!"
>   Here things took an awful turn. The National Guard did not
> hesitate. A fusillade toppled the miserable creature. She fell with a
> great cry. There was a horrified silence at the barricade and among
> the attackers.
>   Suddenly a second woman appeared. This one was younger and
> still more beautiful; she was practically a child, barely seventeen.
> What profound misery! She, too, was a public whore. She raised
> her dress, showed her belly, and cried: "Fire, you bandits!" They
> fired. She fell, pierced with bullets, on top of the other's body.
>   That was how this war began.
>   Nothing is more chilling or more somber. It's a hideous thing,
> this heroism of abjection, when all that weakness contains of
> strength bursts out; this civilization attacked by cynicism and de-
> fending itself by barbarism. On one side, the people's desperation,
> on the other the desperation of society. [31:365–66]

It's impossible to determine how accurate this is; though it purports
to be an eyewitness account, it differs in its details—and, particularly, in its most striking detail: the women's gesture—from other

descriptions of what must be the same encounter.[5] But regardless of whether the provocative actions it reports took place or were a supplementary invention of Hugo's, there can be no doubt about how intensely stylized this telling of the story is. The managing of local rhythmic sequences (e.g., in the original, *une femme jeune, belle, échevelée, terrible*), the dreamlike abruptness with which the women are made to appear, the fairy-tale progression (first one young woman, then another younger still: one almost expects a third—the Cinderella of the barricades), the strong centripetal pull toward that meaningfully terse one-sentence paragraph ("That was how this war began")—all this heavy codification marks the anecdote as "representative," the story of a beginning that is intended as a revelation of essence. But the point is made in a still more telling way, one that has disappeared in translation. The feminine gender of the word for an uprising—*une émeute*—allows for a startling double-entendre to develop, retroactively, in the second sentence: *Elle montra subitement à la societé épouvantée des formes monstrueuses et inconnues.* What the revolution is said to be doing figuratively is precisely what—in a moment—each of the women will be represented as doing literally, suddenly displaying monstrous and unknown forms to a horrified society. Or rather, to say that the women are doing "precisely" that is to submit to the spell of this lurid equivocation: between the first paragraph and the sentences describing the women's gesture a teasing relation is established that holds out the possibility of conflating the two actions. Once that possibility is glimpsed, then a number of sentences further along are rendered similarly *louche*. What was translated as "Here things took an awful turn" is, in French, "*Ici la chose devint effroyable*" (Here the thing became terrifying), a note that is repeated in the last paragraph's "It's a hideous thing" (*C'est une chose hideuse*), a glance back at the *formes monstrueuses et inconnues*. A context has been created in which the most abstract characterization of the revolution's essential meaning—"all that weakness contains of strength bursts out"—can be read as a final, oblique allusion to the source of the power of the women's gesture: this becomes a *chose vue* with a vengeance.

One's warrant for reading the Hugo passage in this way is provided, of course, by Freud's notes on Medusa's head:

> We have not often attempted to interpret individual mythologi-
> cal themes, but an interpretation suggests itself easily in the case of
> the horrifying decapitated head of Medusa.
>
> To decapitate = to castrate. The terror of Medusa is thus a ter-
> ror of castration that is linked to the sight of something. Numer-
> ous analyses have made us familiar with the occasion for this: it
> occurs when a boy, who has hitherto been unwilling to believe the
> threat of castration, catches sight of the female genitals, probably
> those of an adult, surrounded by hair, and essentially those of his
> mother. . . .
>
> If Medusa's head takes the place of a representation of the female
> genitals, or rather if it isolates their horrifying effects from the
> pleasure-giving ones, it may be recalled that displaying the genitals
> is familiar in other connections as an apotropaic act. What arouses
> horror in oneself will produce the same effect upon the enemy
> against whom one is seeking to defend oneself. We read in Rabelais
> of how the Devil took to flight when the woman showed him her
> vulva.
>
> The erect male organ also has an apotropaic effect, but thanks to
> another mechanism. To display the penis (or any of its surrogates)
> is to say: "I am not afraid of you. I defy you. I have a penis." Here
> then, is another way of intimidating the Evil Spirit.[6]

Freud describes a gesture similar to that of Hugo's women and
offers a compelling account of why that gesture would come across
as, in Hugo's language, *glaçant*, "chilling." In this interpretation,
the strength contained in the woman's weakness is the power to
frighten the man by revealing to him the possibility of his castration. At the barricades, the women's—or the revolutionaries'—lack
of "property" betokens the soldiers'—or society's—risk.[7].

But Freud is as concerned with counterphobic or apotropaic effects as he is with castration anxiety proper. Indeed, the interest of
these notes, as Jean Laplanche has pointed out, is in the deftness
with which they do justice both to the affect of fear and to the
mechanisms of its mitigation. Here are the third and fourth paragraphs in Freud's text, elided in the citation above:

The hair upon Medusa's head is frequently represented in works of art in the form of snakes, and these once again are derived from the castration complex. It is a remarkable fact that, however frightening they may be in themselves, they nevertheless serve as a mitigation of the horror, for they replace the penis, the absence of which is the cause of the horror. This is a confirmation of the technical rule according to which a multiplication of penis symbols signifies castration.

The sight of Medusa's head makes the spectator stiff with terror, turns him into stone. Observe that we have here once again the same origin from the castration complex and the same transformation of affect! For becoming stiff means an erection. Thus in the original situation it offers consolation to the spectator: he is still in possession of a penis, and the stiffening reassures him of the fact.

Laplanche's commentary draws attention to the multiple—in some cases, contradictory—associations that are brought into concentrated focus in the symbol as Freud unpacks it: following one strand of associations, for example, the snakes curling around Medusa's face are penises; following another they are the pubic hair surrounding the castrated (and—to the terrified boy—castrating) sex of the mother. The symbol wouldn't function *as* a symbol, he reminds us, if such condensation and concentration weren't operative; further, in addition to the effects of "consolation" Freud attributes to specific elements in the mix (as when Medusa's grim powers of petrification are translated, reassuringly, into the stiffening of an erection, or her snakes into replaceable parts), Laplanche insists on the primary apotropaic power of symbolic concentration itself. The symbol of the Medusa's head is reassuring not only because its elements can be read in those ways, but because it is a symbol. Here Laplanche's analysis of Freud's notes rejoins one of the main currents of his own thought about the castration complex, his insistence on the reassurance implicit in any scenario (however scarifying) that structures anxiety and, more particularly, in a scenario which links a theory (of how women got that way) with a perception (of what their bodies look like). "It goes without saying," he remarks, "that castration is precisely not a reality, but a thematization of reality. A certain theorization of reality which, for Freud, is so anchored in perception that to deny castration is finally the same thing as denying the perceptual experience itself. . . ."[8] Those final dots appear in Laplanche's text: the paragraph ends with that nuance of inconclusiveness, partly, I suspect, because Laplanche wants to leave the referent of "the perceptual experience itself" (*ce serait finalement la même chose de dénier la castration que de dénier l'expérience perceptive elle-même* . . .) ambiguous. He is certainly referring to the specific perceptual experience Freud's little boy is said to have of his mother's body; but beyond that Laplanche would claim more broadly that perception and castration are ineluctably linked, and linked by way of the child's narcissism, by the intensity of his investment in representations of himself and by the predominance of his penis among such representations.

Laplanche's discussion of anxiety can help us to formulate a litany of nervous questions that may be imagined as the murmured subtext of writing like Hugo's, questions that give expression to epistemological anxiety (can I trust my eyes?), to narcissism (can I hold myself together?), to sexual anxiety (can I hold on to my penis?), to—beyond that—social and economic fears about property and status (can I hold onto anything, including representations of myself?) or—put more grandly by one of this century's grand hysterics—Can the center hold? or is mere anarchy to be loosed upon the world?

To return to Victor Hugo, we can say that his choice to concentrate his account of the beginnings of the June Days as he does, by focusing on the gesture of those two women, is equivalent to the acts of condensation and focusing that went into the production of the Medusa's head as a powerful symbol. It is appropriate that Hugo writes of the uprising that it "presented strange lineaments": the lineaments may be strange, they may indeed, in the next sentence, be transformed into "monstrous and unknown forms," but that they are namable as "lineaments" gives them a physiognomic legibility that is reassuring. Hugo's anecdote is about horror, but it is shaped into an apotropaic emblem.[9]

I have said nothing about that odd phrase in which Hugo apologizes, after a fashion, for not being able to report the first woman's speech quite accurately, when she "pulled her dress up to the waist and cried . . . in that dreadful brothel language that one is always obliged to translate (*dans cette affreuse langue de lupanar qu'on est toujours forcé de traduire*) 'Cowards! Fire, if you dare, at the belly of a woman!'" The gesture might seem merely prim on Hugo's part, or else unpleasantly, leeringly allusive. More likely this is as close as Hugo will come in this text to betraying an uneasy self-consciousness about the activity of representation he is engaged in. Here it is productive of a momentary qualm; in the next selection we shall be examining, from Maxime du Camp's polemical account of the Commune, we shall find a more elaborate excursus into aesthetic theory—specifically into a theory of representation—bound up with a still more explicit linking of what is politically dangerous to feelings of sexual horror and fascination.

II

Maxime du Camp—*littérateur*, photographer, member of the Académie Française, friend of Flaubert, man about town—was sufficiently disturbed by the events of 1870–71 to publish, ten years later, a four-volume denunciation of the Commune and defense of the actions of the forces of order. He entitled it *Les Convulsions de Paris* and in it he included an attack on the painter Courbet for his role in the destruction of the Vendôme column, the Napoleonic monument to the victories of the Grande Armée. Whether Courbet was in fact responsible for this was a matter of some debate: Courbet denied it, but he was nevertheless found guilty by the investigating panel, heavily fined, and driven into exile.[10] Du Camp is writing after the fact to justify the verdict on circumstantial grounds, claiming that both in his theory of painting and in his practice Courbet revealed himself as just the sort of person who would get mixed up in just this sort of thing: "The man who . . . could degrade his craft to the point of abjection is capable of anything."[11]

> Every weak case may be contested, and this poor man did what he could, before the military tribunals, to fend off, or at least to attenuate the accusation that weighed on him. He was a conceited man whose self-love had drawn him into a path that was not his

own. His works, too much praised and too much denigrated, made him well-known and provided him with a comfortable living. His absence of imagination, the difficulty he experienced in *composing* a painting, had forced him to limit himself to what has been called realism, that is, to the exact representation of natural objects, without discernment, without selection, just as they offered themselves to view: Thersites and Venus are thus equally beautiful simply because they exist; the humpback of the one is equal to the bosom of the other. This is the theory of impotent men, who erect their defects into a system; everyone knows the fable of the fox whose tail was cut off. [p. 184]

The rhetoric of political confrontation, like that of any specular facing-off, is inclined to draw its force from figures of reversal: so, for Hugo, the effect of the woman's gesture—or of the *émeute* "herself"—could be caught in that phrase, "all that weakness contains of strength." To speak of realism as "the theory of impotent men, who erect their defects into a system" is to draw on the same resources: du Camp is locating Courbet and his school where Hugo had placed women or the unpropertied classes—impotent, with nothing to show for themselves, no natural talent, they would instead display a theory in its place. Du Camp's language finds *its* place somewhere between Freud's description of an apotropaic gesture ("To display the penis [or any of its surrogates] . . .") and the metaphors with which Burke castigated the revolutionaries of 1789: "Is it then true . . . that it was of absolute necessity the whole fabric should be at once pulled down, and the area cleared for the erection of a theoretic experimental edifice in its place?"[12] In this view a system—a "theoretic experimental edifice"—whether it's a system of government or a system of aesthetics, is phallic or—more properly—fetishistic: it is an ersatz thing-in-itself which can be erected, narcissistically invested, and then brandished in self-defense. Hence the castration jokes Maxime du Camp feels he can make at the Realists' expense.

Nor are the Realists the only fetishists in this text: the accusation is made explicit in du Camp's account of the toppling of the column. "This rage to take it out on material things, this reversed fetishism (*ce fétichisme à l'envers*) which is the height of fetishism, which was the sickness of the Commune, appeared in all its inten-

Figure 2. *Paris sous la Commune. Chute de la colonne Vendôme.* Reprinted from *L'Illustration,* Paris, May 27, 1871.

sity at the moment of the column's fall (*lors du renversement de la colonne*)" (p. 209). Figures of reversal, including this image of a literal *renversement* (figure 2), coexist here with a polemical stance that is both given to and braced against *tu quoque* retorts:

> The materialism which darkened the mind of these people led them to attach importance only to the exterior, to the materiality of things. . . . In this respect, as in many others as well, the men of the Commune were medieval men. To set up an idol, to pull down an idol, to be a idolator, to be an iconoclast—it's all the same; it is to believe in the idol. [p. 183]

It is part of the logic of such encounters that du Camp should himself sound somewhat overwrought here, just as, in a more in-

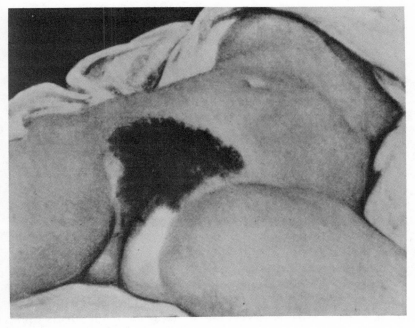

Figure 3. Gustave Courbet. *L'Origine du monde,* c. 1866. Museum of Fine Arts, Budapest [?].

teresting moment in his text, he seems peculiarly overexcited by what he finds obscene in a work of Courbet's:

> All that one may ask of a man—outside of the grand principles of morality which no one should neglect—is to respect the art he professes. He can be lacking in intelligence, in learning, in wit, in politeness, in urbanity, and still remain honorable, if he maintains the practice of his art aloft and intact. Now this elementary duty, which constitutes professional probity, Courbet ignored. To please a Moslem who paid for his whims in gold, and who, for a time, enjoyed a certain notoriety in Paris because of his prodigalities, Courbet, this same man whose avowed intention was to renew French painting, painted a portrait of a woman which is difficult to describe. In the dressing-room of this foreign personage, one sees a small picture hidden under a green veil. When one draws aside

171

the veil one remains stupefied to perceive a woman, life-size, seen from the front, moved and convulsed, remarkably executed, re-produced *con amore*, as the Italians say, providing the last word in realism. But, by some inconceivable forgetfulness, the artist who copied his model from nature, had neglected to represent the feet, the legs, the thighs, the stomach, the hips, the chest, the hands, the arms, the shoulders, the neck and the head.

The man who, for a few coins, could degrade his craft to the point of abjection, is capable of anything. [pp. 189–90]

I have reproduced Courbet's picture here (figure 3) to document that there is a certain degree of overkill in Maxime du Camp's account of it: the artist hadn't, it would appear, entirely neglected "the thighs, the stomach, the hips" or "the chest." The intensity of focus, that zeroing-in on the woman's genitals, is the work of the beholder in this case, and it is coordinate with other features of his text: its disingenuous air of moral indignation, the coyness of its negative anatomy ("not this, not that . . . but you know what!"), its dragging-in of those innocent Italians, presumably so as to mo-tivate the appearance of the word *con,* so that du Camp can surrep-titiously name what is "difficult to describe" without openly using what Hugo called "that dreadful brothel language that one is always obliged to translate." It would be wrong to suggest, however, that behind all this periphrasis and moral outrage lies no more than the prurience of a closet voyeur: du Camp's dismay is as genuine and as powerful as his fascination. Together they produce an ambivalence that informs his discussion of the Commune and the aesthetic theo-ries of the Realists as much as it does his response to Courbet's nude. To describe her body as "convulsed," for example, is to assimilate her horrid appeal to that of the political "convulsions" du Camp is charting in Paris. But the links among erotic, political, and aesthetic attitudes go deeper than that, and they become easier to discern when one collates the apparently contradictory statements these pages on Courbet contain. It is because Courbet had difficulty "*composing* a painting," du Camp insists, that he was forced into realism, "the exact representation of natural objects . . . just as they offered themselves to view." And yet "the last word in realism" turns out to be this representation of a woman's genitals "just as they offered themselves to view," yet still *composed,* selected and focused—in du Camp's account—with an intensity that would be hard to match. Here the traditional paradoxes about what it means for a painter to copy "Nature" are energized by the ambivalence—sexual and epistemological—that inheres in fetishism: What is there to be seen in the object? How passive—or how willfully system-atic—is that seeing? How is what one sees shaped by what one thinks one has or fears to lose? There are the urgencies that are played out in Maxime du Camp's pages: it is not unreasonable that his hatred of the Commune should have led him, by something like free association, to Courbet's nude.

III

Confronted with such extravagant responses, we may decide to grant Victor Hugo the license of a poet and novelist and to write off Maxime du Camp as not much more than a panicky *arriviste,* the Norman Podhoretz of the Second Empire.[13] But what of a serious historian? Let us look now at Tocqueville's recollections of the events of 1848, as he set them down in his posthumously published *Souvenirs.* Although not a republican, Tocqueville was nevertheless not displeased when Louis-Phillipe was overthrown in February. Like Hugo, he momentarily hoped that a regency could be estab-lished; when that did not materialize, he adopted an attitude he describes as one of somewhat remote curiosity, but by June he had become disturbed by the turn events were taking, and when the fighting broke out he was very much on the side of the party of order. I quote his account of an incident on June 24, the second day of street fighting, as he made his way to the Chamber of Deputies:

> When I was getting near and was already in the midst of the troops guarding it, an old woman with a vegetable cart stubbornly barred my way. I ended by telling her rather sharply to make room. Instead of doing so, she left her cart and rushed at me with such sudden frenzy that I had trouble defending myself. I shuddered at the frightful and hideous expression on her face, which reflected demagogic passions and the fury of civil war. I mention this minor

fact because I saw in it then, and rightly, a major symptom. At moments of violent crisis even actions that have nothing to do with politics take on a strange character of chaotic anger; these actions are not lost on the attentive eye and they provide a very reliable index of the general state of mind. It is as though these great public emotions create a burning atmosphere in which private feelings seethe and boil.[14]

This is a story with two points. One is about the nature of the June Days: like Hugo's, this is a representative anecdote, in which a woman's gesture encapsulates the meaning of the revolution. But Tocqueville also intends to tell us something about how one comes upon representative anecdotes, about the power of that "attentive eye" to grasp the meaning of a minor, possibly negligible, incident, a power that the author of *Democracy in America* can rightly claim for himself. He knows that an observer thoughtful and canny and experienced enough will "see" the meaning of historical moments in such small details. But perhaps "seeing" is not quite the right verb for what Tocqueville is demonstrating here: rather his power is that of someone who can "read" the meaning of a face in a rapid and unperplexed fashion. For, like Victor Hugo, Tocqueville is interested in the "lineaments"—what he calls *traits,* "features"—of physiognomy, and indeed physiognomy is his chief metaphor for historical interpretation. The *Souvenirs* open with these lines:

> Now that for the moment I am out of the stream of public life, and the uncertain state of my health does not even allow me to follow any consecutive study, I have in my solitude for a time turned my thoughts to myself, or rather to those events of the recent past in which I played a part or stood as a witness. The best use of my leisure seems to be to go back over these events, to describe the men I saw taking part in them, and in this way, if I can, to catch and engrave on my memory those confused features that make up the uncertain physiognomy of my time. [S29/R3]

A page later, describing the last years of the July Monarchy, he writes: "Only the general physiognomy of that time comes readily to my mind. For that was something I often contemplated with mingled curiosity and fear, and I clearly discerned the particular features that gave it its character" (S30/R4). Readers familiar with

Hegel's critique of Lavater in the *Phenomenology*[15] might assume that, forty years later, it would be impossible for serious observers to use the language of physiognomy in anything other than a figurative sense, as Tocqueville does in these two citations: the face that he here contemplates "with mingled curiosity and fear" is one he has conjured into existence and attributed to his "times." But physiognomy's hold on the nineteenth-century imagination was tenacious. Lavater's works continued to sell, and even among intellectuals who might deny their scientific status, the appeal of physiognomic lore in both the interpretation of character and the elaboration of portraits was powerful.[16] So it should not surprise us to find Tocqueville reading the meaning of his times out of the quite literal face of a vegetable woman: literal faces could take on that synecdochic value. But why should it have been a woman's face? Why should that have been the representative anecdote of the June uprising? To answer that we have to follow a number of other threads in Tocqueville's *Souvenirs,* one concerning property, one concerning the place of theory in the events of 1848 and, finally, one concerning women.

Perhaps the first remark to make about Tocqueville on property is that the *Souvenirs* were begun quite literally on his property: facing the opening page of text he had written *Écrite en juillet 1850 à Tocqueville.* We are reading the thoughts of Tocqueville from Tocqueville, and the relation between that signature and that place name is both more interesting and more elusive than that of a pun. If I were to protest that I was writing to you "from the heart"— *Herz von dem Herz*—that would indeed be a pun, but not an especially snappy one. Like all puns it would express a certain willfulness. But it isn't clear that the same accusation applies in this case: Tocqueville himself no doubt hardly gave a thought, as he wrote that line, to the fact that his name was his place. Whatever self-satisfaction inheres in the coalescence of an individual, a family, and some acreage would operate in ways that had, by time, been muted and quasi-naturalized. That Tocqueville's investment in Tocqueville should be strengthened by whatever representative—and self-representative—power the sign held for him, and not depend simply on the value of the real estate, is something we take for granted, even though we grant further that this area—where land, people, and language interact—is a hard one to chart. Tocqueville was himself alert to the ways in which the notion of property had both a natural and a semiotic component. Here, for example, is how he epitomizes the "socialist character of the February Revolution":

> Inevitably [the people] were bound to discover sooner or later that what held them back in their place was not the constitution of the government, but the unalterable laws that constitute society itself; and it was natural for them to ask whether they did not have the power and the right to change these too, as they had changed the others. And to speak specifically about property, which is, so to speak, the foundation of our social order, when all the privileges that cover and conceal the privilege of property had been abolished and property remained as the main obstacle to equality among men and seemed to be the only sign thereof, was it not inevitable, I do not say that it should be abolished in its turn, but that at least the idea of abolishing it should strike minds that had no part in its enjoyment?
>
> This natural restlessness in the minds of the people, with the inevitable ferment in the desires, thoughts, needs and instincts of the crowd, formed the fabric on which the innovators drew such monstrous and grotesque patterns. [S96/R-76-76]

Tocqueville could here be echoing Burke's dictum in the *Reflections* that the "characteristic essence of property, formed from the combined principles of its acquisition and conservation, is to be *unequal*."[17] For Tocqueville as for Burke, unequally distributed property functions as a natural sign of legitimate inequalities and, as such, can be expected to serve not simply as the occasion for material greed but—more subtly and dangerously—as an incitement to a sort of semiotic restlessness: when all the other signs of privilege had been removed, the itch to get past that last sign to bare unaccommodated man, what Burke calls "naked, shivering nature," becomes intolerably strong.

But the semiotics of property are still more complicated, in Tocqueville's view. If the distribution of property establishes a set of natural—and, to that extent, good—signs of inequality, and prompts a natural—and understandable—"restlessness," Tocqueville's account also invokes a more reprehensible set of signs, those

176

that are actively, willfully, traced by "innovators" on the "fabric" provided by the people's restlessness. Like designs sketched on a cloth ground, these are "monstrous and grotesque patterns," rather like the "monstrous and unknown forms" Victor Hugo discerned in the events of 1848. But if the language of Hugo's text immediately associated the "monstrous and unknown forms" with the sight of a woman's body, the path of association in Tocqueville is less rapid and direct: it goes by way of a denunciation of socialist theorizers as furiously energetic, crazed producers of signs:

> It was those social theories, which I have previously called the philosophy of the February Revolution, that later kindled real passions, embittered jealousies, and finally stirred up war between the classes.
>
> After the 25th February a thousand strange systems poured from the impetuous imaginations of innovators and spread through the troubled minds of the crowd. Everything except Throne and Parliament was still standing; and yet it seemed that the shock of revolution had reduced society itself to dust, and that there was an open competition for the plan of the new edifice to be put in its place; each man had his own scheme; one might publish his in the papers; another might use the posters that soon covered the walls; a third might proclaim his to the listening winds. One was going to abolish inequality of fortunes; another that of education; while a third attacked the oldest inequality of all, that between men and women. [S95/R74]

Like Pope's madman who "locked from ink and paper scrawls / With desperate charcoal round his darkened walls," the innovators are here conjured up in a vision of semiotic behavior gone haywire; the paragraphs link socialism to the grotesque proliferation of theories, to irregular publication, to the abolition of inequalities and—in a cadence that should by now seem predictable—to the final, one would have thought ineradicable difference between the sexes. But how, exactly, did Tocqueville get from writing to women? A final quotation should make that clear: it is a vignette of a conversation Tocqueville had, in the spring of 1848, with the writer and socialist sympathizer George Sand:

> Milnes put me beside Madame Sand; I had never spoken to her, and I don't think I had ever seen her before (for I have not lived

177

much in the world of literary adventurers which she inhabited). When one of my friends asked her what she thought of my book about America, she replied: "Sir, I make it a habit only to read the books that are presented to me by the authors." I had a strong prejudice against Madame Sand, for I detest women who write, especially those who disguise the weaknesses of their sex *en système* . . . [S150/R134]

I have left the last two words in French because it's hard to find English equivalents that are both easily colloquial and accurate: that may say something about the long history of Anglo-American difficulties with French systems. Tocqueville's most recent translator writes "especially those who systematically disguise the weaknesses of their sex," but that isn't the point here: Tocqueville is using *en système* in the only way it is generally used in French; that is, in the same way Maxime du Camp is using it when he complains that the Realists are "impotent men, who erect their defects into a system" (*qui érigent leurs défauts en système*): the phrase should read "I detest women who write, especially those who disguise the weaknesses of their sex by producing a system," however awkwardly that strikes the ear. In this respect George Sand serves as a transitional figure between Tocqueville's dismay with socialist theories and the horror he felt when he stared into the face of the old woman.

If his use of *en système* aligns Tocqueville's text with du Camp's, his remark about women who disguise the weaknesses of their sex brings his language close to Hugo's "all that weakness contains of strength." Tocqueville's writing is more considered and less overwrought, but his implication in this tangled set of attitudes toward sexual difference, politics, and knowledge is similar to theirs. All three writers have produced intensely charged passages that are about a confrontation with a woman, a confrontation in which each finds an emblem of what revolutionary violence is all about. To rehearse the chain of associations we have been following in Tocqueville may allow us to see what is at work in the other writers as well. An investment in property, to begin with: property seen as a sign of privilege and set against those other signs marked out by those without property, the systems and theories of socialists. It is they who publish attacks on all inequalities—any old inequality—including the oldest of all, that between men and women. And in this they are like those women writers who convert their weaknesses into systems and would brandish these substitutes apotropaically, defying those possessed of the more natural signs of privilege, of which property is the most fundamental. This would seem to be in defense of Tocqueville as a man of property, Tocqueville from Tocqueville. But it is also a defense of Tocqueville as the author of this resolutely nontheoretical account of what is happening in the world, a physiognomic reading of the confused features of his time which, though he contemplates them with mingled curiosity and fear, he nevertheless imagines to be *viewable*, composable into features of the same face, if not characters of the great Apocalypse. I'm suggesting that it is this belief—that one can see history as the features of a face, read it off a composed physiognomy—that Tocqueville must defend, chiefly by casting out something that resembles it a bit too closely for comfort: that production of "unnatural" systems which interpret the historical world with a willed and artificial coherence, and which are manifestly invested by their creators with the narcissistic charge of something like property. They are threatening to the extent that they raise doubts about one's own more natural ways of looking at things; and it is that threat that prompts these powerfully rendered Medusa fantasies when they are offered as substitutes for a more patient, inclusive account of political conflict.

A Vermiform Appendix: The Phrygian Cap

When I first presented this material to an audience at Johns Hopkins, Beatrice Marie, of the Humanities Center, suggested that some connections might be drawn between the complex of sexual, proprietary, and epistemological investments I had associated with the appearance of Medusa fantasies in political contexts, on the one hand, and, on the other, the adoption, during the French Revolution, of the Phrygian cap as an emblem of Liberty. She had in mind the droopy-phallic look the cap takes on when its crown falls for-

Figure 4. *Louis XVI en bonnet de la liberté,* 1792. Paris, Bibliothèque Nationale.   Photo: Bibliothèque Nationale.

ward or to one side, as it does in a mocking portrayal of Louis XVI
(figure 4) obliged to wear the cap (apotropaically, but—as it turned
out—ineffectively so) in June 1792; and she wondered if the cap
might not consistently, if surreptitiously, be associated with the
threat of impotence or castration. I had no ideas on the subject at
the time, but I've since had a chance to read around in histories of
costume and of iconography, and this reading would seem to confirm Ms. Marie's hunch. It also provides a further illustration of the
odd now-you-see-it/now-you-don't logic with which these motifs
appear and disappear, come together and disperse, in historical en-
actment and in historical interpretation.

The usual understanding of the *bonnet rouge de la Liberté* is as an
unequivocally political symbol. The cap was taken to stand for
liberty because it had stood for liberty in Rome: under the Empire
it had been awarded to slaves on the occasion of their manumission;
earlier still, it had been mounted on a staff and paraded through the
streets of the city by Caesar's assassins. I cite a recent summary of
this account from an article by Jennifer Harris:

> Along with other symbols borrowed from the period of classical
> antiquity (such as the Roman *fasces* denoting Unity and Indi-
> visibility), [the *bonnet rouge*] early enters revolutionary iconogra-
> phy as a symbol of liberty, having been worn in Rome by
> freedmen as a sign of their new position, although it was also worn
> by several different nations of antiquity and by various individu-
> als. It is associated, for example, with the dress of Paris who is
> shown wearing it in David's 1788 painting *Paris and Helen*. In Rome
> it does appear to have stood for liberty in the same way that it was
> to in France after 1789, for it is represented on a coin of Brutus,
> issued in Asia Minor in 44–42 B.C., positioned between two dag-
> gers and recalling the Ides of March.[18]

But here a slight complication develops: the cap on the coin Harris
is referring to (figure 5) doesn't look like a Phrygian cap—it lacks
the droop. Does that matter? Apparently it does, at least to some
historians, ancient and modern: as one reads further in French accounts of the *bonnet rouge* and in descriptions of classical headgear,
the question of what the Roman cap of liberty actually looked like
(and what sorts of cap it was to be distinguished from) gets inter-

Figure 5. Roman coin commemorating the Ides of March, 44 B.C. (greatly enlarged). Redrawn after L. Olschki, *The Myth of Felt* (Berkeley: University of California Press, 1949), pl. 3.   Courtesy of Lorna Price.

estingly tangled and generates more vehemence than you would think a hat properly should. It will be worth our while to look at some discussions of Phrygian, Greek, and Roman versions of the cap before returning to modern France.

Harris cites the Pauly-Wissowa *Encyclopädie,* which, under *pilleus,* describes a cap that, in Rome, became so firmly associated with "liberty" that one could speak of "attaining the *pilleus*" or "conferring the *pilleus*" when a slave earned or was granted his freedom.[19] This *pilleus* was rounded, like the one pictured on the coin; there is no mention of a droop, nor of any Phrygian associations; the cap's origins would seem to be Etruscan and its connotations political or, when religious, associated with the official Roman priesthood. The *Phrygian* cap, on the other hand, according to Pauly-Wissowa, is not properly a *pilleus* but a variant of the old

Persian *tiara*.[20] In the words of one of the scholars whose work the *Encyclopädie* draws on, "this *tiara* was well known to the Greeks; they used it to designate not only Persians but Orientals in general: Scythians, Amazons, Trojans, and other Easterners. It consists of a high cap, apparently of felt, with a rounded peak which nods forward; to its lower edge a pair of lappets and a broad neckpiece were attached."[21] It appears as an attribute of a variety of Asiatic figures in Greek and Roman art—of Ganymede, of Paris, of Mithra, and of Attis, among others. If we accept the authority of Pauly-Wissowa, there is no connection to be made between the uses or symbolic values of these two quite distinctly shaped caps: the two encyclopedia entries—*pilleus* and *tiara*—are not cross-referenced, nor does either allude to the other. It may be, then, that the French revolutionaries simply made a mistake; lacking the perspective of modern scholarship, they confused the two caps and conferred on the droop of the one the political meanings of the other. This conclusion would be endorsed by a number of contemporary historians of costume and of symbolism;[22] indeed it was even put forward—and forcefully, as we shall see—by a French antiquarian writing in 1796.

But the situation—at least, as it appears to an amateur, reading out of his field—may be more complicated than this conclusion would suggest. For "modern scholarship," even modern German scholarship, is not of one mind on the subject. The *Encyclopädie* discussion of the *tiara* was revised in 1974; in 1978 Eleanore Dörner, an interpreter of Mithraic symbolism, published an article entitled "Deus Pileatus" in which she traced a line of descent from the Persian *tiara* through the "soft-falling" (*weichfallende*) Phrygian cap worn by Mithra down to the *pileus libertatis* of Rome and on to the *bonnet rouge* of 1792.[23] Can Dörner, like the eighteenth-century promoters of the Phrygian cap, be ignorant of more recent archeological findings? That is possible, but less likely in her case: her footnotes refer to current scholarship, her manner of proceeding is cautious, she likes to point out what is "extraordinarily hard to decide" or what is "especially unclear." Indeed, her article is distinguished by two things—the care with which she weighs the materials she chose to include and, considering that care, the puzzling omission of another set of iconographic associations that would seem to pertain to her subject, those connected not with the cult of Mithra but with that of the Magna Mater—the goddess Cybele—and her lover Attis.

Both cults were among the half-dozen Eastern mystery religions tolerated under the Roman Empire;[24] both gods were depicted in recognizably oriental dress, wearing the *tiara* with its rounded peak nodding forward. Furthermore, the two cults coexisted, as one scholar puts it, "in intimate communion,"[25] so that their monumental traces are frequently found mingled with one another, to the point where it often takes considerable archeological and epigraphical skill to establish which of the two gods is being represented in a particular statue.[26] But if busts of Mithra and Attis could be mistaken for one another, it would be harder to confuse the adherents of the two cults, or their religious practices. Mithraic ceremonies were secret, austere, and restricted to male adepts (the cult was widespread among the Roman legions), whereas the followers of Cybele and Attis included both men and women, as well as a group of *semivirs,* eunuchs who had castrated themselves in fervid emulation of their god. For the legend of Attis is that of a dying and rising god, a Phrygian shepherd beloved by the Great Mother who, in a moment of erotic frenzy, mutilates himself, dies, then rises deified and restored to his virility. In the ceremonies commemorating his passion, death, and rebirth—held in Rome in March—some of the devout would mark the seriousness of their devotion by sacrificing their genitals to the goddess.[27] Thus initiated, these *galli,* as they were called, were recognizable thereafter in the streets of Rome by the "Asiatic" extravagance of their dress: they wore colored robes belted at the waist in what, to the Romans, was a feminine fashion, earrings, other ornaments considered effeminate and, tied under the chin, a Phrygian cap.[28]

This digression on the cult of Attis is meant to supplement—and complicate still further—Dörner's conclusions on the *pilleus* and the *tiara.* Suppose she is correct in believing that the cap awarded to freed slaves resembles the headgear of Mithra; then it would also resemble the headgear of Attis and of the *galli.* And while the gods themselves might only appear in representations of one sort or another, their followers might be seen walking about the streets of Rome, wearing hats which, if not precisely identical to those of the freedmen, would be noticeably similar. Did anyone in fact notice? And, if so, what, if anything, was this taken to mean—either at the time, by the Romans accustomed to the sight, or later by historians seeking the significance of these signs of status and allegiance? Did anyone ask why the cap that meant "liberty" could also mean "castration"?

Dörner, who isn't concerned with Attis, has nothing directly to say to these questions, but her article does suggest some ways to approach them. She tentatively proposes that a connection might have existed, in the minds of Roman worshipers of Mithra, between the egalitarian tenets of their cult—they chose to think of themselves as *fratres,* united in brotherhood regardless of their social rank in the city—and their wearing a cap which, in another context, signified the raising of a slave to the dignity of civic freedom. The Phrygian cap, then, would in both cases connote the dissolution of hierarchical difference. This is plausible, if hypothetical: Dörner cites no explicit testimony to this way of thinking about the cap. But she does quote, from Servius' fourth-century commentary on Virgil, some remarks that could be taken as an attempt to assert—in the face of the possibility of confusing one sort of hat with another—a clear-cut distinction between the sort of cap appropriate for men and the sort for women. Virgil had, at certain points in the *Aeneid,* used the noun *mitra* to designate a style of hat, and Servius is explaining that the *mitra* is a Phrygian or Lydian item, a curved *pilleus* with pendant laces, a feminine cap, not by any means to be confused with the true *pilleus,* which is worn by men. It is clear from the context in Virgil and Servius that this moment of decisiveness is coordinate with the scorn Romans directed at everything that seemed sexually equivocal or positively effeminate about "the East," including its gods, their followers, and their headgear.[29] The Phrygian cap could become a target for this scorn: phallic but not erect, it could function as what Lacan might term a drooping signifier, eliciting uncertainties about the stability of sexual difference, uncertainties that could resonate with those developing out of the blurring of differences in social status— between, for instance, citizens, freedmen, and slaves.

All this is speculative and depends, as I've indicated, on accepting Dörner's assumptions about the look of the freedman's *pilleus* rather than those of the scholars who would insist that the *pilleus* and the Phrygian cap were obviously distinct and unconflatable. It could be that the distinguishers are right, and that Dörner is repeating, uncritically, a mistake the French made in the 1790s. But as we shall see when we turn to the French, the act of insisting on distinctions here can take on its own ideological charge: scholars as well as other historical agents can get caught up in the drive to see things clearly and distinctly.

When Voltaire's *Brutus* was performed at the Théâtre de la Nation in March 1792, a *bonnet rouge* was ceremonially placed on the bust of the playwright: Jennifer Harris recounts the incident and reprints a drawing commemorating this crowning of Voltaire as patron saint or poet laureate of tyrannicide.[30] However—and this is one reason for its longevity as a symbol—the cap was also available for less bloody-minded iconographic uses: if you look back at that anti-revolutionary document, "The Contrast" (figure 1), also worked up in response to what was happening in Paris in 1792, you will find the Phrygian cap not on the head of the Gorgon—the snakes would make that difficult—but in the other vignette, calmly taking its place among the benign attributes of British Liberty, propped on a rod beside her throne. This can serve as a synchronic instance of what Maurice Agulhon, in the most comprehensive and subtle account of the cap's vicissitudes in France, has referred to as "the wavering of political imagery between the notion of popular, dynamic, even vehement struggle and one of serene power established in the wake of victory."[31]

Because it had been settled, by the end of the Revolution, that figures representing Liberty, or the Republic, or France, would be female,[32] the political themes played out in this wavering fashion could draw, consciously or subliminally, on attitudes toward sexual difference for their affective force. A straightforward example of this can be found in an editorial Agulhon cites from *L'Artiste* of March 1848: "The Republic will wear no red cap," it decrees, "she will be no camp-follower but a serene, glorious and fertile mother who will hold festivals and shed smiles upon her children."[33] But more bizarre and, for our purposes, more telling evidence that the Phrygian cap carried a high sexual charge can be found in a pamphlet entitled *De l'Origine et de la forme du bonnet de la Liberté* (1796). Its author, Esprit-Antoine Gibelin, identifies himself as a *Peintre d'histoire,* but he must also have been a reader of considerable range, capable of rapidly surveying the uses the cap was put to from classical times through the Renaissance. But chiefly he writes as a distinguisher, someone anxious to disseminate the "true meaning" of the *bonnet rouge* by insisting that its "true form" is that of the simple, rounded *pilleus,* just as it appears on the coin of Brutus: semi-oval, chaste, and droop-free. I cite at length, to convey the urgency of his insistence and the sexual polemic which informs it:

> our French artists, in the many paintings, sculptures, and engravings made since the beginning of the revolution, have used the form of the Phyrgian cap to adorn the head even of the figure of Liberty. Seduced by the refined turn of this effeminate cap (*Seduits par le galbe recherché de ce bonnet efféminé*) that ancient monuments have preserved for us on the graceful heads of a Paris and of a Ganymede, they have not considered that nothing is less appropriate to designate liberty than the Phrygian cap; that it is an Asian headgear; that liberty never dwelt in those lands; that even the Asiatic section of Greece was unable to preserve its own liberty and that the enslaved kings pictured on Roman arches of triumph wear an almost similar cap.
>
> In truth, when the semi-oval form of the ordinary cap is a little elongated, the part that exceeds the crown of the head folds and falls, sometimes forward, sometimes back. Then it more or less imitates the form of the Phrygian cap; and the caps of those enslaved kings, placed in Rome on the arch of triumph of Constantine, and on the stairway of the Farnese palace, seem to be of that sort. But, once again, this is not the true cap of Liberty as it is represented on ancient medals and monuments.
>
> It must be semi-oval, and if artists may permit themselves, in their imitation, to give it a little bit more fullness, in order to obtain picturesque folds, they must never, running to excess, expose to our view a Phrygian cap as a cap of Liberty (*il ne faut point*

que, donnant dans l'excès, ils exposent à nos regards un bonnet Phrygien pour un bonnet de la liberté).

It is especially essential, in a symbolic representation of this sort, to avoid anything that can mislead the imagination by associations that are seductive (*d'éviter tout ce qui peut égarer l'imagination par des rapports séduisans*) and contrary to the goal proposed by the majority. It is necessary to determine (*fixer*) a just idea of the emblematic meaning of each form.[34]

The dangers to be avoided here are indeterminately political, sexual, and epistemological. Enslavement, seduction, the loss of manhood, and the unfixing of determinate ideas of what things mean are held up as equivalent threats, and these baleful consequences inhere in the overly refined turn of the top of a cap, or—more theatrically—in the possibility that, looking for Liberty (or for the Republic, that "serene, glorious, and fertile mother"), we may find, exposed to our glance, the droop of the Phrygian cap. This is the rhetoric of male hysteria, playing out, with an only slightly different set of images, the Medusa fantasies we have been considering. And I suspect that it is in these terms that we can best understand an otherwise puzzling moment in Agulhon's history. Here again he is citing *L'Artiste,* this time a set of instructions, published in April 1848, on how properly to represent the figure of the Republic. She should be seated, thus expressing, as Agulhon notes, calm and order; she should manifest all three of her aspects—Liberty as well as Equality and Fraternity—hence she should wear the cap, but with a difference:

> I nearly forgot to mention the cap. I indicated above that the Republic should sum up the three forces of which her symbol is combined. You are therefore not in a position to remove this sign of liberty. Only do find some way of transfiguring it.

Agulhon quotes these lines then wonders, in a footnote, what they can mean, exactly: "Although the intentions are clear, the concrete instructions are less so. How can one 'transfigure' a cap but 'not make it disappear' in its accustomed form?"[35] I think the answer is simple: remove the droop and you transfigure the cap. The author of those instructions shared, no doubt unconsciously, Gibelin's

188

feelings about the proper look, the "true form" of the cap of Liberty.

Untransfigured, the Phrygian cap aroused strong feelings; indeed, after the Commune it became, in Agulhon's words, "an object of official loathing," and the last chapters of his book chart the intensities of opposition during the 1870s and 1880s. I have been implying that, whatever its political sources, some of that intensity was psychosexual in origin, the result of the cap's signifying, equivocally, both the possession and the lack of phallic power.[36] Just as Gibelin urgently repeats his identification of the effeminate cap with that of "the enslaved kings pictured on Roman arches of triumph," so nineteenth-century men of property could read in the cap the provocative lineaments of power and abjection, both "all that weakness contains of strength" and, proleptically, all that their own strength might conceal of weakness. For if caps can be removed, so can heads; and, not so long before, a certain number of heads *had* been removed by people wearing those very caps. Shortly after Louis XVI's execution, a print appeared showing his head held aloft like Medusa's (figure 6). Beneath it are two revolutionary emblems, the cap of Liberty and the Masonic level, the sign of Equality. Supported by the level, the cap has been carefully aligned with the king's head, so that its tip, soft-falling to the right, echoes the fall of the king's hair. Detached in this way, the cap functions as a mini-Medusa, and it seems to have been capable of producing something of the same *frisson*.

Agulhon, who is wary of psychoanalytic interpretations, and who would no doubt find this association of the *bonnet rouge* with Medusa both far-fetched and tendentious,[37] nevertheless provides further evidence of its plausibility in the chapter on the early 1870s. He describes, in fascinating detail, the conservative polemic against republicanism, the attempts to keep representations of the Motherland free of any taint of revolutionary imagery, attempts which included the destruction of a statue wearing the Phrygian cap, as well as official proclamations condemning the cap as a violent and "seditious" emblem. In this context he takes up a painting produced in 1872, "a representation of Evil entitled 'The Fatal Fall'" which depicts Mankind toppling into the abyss, apparently pro-

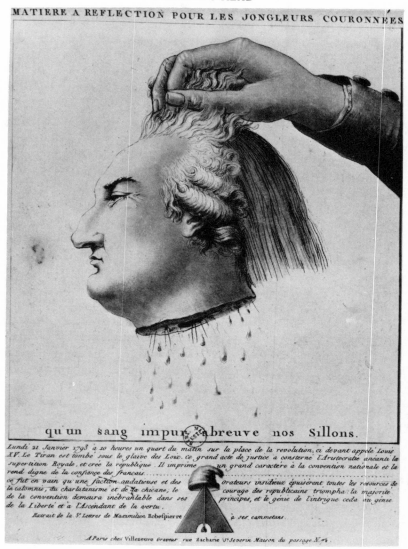

Figure 6. "Matière à Réflection pour les Jongleurs Couronnées," 1793. Paris, Bibliothèque Nationale.   Photo: Bibliothèque Nationale.

pelled there by the powerfully malign influence of three allegorical personages, a sophistic Blakean "Human Reason" and two bad women, whom Agulhon describes in these terms:

> One of them lies there naked, in a state of abandon, with a wine-glass in her hand—she clearly represents Evil in private life; the other, whose upper body only is naked, must be Evil in social life, namely Revolt. In her left hand she holds a torch and in her right a dagger. We cannot fail here to recognize the accessories that have become so familiar to us in their classic reactionary interpretation. The torch of Enlightenment has become the brand that set Paris alight and the sword of political conflict has shrunk to an assassin's dagger.
>
> We are bound, in all honesty, to admit that this fury is not wearing a Phrygian cap. Her heavy locks could be interpreted rather as the serpents of discord—a motif which is, after all, close to it.[38]

Close enough, I would agree.

One final example: in 1797 Antonio Canova began work on a statue of *Perseus Triumphant,* holding at arm's length the head of Medusa (figure 8); customarily such depictions of Perseus— Cellini's, for example (figure 7)—show him wearing the helmet given him by Hades, the helmet of invisibility. In Canova's statue he is wearing an odd conglomerate headpiece, combining the traditional winged helmet with the lappets and the droop of the Phrygian cap. Perhaps there was precedent for this, but I doubt it; it seems unlikely that Perseus could have been represented in this way before 1793—that is, before the guillotining of the king. Canova has also departed from Cellini's example by having Perseus rotate the head so that it is almost—almost, but, for safety's sake, not quite—facing him. The result is to fix in marble an emblem of the political and sexual specularity we have been considering, the inter-changeability of the Phrygian cap and the head of Medusa.

Figure 7. Benvenuto Cellini. *Perseo,* 1545. Florence, National Museum. Photo: Alinari/Art Resource NY.

Figure 8. Antonio Canova. *Perseo Trionfante,* 1797–1801. Rome. Vatican Museum. Photo: Alinari/Art Resource NY.

POSTSCRIPT (1985)

If the argument of these pages carries conviction, it might lead one to expect that Courbet, that producer of Medusas, might also have been partial to the Phrygian cap, and indeed Agulhon mentions a work of his—a bust of Liberty sculpted in 1875—wearing the cap. A richer and more surprising instance has been drawn to my attention, since the publication of this article, by Michael Fried. Preserved in the Bibliothèque Nationale is a copy of a privately printed manifesto, entitled *Lettres de Gustave Courbet à l'Armée allemande et aux artistes allemands: Lues à l'Athenée dans la séance du 29 octobre 1870* (Paris, 1870), a long and, in places, accusatory address to The Enemy which ends on this bizarre note of proffered reconciliation. Here, translated, are the document's last three paragraphs:

> An idea:

> Listen: leave us your Krupp cannons, we'll melt them down together with our own; the last cannon, mouth in the air, topped with a Phrygian cap, will be planted on a pedestal sitting on three cannon-balls, and this colossal monument which we'll erect together on the Place Vendôme will be our column, yours and ours, the column of the peoples, the column of Germany and of France, forever united in federation.

> The goddess of our liberty, like Venus crowning the god Mars, will string garlands on the pivots of the cannon which project like arms from its sides—bunches of grapes, sheaves of wheat, and hop-flowers.

> G. Courbet
> Rue Hautefeuille, no. 32

Mars disarmed in the lap of Venus, drowsy from all that (French) wine and (German) beer, the threatening cannon-shaft and cannon-balls capped with a droop: Courbet is anticipating here those *gemütlich* reunions of former enemies revisiting battlefields years after the World Wars. The alcohol, presumably, sweetens the relations between these (male) protagonists, as well as dissimulating the cutting edge of the "goddess of our liberty."

193

RESPONSE FROM CATHERINE GALLAGHER

Department of English, University of California, Berkeley

In answering the question posed at the beginning of his essay—why are certain kinds of revolutionary violence often emblematized by a "hideous and fierce but not exactly sexless woman?"—Neil Hertz immediately limits himself to a single interpretation of the Medusa's head. It stands for the vagina, which in turn represents the threat of losing one's penis and, by extension, one's property, one's social and economic power, one's very self-representations. Simultaneously, of course, the display of the vagina reassures one that the threatened castration has *not* taken place. But in both its phobic and its counterphobic effects, the vagina is—always and only—the site and sign of an absence, a terrifying lack that can only gain power by the lurid display of its own weakness.

This analysis allows many extraordinary insights into the texts Neil Hertz has chosen. However, it prevents many others; specifically, it prevents insights that would see the displayed vagina as something other than the sign of an absence. What else besides a lurid and threatening weakness might a "hideous and fierce but not exactly sexless woman" have meant in the context of nineteenth-century revolutionary upheaval?

I'd like, briefly, to suggest another meaning by reinterpreting the same passages from Tocqueville that Neil Hertz has just discussed. And, to maintain symmetry in this confrontation, I'll gather and reweave the very threads in Tocqueville's thought that Professor Hertz has just handled: one concerning property, one concerning women, and one concerning the fear of theory.

In Professor Hertz's account, Tocqueville's thoughts on property include a complex semiotics: property establishes a set of natural signs of inequality. *Tocqueville à Tocqueville* is such a sign. For Professor Hertz it signifies a confluence of person, name, and property that was, he tells us, probably very satisfying to Tocqueville. But he does not mention a fairly obvious fact: that this satisfying confluence of self-representation and property is based on the assumption of legitimacy, biological descent organized within the boundaries of patriarchal property inheritance. The natural signs of inequality are natural only insofar as women's sexuality and reproductive capacities remain proper. The assumed sexual property of women underlies both property relations and semiotics in the world Tocqueville inhabits, a world in which property is acreage and the important self-representation is still the name of the father. "This area," writes Neil Hertz, "—where land, people, and language interact—is a hard one to chart." But it may be named: it is the mother's vagina.

Bearing this in mind, what can we make of the old woman with the vegetable cart barring Tocqueville's access to the Chamber of Deputies? The old woman, cumbered with the severed produce of the land, is a familiar figure in nineteenth-century social reportage, and this female costermonger of Tocqueville's seems to carry the usual emblematic burden of her kind. She is mobile, yet obstructs the "natural" flow of persons through the city; thus she is often associated with the growth of an unnatural and irrational market economy as well as with the discrediting of the assumption that value inheres exclusively in the land and is passed on from father to legitimate son. The costermonger, then, is already a repository of fears about the odd mobility and irrational intransigence of an expanding money economy and about the possible independence of urban life and its forms of wealth from the more traditionally organized countryside. In Tocqueville's story, these commonplace associations mix themselves with the fear of a more violent kind of revolution, and the preternaturally strong costermonger woman becomes the image of the frenzied mother, evoking the possibility of completely chaotic reproduction.

It is precisely this possibility of seemingly disorganized reproduction (of children, of goods, or money, of value) that ignites the fear of what Neil Hertz describes as "semiotic behavior gone haywire." Hertz rightly connects Tocqueville's fear of the uncontrolled mother with his fear of semiotic chaos. But, again, an obvious connecting link is missing: if the mother is not properly constrained then semiotic riot is the result. One's name may mean nothing; one's property may have no natural relationship to one's name. One's self-representations may prove to be mere mental constructions, like the despised systems of George Sand, if one's mother was capable of the biological equivalent of system-making, of generating illegitimate and unprecedented progeny. Thus, Tocqueville's fear of what Professor Hertz calls "the grotesque proliferation of theories" seems to me, not a fear of the weakness of the vagina, but a fear of its reproductive power.

Professor Hertz makes nothing of the specific remark that raises Tocqueville's anger against George Sand: her remark that she only reads books presented to her by the authors. The statement amounts to a demand to see the direct connection between a person and his self-representation, the book, or the child, or the name. And that demand serves as a reminder that woman's biological power gives her the authority to call men's authorship into question.

From 1789 to 1870 French revolutionary violence repeatedly enacted an ambivalent attack on patriarchy. And the emblematic importance of the uncontrolled and luridly sexual woman cannot be separated from that attack. On the one hand the revolutionaries needed to undermine the patriarchal assumptions that buttressed monarchical and aristocratic power. Thus the symbol of liberty who leads the people is female. But liberty, in the iconography of the age, often turns into a whore when she threatens the patriarchal family as such. The sexually uncontrolled woman then becomes a threat to all forms of property and established power. Her fierce independence is viewed, even by revolutionaries, as an attack on the Rights of Man.

I do not wish to suggest that all men deeply fear the generativity of women; I am not trying to substitute one primal anxiety (generativity) for another (castration). But I am suggesting that in a society in which the forms and relations of property are undergoing irreversible changes and into which violent revolution threatens to bring even more radical disruptions, the fear of the Medusa's head can be analyzed as a much more historical and a much less hysterical phenomenon than Professor Hertz makes it seem.

RESPONSE FROM JOEL FINEMAN

Department of English,
University of California, Berkeley

There is in Neil Hertz's paper a dilemma or an irresolution, broached but deliberately left unresolved, that is partially political, partially aesthetic, and, even partially erotic—for Hertz's paper is inevitably written, to some extent (however bad he says the pun is), from his good heart. In this response I want briefly to address both the historical context and the formal reasoning that gives to this dilemma and to Hertz's paper their significance and their pathos. Even more briefly, I want to raise a question regarding the currency of Hertz's paper: namely, whether what I call its dilemma is something novel, possessing an especially contemporary urgency, or, instead, is something perennial, possessing the importance of a traditionary commonplace.

In general terms the paper stages an ongoing confrontation between two perspectival points of view, between two different ways of looking at "things seen." On the one hand, there is a naively physiognomic, natural and naturalizing, point of view, that of the proper and of property. Here things and the significance attaching to them are seen as they are, directly and immediately. If these things are signs, they are signs related by natural necessity to that which they signify. These signs are "self-representative," Hertz says; their semiotic veridicality cannot be overlooked. This, we can say, is a Cratylitic semiosis whereby words are the self-validating images or icons, the *eidola,* of either their referents or their meanings. With regard to politics, Hertz says that this is the point of view of the right, of the reactionary, Fascist, counterrevolutionary right of the sort we are to associate with Tocqueville. With regard to erotics, this is the point of view of Man, of hysterical and sexist Man.

On the other hand, counterpoised against the counterrevolutionary, there is another—or *The* other—point of view that never sees

197

things as they are because, instead, it sees things through the filter or lens of a supplementary "theorization of reality," to use the phrase from Laplanche that Hertz quotes, apparently with approval. From this other perspective, however, "theory"—and the visuality etymologically embedded in "theory" is central to Hertz's paper—is no gratuitously extraneous addition to visual perception. Such mediating and systematizing "scenarios," such symbolic amplifications of the visible, are what enable "things seen" to be seen, and to be seen *as* things, in the first place. From this point of view perception is equal to perception *plus* theory, for the "theorization of reality," as Laplanche says of castration theory (either Freud's theory or the horrified little boy's theory), "is so anchored in perception that to deny [it] is finally the same thing as denying the perceptual experience itself." Moreover, with the registration of this theoretical necessity there comes also the "semiotic restlessness" to which Hertz refers, an unloosing of signs that is occasioned by the realization that things and the signs of things are no longer transparently or necessarily related either to themselves or to what they signify. This theoretical necessity, recognized as such, i.e., recognized as a *need* for theory, bespeaks the arbitrariness of things and signs, their unmotivated, unnatural, or, at least, their denatured significance. This is not, therefore, a Cratylitic semiosis. Quite the contrary, this is an emblematic semiosis, generated by a meaningful but ungrounded compact of a picture and its explanatory caption, by the contingent marriage of a sight and its verbal gloss. Moreover, because such arbitrariness speaks against the propriety of property relations which are secured by natural signs, Hertz associates this point of view with the political left, or, rather, more precisely, with the political left as seen by the political right. That is to say, this is the point of view that the counterrevolution fearfully attributes to that which it opposes: this is how the right imagines revolutionary imagination. In the same way, with regard to erotics, this is the point of view not exactly of Woman but of that which natural Man looks at with erotic dread and fascination. Again, this is a point of view that is more seen than it is seeing, natural Man's salacious, voyeuristic image of the gaze of his unnatural other, the Other to which, as Lacan says, there is no other.

In Hertz's paper these two points of view are provisionally opposed to each other, but the paper's point, really, is that from one point of view they go together. Burke, Hugo, du Camp, Tocqueville, all look "with mingled curiosity and fear" at their uncanny double. All these men see in the theoretical something that, Hertz says, "resembles" (p. 00)—his word here is important—their own natural way of looking at things "a bit too closely for comfort," a simulacrum that raises the specter of the arbitrary nature of their natural signs, a counterspeculation that shows up their natural perspective as being but a limit case of theory. Thus Hertz can explain the fetishistic, eroticized aggression that these men of property direct against their mirror image. The lurid, euphemizing fantasies that they symptomatically invent betray their insight *into* theory, into the thrilling danger that it poses, and this in turn supplies the political and personal motivation that leads these men then to defend the integrity of their motivated signs.

So much for one point of view, for its motifs and for its motives, but what about the other, the other point of view which is the point of view of the Other? In the name of what does this unnatural perspective act if this perspective speaks against the natural propriety of names? This is not much of a problem if we can bring ourselves to imagine that the systematic theoreticians of the left believe in their own theories, for then, however mediated, there is still some deep relation between their signifiers and their signifieds. Such belief, however, will *as* belief, whatever its content, rather collapse the difference between left and right that governs Hertz's paper. According to the logic and the psychologic of what Hertz calls male hysteria, any theoretician will cease to be such to the extent that he commits himself to theory, for in this way he will naturalize his theory by understanding it as something that is positively true. Thus committed, however, even if only to a belief in the arbitrary, even the theoreticians of the left immediately fall prey to the reactive hysterical syndrome that Hertz describes. Because their good faith in theory is held in bad faith, because theory is itself a limit case of a Cratylism always threatened by another Other, the theoreticians of the left will, by nature, breed out of their own insecurity ever more elaborate structures of aggressive defense.

Thus even the exhibitionist woman on the barricades, subject to but also of such male hysteria, is a figure whose apotropaic gesture exposes more than herself. She shows us how the left, as does the right, hysterically girds up its loins against what seems to be *its* other—to a point, however, one that modern political history has surely made familiar, that it becomes difficult to distinguish between the Fascism of left and right.

To some extent, therefore, the "resemblance" that Hertz notices between these two points of view is a knife—in French we might say a *courbet*—that cuts, as Freud would say, both ways.[1] Looking to the left or to the right, we see only the same right-wing point of view. Looking either at man or at woman, we see only sexist man. Does this mean, then, that there is no one who takes up the other and the Other's point of view? Is there no one to speak up for the essential impropriety of the proper? It would seem to be the suggestion of Hertz's paper that Hertz himself does this, for it is Hertz who seems to speak from a critical perspective that places him at one remove from the hysteria he observes. Inevitably there must be some question as to whether such a critical distance can ever be maintained, whether such a Hertzian perspective, looked at closely, is not, instead, a kind of critical vanishing point. Leaving this question to the side, for the moment, we can say that if this is the case, if it really is possible thus to speak against hysteria, then we are once again obliged to raise the question of motivation, namely, in the name of what does this confessedly unnatural perspective act if this perspective, on its own terms, speaks against the natural propriety of names? This would be a trivial or trivializing question if raised as an epistemological quibble, for the kind of radical skepticism here invoked will hardly be undone when told that it too much believes its own suspicions. The question becomes more pointed, however, when the causes and consequences of such a theoretical position are more practically conceived. What kind of action derives, or can derive, from such self-consciously suspicious speculation? What happens to revolutionary ardor—or to any other kind of ardor, for that matter—when it is caught up in the kind of second-order reflections sketched out in Hertz's paper, when the strongest speculations of theory are reduced, *by* speculation, to the merely and the arbitrarily theoretical, when symbolic explanation works to cut the symbol off from what, from a naively theoretical point of view, we might want to call the real? What is the motivation, that is to say, of the politics of the unmotivated sign? What does the semiotic revolution want, and how, in fact, can it want it?

I call this a political dilemma, and it is a real one, as a glance at recent theoretical discussions would immediately reveal. From what Olympian, Archimedean vantage point, for example, does Foucault direct his analyses of discursive, epistemic history toward specific political ends? Alternatively, how does Derrida escape the political constraints imposed upon him by a metaphysical tradition that in a self-serving way predetermines and calls out for Derridean deconstruction? In the same way, we can ask what strategic functions of late capitalist development certain contemporary sophistications of Marxism, despite themselves, fulfill? Similarly, we can ask how a feminist analysis of the fetishistic logic of desire proceeds in turn to desire something else, as though it were possible to have this theoretical cake and also to want it too? Such questions define the contours of a genuine political dilemma, one that is shared by various speculative theorizations, all of which have in common the fact that they make of all activities of representation, including their own, something problematic.

For this reason, however, these questions also define the contours of an analogous aesthetic dilemma, one that is pertinent to the present discussion because it emerges precisely and pressingly in the revolutionary period that Hertz's paper discusses. I refer, of course, to the debates in the nineteenth century regarding realism in the arts, for it is a great, though hardly unremarked, irony that realism becomes an important aesthetic question just at that moment when not only the propriety but also the possibility of representing the real is put into question. Not the least virtue of Hertz's paper is the economical way it joins the political and aesthetic dimensions of this question of the real by focusing on the figure of Maxime du Camp, especially on the rich passage in which du Camp collates Courbet's shocking, realistic painting of female genitals— and of whatever relevantly attaches to these genitals—with Courbet's revolutionary politics. In this connection, however, it is important to recall, as Hertz does briefly, that Maxime du Camp was not only the enemy of the realist Courbet but also the friend (and publisher) of the realist Flaubert. And in the context of Hertz's paper and the political spectrum it sets up, it is important also to recall that if Courbet was on the left, Flaubert was on the right—as if the two of them together meant to illustrate the uncanny "resemblance" to which Hertz refers, but only one direction of which—du Camp to Courbet—he goes on in his paper to discuss.

Courbet-Flaubert is a significant pairing because the two of them together make up, as it were, an allegorical emblem of emblematic semiosis, with the visuality of Courbet, the painter, glossed, so to speak, by the textuality of the writer Flaubert.[2] Pursuing the allegory, we can note also that if Maxime du Camp is remembered for anything, it is for his contribution to the history of photography, the medium in which, as its name suggests, the ontology of the visual and the ontology of the written come complicatedly to coalesce—in the image that the technology of the camera manages to photograph.[3] This is a complicated way of making the point that Maxime du Camp, *as* a photographer, has a conflicted and an ambiguous relationship to the realism that only a tertiary half of him opposes, just as, I want also to suggest, realism has an ambiguous relationship to the politics of left and right. This point can be made more simply, however, by recalling the fact that du Camp was the author of what is usually cited as the first book in which words and photographs are combined, a vaguely realistic book that documents his travels with Flaubert throughout the Middle East—the Middle East which is also the Orientalist origin, via the Turkish ambassador, of Courbet's *L'Origine du monde*.[4]

By themselves these are only anecdotal facts, but in the context of Hertz's paper these and other facts acquire, or so I want to suggest, a larger significance. First of all, we should recall that photography is very much connected to the political history of the Commune, initially because this is one of the first times in history that political action is staged for the camera—as when the communards pose for pictures before and after toppling the Vendôme column. Subsequently when these very pictures are used by the counterrevolutionary police to identify the now defeated terrorists, this is the first time in history that photography becomes an instrument of power.[5] There is more, however, even to this fact, than meets the eye. Given the technology of the camera in the 1870s, the one thing that photography could *not* photograph was action, for the only images the camera could record were frozen images, images immobilized for the extended time required to register an exposure. This is why we have pictures of before and after the toppling of the column but not of the toppling itself, or why the still-life corpses of the executed communards make such perfect photographic subjects.[6] This is an important qualification, for it demonstrates that it was for the purpose of commemorative, not reportorial, documentation that the communards posed for the camera, and the same commemorative impulse lies behind the souvenir photographs illustrating the crimes of the Commune that were widely distributed after the insurrection was suppressed. With one difference between them, however. For, unlike the photographs taken by the communards, the incriminating postrevolutionary photographs retailed by the right were deliberately faked, tendentiously reassembled montages of events whose movement and turbulent restlessness the technology of the camera could never have recorded—a point, moreover, of which the public audience for these pictures was very much aware. In the context of Hertz's paper we can say that the right had learned very well the lesson of the arbitrary nature of the realistic sign, and, moreover, that the right had very quickly learned to put this arbitrariness to use.

Where, then, does Hertz, as disinterested author, stand in relation to such motivated arbitrariness? Here again it is photography that perhaps suggests an answer. In his "Short History of Photography," Walter Benjamin discusses what he calls the "aura" possessed by photographs from the early period of photography, the 1850s, the decade that precedes the industrialization of photography.[7] These early photographic images, contemporary with du Camp's, are rich with the presence of that which they record, in part because the time required for their exposure makes them images of special concentration, as though, Benjamin says, the models for these pictures had grown during the temporal duration of photographic exposure "into the image."[8] Benjamin contrasts this with the decadence of later photography, where, for technological and social reasons, photographs merely simulate the auratic, when the photograph becomes the snapshot. Bearing this history in mind, I want to suggest that Courbet's nude is for Maxime du Camp, and through him for Hertz, a painting of this loss of auratic presence, a picture of the difference between early and late photography.[9] I make this suggestion first to explain why du Camp sees in Courbet's picture the loss of painterly portrait presence, which is precisely the genre that, Benjamin says, photography had stolen from painting. But this also explains why du Camp's reaction to Courbet's realistic painting plays such a powerful role in Hertz's paper. My suggestion is that in the Courbet we see a picture of the modernist pudendum, of the energizing shame occasioned by the loss of the natural sign. But this shame also determines—if we take the exemplary hesitations of Hertz's paper as an example—the dilemma of a post-modernist political project whose agents are poised midway between the auratic and its subversive simulation. This explains, that is to say, as I said at the beginning, both the significance and the pathos of Hertz's paper. Situated between the visual and the verbal, poised between, if I may invoke Lacan against Laplanche, the Imaginary and Symbolic, we encounter in this paper the politics of a broken heart—a rupture that measures the humbling historical distance separating what the paper teaches us to call "Hertz from Courbet."[10]

And yet, if Hertz's paper is governed in this way by the broken identification of its authorial subject with his heroic ego-ideal, this is a fact that is uncannily brought home to us only by the personal touch of the disavowed pun on "Herz von dem Herz," the pun that, according to Hertz, is "willful" and not "snappy." Here we encounter, between the lines, the euphemized Hertz, the presence of an author who, though he says he knows better, nevertheless finds himself writing from the "coeur" he would like to share with Courbet. This arbitrarily motivated Cratylism, obsessional rather than hysterical, exhibits the logic of fetishism as it has been very well summarized by Octave Mannoni in the formula "Je sais bien, mais quand même . . .," for it is as a bad pun, literally half-hearted, that "Herz von dem Herz" takes away with one hand what it gives with the other.[11] And if Hertz enacts this logic even as he resists it, returning to Cratylism after the fact, but as though to the scene of a crime, this suggests that he writes from a displaced place of desire whose erotic exigencies cannot be avoided. And if this is a necessary place, an authorial commonplace, then there is some question regarding the historical novelty of Hertz's point of view. There is not much difference, for example, between what I have called Hertz's dilemma and the self-conscious way that Astrophil, at the beginning of Sidney's sonnet-sequence, looks into his heart to write, and finds there pre-engraved or stelled upon it the image or *imago* of the Stella whom he loves. That is to say, there are no new developments in the history of photography.

IN REPLY

Catherine Gallagher's remarks on Tocqueville are very much to the point. His sense of himself as Tocqueville-from-Tocqueville must indeed rest on his belief that he is legitimate, hence that his mother's sexual behavior and (by implication) that of all women, could be satisfactorily domesticated. Because women have it in their power to unsettle that complacency, they can appear threatening in just the ways Gallagher refers to, and the particular cast of that threat, connected as it is with generativity, can resonate with other forms of dismaying proliferation, as she suggests. The articulation she proposes between one fear and another—"if the mother is not properly constrained, . . . one's name may mean nothing; one's property may have no natural relationship to one's name"—I find convincing. The question remains of how this sense of women's reproductive power is to be related to the recurrent allusions to women's "weakness" that the castration scenario generates, how these (in Gallagher's words) "more historical" elements are connected to the "hysterical" ones I was concerned with. Would Gallagher agree that the clenched specularity of these texts acts precisely to ward off the historical? In each, the field is narrowed to the point where a complex of historical factors can be ignored in favor of a thrilling encounter in which intimations of sheer weakness and sheer power are exchanged. I would grant that this way of thinking about women's sexuality is illusory; but I would argue that the texts we've been considering work to create that illusion, to transform one set of anxieties into another, more manageable one, and that the all-or-nothing logic of castration scenarios is what makes that transformation possible.

Consider, as a further illustration, this well-known anecdote from Machiavelli's *Discourses*. It concerns Caterina Sforza. When her husband, the Count of Forli, was murdered by a group of conspirators, she and her small children were taken prisoner, outside the walls of the citadel. The conspirators hoped to capture the fortress, but its governor, Machiavelli relates, "declined to hand it over." At this point, the countess

> promised the conspirators that, if they would let her go to the citadel, she would arrange for it to be handed over to them. Meanwhile they were to keep her children as hostages. On this understanding the conspirators let her go to the citadel, from the walls of which, when she got inside, she reproached them with killing her husband and threatened them with vengeance in every shape and form. And to convince them that she did not care about her children she exposed herself and said that she was still capable of bearing more. The conspirators, dumbfounded, realised their mistake too late, and paid the penalty for their lack of prudence by suffering perpetual banishment.[1]

Machiavelli's translator has softened the original here: the Italian that he rendered as "exposed herself" is "mostrò loro le membra genitali." She "showed them her genital members." A strange formulation: according to John Freccero it is as unusual in Italian as it is in English to refer to a woman's genitals as "members," whether in the plural or in the singular.[2] But Machiavelli's use of the term has the effect of phallicizing the countess's gesture, of transforming what seems to have been a clear allusion, by the countess, to her own generative power into a more obscurely threatening play of sameness and difference, very much in the Medusa mode. Needless to say, this tells us nothing about the countess' intentions, nor is it evidence for what men "really" find threatening about women's sexuality, any more than Victor Hugo's anecdote tells us anything about the intentions of the women on the barricades or the fears experienced by the guardsmen. But both Machiavelli's text and Hugo's tell us something about how powerfully attractive—to men—these specular scenarios can be.

Joel Fineman describes a "political dilemma" he finds unresolved in my paper, one which he generously (or mock-heroically) claims I share with various other writers on these matters (Derrida and Foucault, for example) who "make of all activities of representation, including their own, something problematic." "What kind of action derives, or can derive," he asks, "from such self-consciously suspicious speculation?" I take the question seriously, but I'm not sure I have to accept the terms in which Fineman puts it. Can political questions be boiled down to a dilemma—that is, in the dictionary's strong sense of that word, to "a situation that requires one to choose between equally balanced alternatives"? The moments that strike me as most suggestive in the political writings of—to stay with Fineman's instances—Foucault and Derrida are precisely those that work to elude symmetrical formulations of this sort. In Foucault these moments are often marked by long lists of plural nouns, which produce the exhilarating sense of just how many factors one must take into account in a particular issue; in Derrida, by the mullings and backings-and-fillings with which he works his way into a problem, his remarkable ability to both fish *and* cut bait.

It is true that these ways of proceeding—the Foucaldian catalogue, the Derridean backward turn—to the extent that they are distinctive traits, little signature tunes, risk degenerating into mere mannerisms, their political or intellectual content diminished in relation to their self-representative function. On the other hand, when these writers are at their most instructive, the signs of self-representation don't so much disappear as turn up scattered over a wide field of invested objects of attention. And it is that sort of distribution of attention that seems to offer a way out of the hysterical overconcentrations of focus I had been attributing to those right-wing authors and which, as Fineman correctly points out, can be found (alas) on the left as well. One assumption of my paper was that a powerful source of such hysteria could be located in the intellectual narcissism implicit in Hugo's or du Camp's or Tocqueville's texts, the wish of each of these writers to produce a representation of a complex political situation which would function simultaneously as a representation of self.[3] I assume that it is this desire that impels them to minimize the play of differences to the most rudimentary distinctions: self or other, strong or weak, or (in the shorthand of the lunch counter) "with" or "without."[4]

One such reduction is performed by Maxime du Camp in the paragraph describing Courbet's nude. Fineman's suggestion about *L'Origine du monde*—that it expresses "the energizing shame occasioned by the loss of the natural sign"—is wonderfully acute, if you grant that the signs of that shame can take other, and more interesting, forms than du Camp's certainly energetic enough reaction.[5] Du Camp's energy seems totally committed to the task of defensive self-representation; it is worth asking whether that is also the case with Courbet, and to do that I'd like to briefly consider *L'Origine du monde* in relation to some other Courbet canvases.

We know Courbet as an artist who painted in many genres and who attempted all sorts of subjects: the catalogue of the centenary exhibit in Paris[6] includes not only the great and (to his contemporaries) startling depictions of village life, but also seascapes and self-portraits, hunting scenes, landscapes, formal portraits, nudes, and still-lifes. His "realism" may not be quite what Maxime du Camp made of it—"the exact representation of natural objects, without discernment, without selection, just as they offered themselves to view"—but it is indeed programmatically concerned with a wide range of differences in the looks of things, as well as programmatically concerned with the particular difference that separates the painter from his canvas.[7] At moments in his work, paintings appear in which this play of differences is experimentally reduced in one way or another—for example, by radically limiting the number of objects in view, or by allowing the paint to dissimulate the distinguishing outlines of objects, or by thematizing within the painting Courbet's own (or his spectator's) relation to the canvas. These pictures form a large and fascinating subset of Courbet's production, interrelated by repetitions of motif, of structure, or of technique. Many of them have, as a focal point, a dark patch close to the center of the canvas: a shaded spot in a landscape; or a somber rock placed in the foreground of a seascape or else so as to interrupt the flow of an inland stream; or the hollowed-out shape of a great wave coming toward the shore; or a heavy human form leaning back somnolently, or seen from behind, seated and watching a small waterfall. Among the most compelling of these works are a series of representations of the source of the Loue, a river that issues from a cave in a rock face at a site close to Courbet's birthplace. In the version I have reproduced here (figure 9), one painted in 1864, Courbet has composed the scene without intervening human fig-

Figure 9. Gustave Courbet. *La Source de la Loue,* 1864. Albright-Knox Gallery, Buffalo, N.Y. George and Jenny R. Matthews Fund, 1959.   Photo: Albright-Knox Gallery.

ures. The stream comes out toward the viewer, moving off to the right, but the viewer's gaze is led back against the flow of the current, into the darkness of the cave, by the converging lines of the strata that form the rock wall and by the lure of the intense black paint itself. And yet, what the eye is drawn to is not exactly a heart of darkness, or "the void"; a rock column in the middle distance divides the cavern into two chambers, left and right, and the reflection of that column on the surface of the stream suggests another division, between the dark waters and the dark rock walls above them. But if this difference is suggested, it is literally indiscernible, a difference without a distinction: for what we *see* are identical strokes of black paint, though some of them render what we "know" to be water, others what we "know" to be rock.

I have been following the viewer's gaze back to this central equivocation, where the wide-open question of the relation between a painter and the world has been narrowed down and played out in terms of two related questions, that of the difference between paint and the surfaces of things, and that of the difference between what the eye sees and what it "knows" to be there. This last question, it should be remarked, is the fetishist's question *par excellence:* it is the source of that "energizing shame" that Fineman has detected in Maxime du Camp's response to Courbet. In Courbet's case, what the shame has energized is not just the desire to get to the heart of the matter—that he shares with du Camp—but the will to patiently explore the matter along the way. The signs of that patience are in his linking of the fetishist's questions (what does the eye see? what does it "know" to be there?) with questions of technique (how can strokes of paint represent the surfaces of things?), and these signs, though they are focused with emblematic intensity at the heart of the cave, in the "difference" between black and black, are in fact spread all over the surface of the canvas. The rock walls that frame the cave, which may seem like an austerely contracted version of "the world," nevertheless allow for astonishingly varied effects of coloring—shades of pink and yellow and grey that have disappeared in our black-and-white reproduction. This variety of texture, and the particular way in which Courbet's application of paint draws attention to itself (not as brushstrokes, but as paint) engages the eye, slowing down and complicating its movement along the lines of the stratified rock toward the "source" itself, and allowing for contrary movements, in which interest is diffused and dispersed across the whole visual field.

An analogous scene can be found in *L'Éducation sentimentale* (1869) and, since Joel Fineman had raised the question of Courbet's relation to Flaubert, it may be helpful to look at that now. The novel's hero, Frédéric Moreau (a figure partly autobiographical, partly based on Flaubert's old friend Maxime du Camp), has just, for the first time, touched the hand of the Older Woman with whom he is in love. (The thematics of the Mother—whether as Older Woman, or Source, or Origin of the World—inheres in these works that bring the logic of fetishism into touch with aesthetic concerns.) He leaves her apartment, walks aimlessly and excitedly through the darkened streets of Paris, stopping finally on the Pont-Neuf. He looks down the river, and Flaubert describes what is to be seen there. I shall cite the French first, since Flaubert's handling of words, like Courbet's handling of paint, is pertinent (and, fortunately, easier to reproduce here):

> Les réverbères brillaient en deux lignes droites, indéfiniment, et de longues flammes rouges vacillaient dans la profondeur de l'eau. Elle était de couleur ardoise, tandis que le ciel, plus clair, semblait soutenu par les grandes masses d'ombre qui se levaient de chaque côté du fleuve. Des édifices, que l'on n'apercevait pas, faisaient des redoublements d'obscurité. Un brouillard lumieux flottait au delà, sur les toits; tous les bruits se fondaient en un seul bourdonnement; un vent léger soufflait.[8]

> (The street lamps stretched away to infinity in two straight lines, and long red flames wavered in the depths of the water. The river was slate-colored while the lighter sky seemed to rest on two great walls of shadow which rose on either side of the flow. The darkness was deepened by unseen buildings. Farther off a luminous mist floated above the roofs; all the sounds melted into one murmur; a light breeze blew.)

"Des édifices, que l'on n'apercevait pas, faisaient des redoublements d'obscurité": this strange sentence can be aligned with the center of Courbet's cave. Here it is the buildings—which, we are told, "one" can't see—that are productive of an equivocally deepened or doubled darkness. And just as all sounds have melted into a single murmur, so visual distinctions have been reduced, yet not so drastically as to preclude effects of muted loveliness (the notation of the slate-colored sky, for instance) or—in the first sentence—of an exquisitely shimmering symmetry, indeterminately the result of the way things happen to look and of the way Flaubert has cannily represented them. The verbs of the two halves of that sentence— "brillaient" and "vacillaient"—echo each other with a rhyming neatness that the actions they refer to cannot approach, although they come out sounding transparently appropriate to their actions. Like the paint rendering the rock walls of *La Source de la Loue,* language such as this, mimetic but self-consciously so, acts to disperse throughout the paragraph (and indeed throughout the novel) what is occasionally concentrated into expressions like *"redoublements d'obscurité";* and the desire to arrive at such reductive moments is both whetted and deferred by the scrupulous virtuosity of Flaubert's prose.

If we now consider *L'Origine du monde* in the context of these other "scenes," what do we see? A powerfully reductive performance on Courbet's part, to be sure, and one that is erotically charged and disturbing, but not for quite the same reasons that Maxime du Camp's account of the picture would suggest. The framing of the image, eliminating the upper body and lower legs, and the foreshortening produced by the angle of vision chosen, have the effect of arranging the model's body into three massive columns of flesh—a diminished torso and two enlarged thighs—which radiate out from the dark central triangle of pubic hair, each column joined to one side of that triangle. The darkness of the paint combines with the pull of erotic fascination to draw the eye to that central patch, but this centripetal movement is impeded, if not entirely checked, by the substantiality of the figure's thighs and torso, by details like the almost uncovered breast at the top of the picture, and by what I take to be (judging from black-and-white reproductions of the painting) Courbet's characteristic care in representing the surfaces of his model's body—the care, at once painterly and mimetic, that can be observed in his rendering of the rocks surrounding the cave of the Loue. The desire to zero in on that central point, the desire that gives Maxime du Camp's prurience its metaphysical tinge, is countered and dispersed in these ways, while the wish to believe that what one is drawn to is *a* center, one thing, *la chose même,* is problematized by a detail that is both realistic and abstract: the curved line that marks the vaginal cleft and that is visible disappearing under the triangle of hair, producing not a single dark focal patch but the erotic version of the equivocations "visible" in the center of *La Source de la Loue. L'Origine du monde* stands in the same relation to other Courbet nudes as *La Source de la Loue* does to other landscapes of his. It explores a powerfully invested set of differences—the difference between paint and flesh, between a male artist and his female model, between sexual desire and the will to representation. If we find it disturbing, it may be for the same reasons that we find *L'Éducation sentimentale* disturbing: that is, for reasons that engage the implicit politics of such performances.

I have juxtaposed Courbet's work with Flaubert's in order to suggest that, at least in certain respects, the allegiance of one artist to the left, of the other to the right, makes very little difference. But this sort of partisanship is not all there is to "politics": it would be silly to claim that the scenes I've been considering have no political significance whatever. Rather, their significance is to be sought in their latent—and sometimes not-so-latent—sexual politics, in the ways in which their explorations of the relations between art and fetishism bear the traces of a period in infancy when elementary acts of representation, of self-representation, and of sexual identification begin to distinguish themselves in the child's mind, and, simultaneously, to become entangled with one another. It is not fortuitous that the thematics of the Mother often surface in the works of these realists, nor is it surprising that these men (and not only these *men:* the same pattern can be discovered in the works of George Eliot) in the course of their work, should display both a profound identification with the women they portray and a defensive misogyny when such identifications come to seem threatening. Realism may draw its energies from the tension between the self-diffusing exploration of surfaces and of the media of expression and the self-consolidating assertions of stylistic identity; and when these latter assertions predominate, gestures of misogyny are close at hand. At such moments of misogynistic scapegoating, the sexual politics of "serious" artists may not be worth distinguishing from what I've been calling the "hysteria" of someone like du Camp. If one continues to find Flaubert and Courbet more interesting than Maxime du Camp, it may be because one comes to appreciate the patience with which their works take up these unsavory matters.

Joel Fineman's concluding remarks on the politics implicit in my own paper are telling. I acknowledge the problem and cannot do much more for the moment than reserve the right not to consider it a full-fledged "dilemma." What one takes away with one hand, after all, may not turn out to be exactly equal to what one gives with the other: the economy of such political gestures has more play in it than that, more room for maneuver. After reading Fineman's comments I found the line I thought would best serve as an epigraph for all these pages—the last line of Catullus's poem about Attis, *alios age incitatos, alios age rabidos*. It is from the poet's concluding prayer to Cybele, which reads, in one translation:

> Grant that this house where I dwell
> May never know the madness thou canst send
> Drive other men to frenzy, drive other men insane.[9]

This is the sort of sentiment one can find in antifanatical Enlightenment texts like Hume's *Natural History of Religion*. Hume, of course, would have meant it; presumably Catullus means it too; and so do I, "half-heartedly."

Figure 10.   Gustave Courbet. *La Grotte de la Loue,* c. 1865. National Gallery of Art, Washington. Gift of Charles L. Lindemann, 1957.   Photo: National Gallery.

10.
AFTERWORD:
THE END OF THE LINE

 ON THE OPPOSITE PAGE I've reproduced another one of Courbet's views of the source of the Loue (figure 10), this one including in the composition a human form, that of a boy or young man, standing on a wooden pier that projects into the stream from the left, and facing toward the cave, a space at once compellingly concentrated and doubly divided—into two chambers, as well as into an upper and a lower area, the dark rock walls and the dark waters reflecting them.

I offer this illustration as a means of focusing some of the concerns of the essays collected here. Most immediately, I would refer back to the version of *La Source de la Loue* discussed on pp. 209–11 above. The pictures are almost identical in structure. Here again the eye is drawn into the cave, moving back against the current, and again is involved in a play of what can be seen in the depths against what one "knows" to be there; once again a range of visible differences is reduced to the minimal difference between black and black. But the painting-in of that figure introduces a further difference: it locates—hence, thematizes—a position that was implicit in the other canvas, that of a surrogate viewer, or, if one chooses to read the figure as an oblique self-representation, a surrogate painter. (This latter choice is assisted by the staff or rod the youth is holding, which projects beyond his uplifted right hand, suggesting a brush poised above the black paint at the canvas's center.)[1] The structure can now be thought of as triangular, or—more accurately—as a sort of capital T lying on its side:

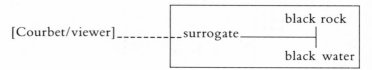

The shaft of the T is the axis along which the play of subject and object develops, a play of identification and distancing joining painter (or viewer) to the landscape or to its representation on canvas; the crossbar indicates the splitting or doubling of that object—it is the axis along which the residual tension of minimal difference, of black against black, is felt. The lure of the structure is in its suggestion that the two axes, the two modes of difference, are not unrelated, that the difference between black and black, for example, can serve as an emblem of tensions that join and separate the viewer (and painter) outside the frame from their surrogates within the frame as well as from the "scene itself," in this case the cave. Here, we can say, is a painting in what Kenneth Burke has named the "to-the-end-of-the-line mode."[2]

That a differential play of subject and object can find its echo and emblem "within" the nominal object is a lesson that may also be read out of Wordsworth's lines on the Boy of Winander, where the transfer of natural sounds and sights "far into [the Boy's] heart" or "unawares into his mind" is repeated in a gently animated vector within the scene itself, when "that uncertain Heaven" is "receiv'd / Into the bosom of the steady Lake."[3] If we assimilate the poem to our diagram, it looks like this:

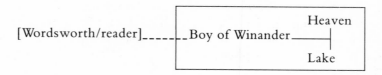

In this context we should turn back to consider another Wordsworthian example, that of the Blind Beggar in book 7 of *The Prelude* (see pp. 57–60, above). There Wordsworth—or his repre-

218

sentative in the poem—moves through the London crowd, an indiscriminate mix of faces and texts, and then is brought to a halt before an "unmoving man," a figure whose fascination seems to lie in the minimal difference between the "Label" on his chest and the "fixed face and sightless eyes" (7.621–23) above it.

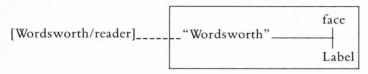

Could we characterize the relation of the label to the face as one of "representation," just as, in our two other instances, the surface of the water (Wordsworth's lake, Courbet's stream) "represents," by reflection, what is positioned above it? Yes and no. The clarity with which these diagrams make the term in the lower right corner look like a "representation" of the term in the upper right corner is achieved by oversimplifying what is, in each case, a more equivocal relationship. In the case of the painting, I pointed out some of those equivocations in my earlier discussion of the Albright-Knox version of the cave. Wordsworth's texts are no less disorienting. The unexpected reversal of adjectives in the one (why should it be "Heaven" that is "uncertain" and the "Lake" that is "steady"?) is paralleled, in the other, by the way in which the Beggar's face is made to seem as fixed and inanimate, as much like reading matter, as the text on his chest. In all three of these examples what one is drawn to is not a clearly oriented reflection, a *mise en abyme* of the artist's representational project, but an engagement with the act and with the medium of painting or writing condensed almost to the point of nonreflective opacity. That expression may be taken quite literally to describe the center of Courbet's canvas; figuratively it can serve to indicate whatever resists the reader at equivalent moments in written texts—difficulties of syntax or of figuration, apparent irrelevancies of association, any verbal play that shadows the referential appeal of the work—whatever keeps reading from being reducible to seeing.

In one way or another all the essays in this volume gravitate toward such points of opacity which, borrowing Burke's expression, I call "the end of the line." The earliest ones are readings of the literature of the sublime, where one would expect such intense and reductive moments, exemplary entanglings of a writer's thematic concerns with issues of epistemology and rhetoric. The interpretative procedures brought to bear on passages from Longinus or Kant, Milton or Wordsworth, were then tried out on some nominally "realist" works, novels by Flaubert and George Eliot: in particular, I was curious to see what could be learned from the appearance in nineteenth-century fiction of two trademarks of the sublime—condensed, epistemologically loaded confrontations, and characters designated as surrogates of their authors' activity. Hence, the reading of chapter 20 in *Middlemarch* dwells not just on the ways Dorothea's encounter with Rome is articulated with her recognition of her husband, but on the narrative's wavering in relation to Dorothea, a wavering that produces the end-of-the-line language about the "roar which lies on the other side of silence" (see pp. 88–96 above). Similarly Jules's experience of a sublime landscape and a grotesque dog, in the 1845 *Sentimental Education,* is read as an allegory of the vicissitudes of Flaubert's self-representation as Jules (see pp. 66–74).

One may be led into such double readings by noticing some resemblance between author and character—sometimes obvious, sometimes less pronounced—but once having begun what one discovers is that the necessity for double reading arises not from the presence of a discernible surrogate within the novel but rather from the requirements of any reading. In terms of our diagram, we could say that because the frame separating the author/reader from the work is permeable—and has to be, if the work is to be read at all—a play develops between author/reader and text, regardless of the degree of autobiographical likeness with which a particular surrogate is represented, indeed regardless of the "visibility" of such a surrogate. This proposition can be tested at a glance: if you look back at the two Courbet caves—one including a human figure, one not—you will notice that the painting-in of that figure makes some difference, but not very much: his "position" is an unavoidable one—the viewer occupies it whether it is marked out for him or left empty.

The scene from *L'Education sentimentale* that I have set alongside the Courbet caves (see pp. 211–14 above) is still more dramatic evidence that, while the *position* of surrogate is a structural necessity, its *occupant* may be attenuated to the point of invisibility. For there can be no doubt that Frédéric Moreau serves as Flaubert's surrogate in the novel, and no doubt that it is he who is to be imagined standing on the Pont-Neuf looking down the river at those *redoublements d'obscurité* that can be read as a figure for end-of-the-line opacity. That is, the scene would seem to lend itself readily to our schematization:

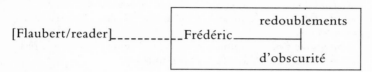

Yet if we look at that paragraph in its context we may wonder if "Frédéric" is the right name for whoever is seeing what is there to be seen. Here is the passage again, in French, with the sentences surrounding it. Frédéric is very much in evidence in both the preceding and following paragraphs; the excitement he feels at having touched the woman he loves drives him, in a trance of narcissism, first through the streets of Paris, then home to his bedroom mirror; yet at the critical moment he seems to have faded out, his foolish self-consciousness replaced by the pronoun *on:*

> Il n'avait plus conscience du milieu, de l'espace, de rien; et, battant le sol du talon, en frappant avec sa canne les volets des boutiques, il allait toujours devant lui, au hasard, éperdu, entraîné. Un air humide l'enveloppa; il se reconnut au bord des quais.
> Les réverbères brillaient en deux lignes droites, indéfiniment, et de longues flammes rouges vacillaient dans la profondeur de l'eau. Elle était de couleur ardoise, tandis que le ciel, plus clair, semblait soutenu par les grandes masses d'ombre que se levaient de chaque côté du fleuve. *Des édifices, que l'on n'apercevait pas, faisaient des redoublements d'obscurité.* Un brouillard lumineux flottait au dela, sur les toits; tous les bruits se fondaient en un seul bourdonnement; un vent léger soufflait.
> Il s'était arrêté au milieu du Pont-Neuf, et, tête nue, poitrine ouverte, il aspirait l'air. Cependant, il sentait monter du fond de lui

même quelque chose d'intarissable, un afflux de tendresse qui l'énervait, comme le mouvement des ondes sous ses yeux. A l'horloge d'une église, une heure sonna, lentement, pareille à une voix qui l'eût appelé.

Alors, il fut saisi par un de ces frissons de l'âme où il vous semble qu'on est transporté dans un monde supérieur. Une faculté extraordinaire, dont il ne savait pas l'objet, lui était venue. Il se demanda, sérieusement, s'il serait un grand peintre ou un grand poète;—et il se décida pour la peinture, car les exigences de ce métier le rapprocheraient de Mme Arnoux. Il avait donc trouvé sa vocation! Le but de son existence était clair maintenant, et l'avenir infaillible.

Quand il eut refermé sa porte, il entendit quelqu'un qui ronflait dans le cabinet noir, près de la chambre. C'était l'autre. Il n'y pensait plus.

Son visage s'offrait à lui dans la glace. Il se trouva beau; et resta une minute à se regarder. [Emphasis added.]⁴

The fluctuation of Frédéric's "presence" in these lines is the diachronic equivalent of the possibility of Courbet's producing versions of his cave either with or without a figure in the foreground—or of Wordsworth's rendering his autobiographical experiences sometimes in the first person, sometimes in the third.⁵ It is as if the consistency of that represented subject or the stability with which it is located in the surrogate's position didn't really matter very much. Or rather that it is precisely the *in*consistency of the subject occupying that position that matters. The diagrams allow us to mark the position and to gauge the substantiality of the figure located there. They make it easier to notice that what is repeatedly represented, at the end of the line, is a practically (but not quite) dispensable "subject" confronting a split or doubled "object."

Paul de Man offered the most succinct characterization of these matters when he described autobiography as "not a genre or a mode, but a figure of reading or of understanding that occurs, to some degree, in all texts," and went on to name this "autobiographical moment" as "an alignment between the two subjects involved in the process of reading in which they determine each other by mutual reflexive substitution."⁶ To call attention to end-of-the-line structures then, is no more than one way—one somewhat excited way—of talking about what happens when one reads; the particular opacity I've attributed to these regions in texts is what de Man would call the mark of their "unreadability."

I have said little so far about what becomes of these moments, of what comes *after* the end of the line. For there is always an "after": the structures we have been examining never coincide with the conclusions of the particular texts in which they figure. Typically the poised relationship of attenuated subject and divided object reveals its inherent instability by breaking down and giving way to scenarios more or less violent, in which the aggressive reassertion of the subject's stability is bought at some other subject's expense. We have seen a hint of this in the paragraphs from Flaubert, where Frédéric's recaptured self-satisfaction is coordinate with his slightly contemptuous dismissal of his closest friend (*"C'était l'autre"*), asleep in the next room.

Paul de Man was aware of the violence associated with "the auto-biographical moment," although he was not fascinated by it: he wrote of such goings-on—in Rousseau or Shelley or Words-worth[7]—as if he took it for granted that a problematical self seeking to tell or to read the story of itself, to locate itself within a rhetorical field, would of course leave the field littered with the remains of acts of mutilation and sacrifice. The real action, he seemed to im-ply, lay elsewhere. Thus he was curious about the specularity of reading, but left it to others to follow up the ways that structure devolved into narcissistic dramas of power. In the most recent of the essays collected here I have tried to trace a few such scenarios, tracking a self reading its way into a historical scene—Freud engag-ing with his patients and disciples, a teacher stigmatizing a pla-giarizing student, participants in Parisian uprisings interpreting their times—so as to test the assumption that the same operations that can be found concentrated at end-of-the-line moments in works of art will turn up producing the acts and the actings-out of historical experience. Others will judge the persuasiveness of these readings; for the moment I'd like to return to some literary exam-ples and look more closely at their economies. At the end of the line, who pays? and why?

Questions of gender enter here: when these dramas turn violent, women are frequently the victims of choice—are they bound to be?

Imagine, for example, a slide show in which the three Courbet canvasses discussed in these pages were flashed on the screen, rapidly, in this sequence: *La Source de la Loue, La Grotte de la Loue, L'Origine du monde*—first the cave, then the boy facing the cave, then the truncated body of a woman. What story would that tell? Wouldn't it be the story of how the violence practiced on the woman—first by the painter's choice of angle and framing, then by the aggression of voyeurs like Maxime du Camp—was an inevitable outcome of the earlier movement of self-location that painted the boy into the picture in an attempt to stabilize a position that was as natural—and as divided—as the interior of the cave? But is this the only story that can be put together about these paintings? It is with questions of this sort in mind that I want to turn first to a central passage in a novel of George Eliot's, then to an equivalently important "autobiographical moment" in Wordsworth.

Late in *Daniel Deronda* its hero is summoned from England to Genoa to meet his mother, who had abandoned him when he was a child and had gone on to pursue a flamboyant career as a singer and actress. Within the frame of the fiction, these interviews with "the Princess" (as she is called) are critical for Daniel: they dissolve the mystery surrounding his origins (he had been raised as the nephew of a British aristocrat) by revealing that he was born a Jew, thus confirming him in an identity he has been seen tentatively consolidating throughout the novel. But the representation of Daniel's meetings with his mother seems to have been just as important for George Eliot, both as a means of bringing her plot to a conclusion and as a brief but intense experiment in writing herself into her text. And out of it again. For at the end of the second interview, when Daniel's mother removes herself from his life, her disappearance may be read as an exorcism, a scapegoating after an ambivalent celebration. We are dealing here with a structure common in Eliot's novels, of double surrogation, in which the author's investment in her characters is split into "good" and "bad" versions, and the valued imaginative activity of the "good" surrogate is purchased by the exiling of the "bad." I analyzed an instance of this in "Recognizing Casaubon" (see pp. 75–96 above), where Dorothea and her husband occupy those two positions; elsewhere in

Middlemarch, Dorothea can be seen paired off with Rosamund in a similar ternary structure. In *Adam Bede,* Dinah and Hetty are thus paired, while in *Daniel Deronda* the roles are taken now by Daniel and Gwendolen, now by Daniel and his mother.

Eliot's recent interpreters have drawn attention to the language that marks the Princess as an autobiographical figure, a more explicit portrait of the artist than Maggie Tulliver or Dorothea Brooke.[8] Indeed, she can be taken as offering a critique of those earlier portrayals of serious young women: when Daniel, for instance, proposes, sympathetically, to "enter into the painfulness of [her] struggle" and adds, very much in the manner of Dorothea, "I can imagine the hardship of an enforced renunciation," the Princess rejects the gesture: "No . . . You are not a woman. You may try— but you can never imagine what it is to have a man's force of genius in you, and yet to suffer the slavery of being a girl" (3.131).[9] At another point in their first interview she is described as someone who "had cast all precedent out of her mind. Precedent had no excuse for her, and she could only seek a justification in the intensest words she could find for her experience" (3.124). "I cared for the wide world," she exclaims, "and all I could represent in it" (3.130), in an equivocal phrase that blends self-aggrandizement with the specific ambition of the mimetic artist. For it is less the vicissitudes of life—even of a woman's life—than the experience of representing life that Eliot would represent in the Princess:

> The varied transitions of tone with which this speech was delivered were as perfect as the most accomplished actress could have made them. The speech was in fact a piece of what may be called sincere acting: this woman's nature was one in which all feeling— and all the more when it was tragic as well as real—immediately became matter of conscious representation: experience immediately passed into drama, and she acted her own emotions. In a minor degree this is nothing uncommon, but in the Princess the acting had a rare perfection of physiognomy, voice, and gesture. It would not be true to say that she felt less because of this double consciousness: she felt—that is, her mind went through—all the more, but with a difference: each nucleus of pain or pleasure had a deep atmosphere of the excitement or spiritual intoxication which at once exalts and deadens. [3.127–28]

Here we may begin to gauge the burden the Princess is made to bear within the economy of the novel, and why she must ultimately be cast out of it. The language dwells on the "double consciousness" that is the instrument of her art, rehearsing its duplicity in a carefully nuanced series of pairings (pain or pleasure, excitement or spiritual intoxication, exalts *and* deadens) so as to guarantee that the paradoxes of representation will be registered as specifically *moral* equivocations. The Princess thus serves to focus or embody a set of problems that need not be thought of initially as moral problems or even, as we shall see, as problems of mimesis, but which are nonetheless disturbing for all that.

How these issues are converted into moral problems, laid on the back of the Princess, and sent packing is what we must turn to now. And we are helped in this by a pair of remarkable paragraphs that serve to introduce the Princess into the novel. They describe Daniel "in his suspense," arrived in Genoa and waiting to hear further from his mother. We can trace in them a movement of funneling that begins by taking notice of a wide range of differences, the stock-in-trade of the mimetic artist, narrows them down to the items impinging on the consciousness of a central character, pursues that consciousness through a subtle meditation on difference that gradually redefines difference as doubleness, then doubleness as duplicity and equivocation and finally gives equivocation a very local habitation—the end of the line—and a name, that of "the mother." At that point, the novel is ready to receive—and be received by—the Princess.

The passage opens with a rapid gesture in the direction of world history: we are in the early summer of 1866, "and every day was a hurrying match of crowded Time towards the world-changing battle of Sadowa" (3:116–17). But in the next, long sentence the vector of history appears to lose its point and the panorama of "Europe" is replaced first by an exquisitely various but miniaturized version of itself—the "hurrying march" reappears as the "hurry of pleasure," the battle as the peaceful heights surrounding Genoa, "crowned with forts"—then, as the oncoming night reduces visibility, by a scene of fewer and fewer differences, until at last "nothing shone but the port lights of the great Lanterna in the blackness below, and the glimmering stars in the blackness above":

226

Meanwhile, in Genoa, the noons were getting hotter, the converging outer roads getting deeper in white dust, the oleanders in the tubs along the wayside gardens looking more and more like fatigued holiday-makers, and the sweet evening changing her office—scattering abroad those whom the mid-day had sent under shelter, and sowing all paths with happy social sounds, little tinklings of mule-bells and whirrings of thrumbed strings, light footsteps and voices, if not leisurely, then with the hurry of pleasure in them; while the encircling heights, crowned with forts, skirted with fine dwellings and gardens, seemed also to come forth and gaze in fulness of beauty after their long siesta, till all strong colour melted in the stream of moonlight which made the streets a new spectacle with shadows, both still and moving, on cathedral steps and against the facades of massive palaces; and then slowly with the descending moon all sank into deep night and silence, and nothing shone but the port lights of the great Lanterna in the blackness below, and the glimmering stars in the blackness above. [3:117]

Now Daniel makes his appearance as a suspended observer and, the text insists, a nonwriter and nonreader:

In his letters to Mordecai and Hans, he had avoided writing about himself, but he was really getting into that state of mind to which all subjects become personal; and the few books he had brought to make him a refuge in study were becoming unreadable, because the point of view that life would make for him was in that agitating moment of uncertainty which is close upon decision. [3:118]

Neither reading nor writing, Daniel is poised in uncertain relation to his author, in an end-of-the-line structure that reproduces that of Courbet's caves or of the night scene in L'Education sentimentale:

Thus located at the window, Daniel begins another sort of reading, tracing in that spare paradigm the elements of his life:

Many nights were watched through by him in gazing from the open window of his room on the double, faintly pierced darkness

227

of the sea and the heavens: often, in struggling under the oppressive scepticism which represented his particular lot, with all the importance he was allowing Mordecai to give it, as of no more lasting effect than a dream—a set of changes which made passion to him, but beyond his consciousness were no more than an imperceptible difference of mass or shadow; sometimes with a reaction of emotive force which gave even to sustained disappointment, even to the fulfilled demand of sacrifice, the nature of a satisfied energy, and spread over his young future, whatever it might be, the attraction of devoted service; sometimes with a sweet irresistible hopefulness that the very best of human possibilities might befall him—the blending of a complete personal love in one current with a larger duty; and sometimes again in a mood of rebellion (what human creature escapes it?) against things in general because they are thus and not otherwise, a mood in which Gwendolen and her equivocal fate moved as busy images of what was amiss in the world along with the concealments which he had felt as a hardship in his own life, and which were acting in him now under the form of an afflicting doubtfulness about the mother who had announced herself coldly and still kept away. [3:118–19]

A mimetic artist's world of differences has been drastically reduced—in Eliot's case, as in Courbet's, to the difference between blackness and blackness. What makes Eliot's text especially pertinent, however, it that it allows us to trace in some detail the elaboration of this particular mimetic image in relation to the mini-narrative that forms its context—the representation of Daniel's thoughts, if not in sequence, at least in some order. If we now attempt to follow that development, we may be able to determine at what point questions of gender begin to matter, and why.

What starts out as a visual notation ("the blackness below, and . . . the blackness above") reappears, in the next paragraph, in a series of transformations:

1. As "double . . . darkness": a slightly conceptualized rendering of the same perception (you can't exactly "see" double darkness, the way you can see blackness below and blackness above, although the phrase's phenomenal referent remains clear). The expression functions in much the same way as Flaubert's *redoublements d'obscurité:* as a figure for "opacity" and as an instance of it. Both

expressions, by their alliterative beat, call attention to the phonic medium and away from straightforward mimetic adequacy.

2. As "a set of changes which made passion to him, but beyond his consciousness were no more than an imperceptible difference of mass or shadow": the "same" figure, this time applied to the uncertain status of Daniel's "particular lot."

3. As allusions to Gwendolen's "equivocal fate" and to "the concealments he had felt as a hardship in his own life": more commonplace terms for the uncertain or duplicitous. Here the language is moving past the neutrality of "an imperceptible difference of mass or shadow" and toward intersubjective scenarios in which women are, indeterminately, the victims or the agents of equivocation or concealment, available for sympathetic identification (as Gwendolen is) or as sources of puzzled resentment (as Daniel's mother, the prime instigator of the concealments in his own life, would seem to be).

4. As "an afflicting doubtfulness about the mother who had announced herself coldly and still kept away": a phrase that links—in specular fashion—Daniel's skepticism and ambivalence to his mother's puzzling behavior. Here doubleness is at last focused.

The paragraph—it is one long sentence—can be seen to be heading toward that final identification—of Daniel's doubtfulness or skepticism, of that in him which feeds on equivocation and finds it everywhere, with his mother when she is taken as the embodiment of "double darkness." Once that identification is made, the mechanism of scapegoating is in place: the language that characterizes the Princess in subsequent chapters reiterates the figure in various ways. We have already noted its reappearance, transformed into her theatrical "double consciousness"; we should add the account of Daniel's last look at her face: "her brow was contracted in one deep fold" (3.185–86).

But what, exactly, has been exorcised from the novel when the Princess disappears into that deep fold? And how is her gender, her being "the mother," linked to her serving as scapegoat? We are obliged once more to offer a double reading: for if the Princess's exorcism reduces a difference at the end of the line, it does so both on behalf of Daniel, in his surrogate's position, and on behalf of his author, hovering outside her fiction, one step down the dotted line:

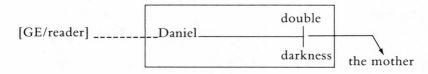

From Daniel's point of view, what is cast out of the world he inhabits is a generalized "afflicting doubtfulness," that combination of skepticism and generously diffused sympathies that had made it impossible for him to act purposefully in the past. His interview with his mother seals his identity as a Jew and a proto-Zionist, and allows him to move from a "suspended" state into what the novel claims is genuine activity. In psychoanalytic terms, Daniel puts a pre-Oedipal mother aside when he enters the symbolic order and takes his place under the sign of his Jewish grandfather.

But what of Daniel's author? What does she stand to gain by this reduction of difference to doubleness and doubleness to the mother? Here some recent turns of psychoanalytic theory may prove helpful. In the essay on sublime blockage, in the course of rehearsing some formulations of Thomas Weiskel's (see pp. 49–53, above), I suggested that both the authors of the literature of the sublime and their interpreters had an investment in moving from the murkier regions of the pre-Oedipal or maternal into the clearer light of what Weiskel reads as a "secondary oedipal system" and what I would call "the sublime of conflict and structure," where the positions of Father, Mother, and Child are more firmly triangulated—at considerable cost, but in a reassuring fashion. I wished to give Weiskel credit for dwelling as long as he did on the puzzles and anxieties of the pre-Oedipal, while also calling attention to the relief he seemed to have experienced as an interpreter in at last bringing it all home to the Father. Since 1976—when *The Romantic Sublime* was published—developments within psychoanalytic practice have converged with the work of feminist and post-structuralist theorists in providing counterirritants to those anxieties and encouraging more, and more varied, exploration of the earliest stages of infancy. In particular, the concept of narcissism has been expanded and generally reworked, both by American psychologists of the "self" and—more interestingly, to my mind—by French writers drawing on Lacan's and Derrida's rereadings of Freud. Of this recent work, an article by Julia Kristeva entitled "L'Abjet d'amour"—"The Abject of Love"—offers an account of the pre-Oedipal that seems peculiarly appropriate to the texts and paintings we have been considering.

Kristeva is struck by the ubiquity of narcissism in Freud's thought and by his description of its particular structure—not a dyadic relation of infant to mother but that relation complicated by a third instance, in her terms "a structuring that is already ternary but otherwise articulated by comparison with the [Oedipal] triangle of ego-object-Other."[10] How are we to understand this non-triangular ternary structure? I'm inclined to say, a little too rapidly: by looking at the diagrams I've sketched in these pages. But let us follow Kristeva's account more patiently. Like Weiskel, Kristeva works by juxtaposing the formulations of post-Saussurian linguistics with those of psychoanalysis: in this article she notes the resemblance—and what is, for her, more than a resemblance—between the bar or gap separating signifier and signified in Saussure's theory (what has become known, formulaically, as the "arbitrary nature of the sign") and the primal separation or blankness or emptiness (the term in French is *vide*) experienced by the infant, the subject both of psychological development and of the acquisition of language. In Kristeva's words, "this *vide* constitutive of the beginnings of the symbolic function is what appears as the first separation between what is not yet an *ego* and what is not yet an *object*" (p. 19). In this rendering of the narcissistic formation three elements go to make up that nontriangle: (1) the child, a sort of "subject," not yet the Freudian *ego;* (2) the mother, whom Kristeva will rename "the abject," to distinguish her role at this point from what she will become, an invested object of love; and (3) the gap itself—not yet Lacan's Symbolic Father, and not even gendered, but "an archaic modality of the paternal function" (p. 18), a placeholder whose role is to maintain the separation between infant and mother that is the guarantee of the infant's acquisition of an identity and of language, for this is also the gap between signifier and signified, the gap that makes language possible.

Readers to whom psychoanalysis does not appear simply as an outmoded means of enforcing patriarchy but rather as an aid in thinking one's way through and around it, may differ in judging the political bearings of Kristeva's formulations, some finding them more conservative or phallocentric than others. Their differences will turn on each reader's sense of how rapidly, and with what necessity, that pre-Oedipal "gap" is given a name, and the figure of the Father trundled into place. For our purposes, the value of the article lies in its emphasis on the rudimentary nature of both "subject" and "object" in narcissistic configurations, and in Kristeva's account of the vicissitudes of this nonobject, what it is that makes her assign the term "abject" to it.

Kristeva understands narcissism to be a means of covering over— to mask, but also to protect—the *vide* or separation that offers the infant the possibility of speech and individuation; without this complicity or, as Kristeva puts it, this "solidarity" between the infant's narcissism and the *vide,* "chaos will take away all possibility of distinction, of a trace and of symbolization, leading to the confusion of the limits of bodies, of words, of the real and the symbolic" (p. 20). It is to stave off that confusion that the infant, in Kristeva's reading of Freud, performs a double gesture: on the one hand linking itself, through a quasi-identification, with the "archaic modality of the paternal function," and, on the other, simultaneously rejecting "that which could have been a chaos and which now begins to become an *abject*" (p. 22), for it is only through this gesture of dismissal or abjection, Kristeva argues, that the place of the Mother can emerge as such, "before becoming an object correlative with the desire of the *ego*" (p. 22). We should notice the equivocation inherent in the gesture Kristeva describes: the casting out of the "abject," of "that which could have been a chaos" would seem to be the magical complement of that identification with a gap, with residual difference, that she takes as enabling. To identify with that gap, to link one's narcissism to the *vide,* is, in Kristeva's account, to acknowledge difference by defusing it of the terrors of primal separation, by seeming to choose separation, as if one might *endorse* "the arbitrary nature of the sign." Something similar may be seen at work in *Daniel Deronda:* the casting out of the Princess, her abjection, is intended not to collapse the distance between author and surrogate, but to stabilize it as a chosen separation and thus to ground the multiple gestures of mimesis that make up the novel. Kristeva's analysis allows us to see why we should not be surprised that it is "the mother" who is cast (and cast out) in this role. But it also sets forth the linguistic basis for this scapegoating, so that we should not be surprised (on the other hand) to find—as we did in our reading of *Middlemarch*—that the position of the "abject" may be occupied by someone like Mr. Casaubon: gestures of misogyny, though deeply motivated, may not be absolutely foundational in these scenarios of end-of-the-line signification.

A still more puzzling overlapping of the question of gender with motifs of suspension, imaginative activity, and self-location can be discerned in and around some famous lines from the opening of book 2 of *The Prelude,* where Wordsworth, musing on the sense of distance he experiences as he writes about his childhood, produces what has been read as an epitome of his autobiographical project:

A tranquillizing spirit presses now
On my corporeal frame, so wide appears
The vacancy between me and those days,
Which yet have such self-presence in my mind
That sometimes when I think of them I seem
Two consciousnesses—conscious of myself,
And of some other being.   [1805 text, 2.27–33]

Reproduced in this way, detached from its context, the passage has allowed any number of commentators to point to the doubling of consciousness they took to be peculiarly Wordsworthian.[11] Here, it would appear, is an end-of-the-line structure of pure self-reflexivity: a poet presents a surrogate of himself, the "I" who says "I think," discovering that the object of his reflection is necessarily split:

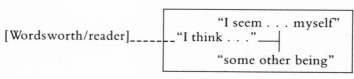

233

We might wish to know why this discovery should feel "tranquil-lizing" rather than dismaying. Thomas Weiskel, in a thoughtful commentary on these lines, suggests that the success of the passage, the way it functions as a "solution" for Wordsworth, lies in its rewriting a more indeterminate and troubling "vacancy" as the gap between a past and a present self.

> The "Two consciousnesses" are here defined by their objects. Both "myself-as-I-am-now" and the "some-other-Being" of the child-hood past are objective states of the self, identities that can be recognized and compared. The vacancy stretches between two known points and thus becomes an extensive attribute of the im-plicit identity that subsumes both states and whose medium is time. This was Wordsworth's great solution. The myth (or plot) of memory is not a problem but an answer. The vacancy, the absolute insufficiency of the *now*, is objectified as the distance between iden-tities which can be signified. . . . Without the myth of memory, Wordsworth's self-consciousness can not be formalized and re-mains outside the discourse.[12]

This points to what lends the passage stability, but without engag-ing the question of how long that stability is allowed to last. For if one reads on, past the period, to what is here quite literally the end of the line, the end of line 33, one encounters an effect still more Wordsworthian, the flickering awareness of an apposition (being:stone) created over against the syntactically controlled sense:

> I seem
> Two consciousnesses, conscious of myself,
> And of some other being. A grey stone
> Of native rock, left midway in the square
> Of our small market-village, was the home
> And centre of these joys; and when, returned
> After long absence, thither I repaired,
> I found that it was split and gone to build
> A smart assembly-room . . .   [2.31–39]

The slight hesitation induced by the line-ending retroactively weakens the period after "being" and invites a reading that draws the referent of "some other being" away from the familiarities of "consciousness"—present and adult or distant and childlike—and assimilates it to the alien inanimacy of "stone." The finality of the end-of-the-line structure gives way here to a slow drift, as the poet's thought slips from being to stone, then from the stone to its splitting and from that to the old woman:

> and when, returned
> After long absence, thither I repaired,
> I found that it was split and gone to build
> A smart assembly-room that perked and flared
> With wash and rough-cast, elbowing the ground
> Which had been ours. But let the fiddle scream,
> And be ye happy! Yet, my friends, I know
> That more than one of you will think with me
> Of those soft starry nights, and that old dame
> From whom the stone was named, who there had sate
> And watched her table with its huxter's wares,
> Assiduous through the length of sixty years.   [2.36–47]

Here the verse comes to rest, with the old woman sitting "assiduous," a phrase that matches—in its redundant expression of sheer immobility and the pathos of belonging—the earlier formulation "a stone of native rock." Stone and woman share a proper name (in a rejected draft Wordsworth included the name: lines 38 f. were to read "Gone was the old grey stone; that 'Stone of Rowe' / Split into fragments . . .");[13] both seem—by metonymy—obscurely associated with that "other being" whom Wordsworth discerned at the end of the line. Indeed, the two rambling sentences with which the verse paragraph concludes read like an oblique and loosely textured rehearsal of lines 27–33: "I found that it was split," for example, might almost be describing the poet's discovery of the gap between his "two consciousnesses," while the calm with which Wordsworth dwells on the thought of "those soft starry nights, and that old dame" feels like one more instance of the "tranquillizing spirit" that descended on him earlier. What was it about lines 27–33 that prompted this repetition-with-a-difference?

Suppose we pursue those resemblances. The split the poet recognizes between his present and his past self we know—and he knows—to be unavoidable; he registers it with wonder ("so wide" . . . "such self-presence") but undismayed. But what of the stone? *That* fragmentation is made to seem both avoidable and deplorable: the sarcasms directed at the "smart assembly-room" and the awkward *ressentiment* of "But let the fiddle scream, / And be ye happy!" betray a certain animus. Is that simply contingent, a distaste for the newfangled? Or is the blame heard there displaced from the other moment of splitting? And, if it is, what might there be to be blame in that case? And why might it not have found more direct expression?

Kristeva's discussion of narcissism can come to our aid here by suggesting that we may be considering still another tale of abjection. An attenuated subject—the "I" who says "I think"—is set over against a "vacancy" between two objects, versions of the poet's self momentarily fixed in a wondering contrast, a structure not of desire but of rudimentary differentiation. That poised structure then gives way, first to a scene of violence—the splitting of the stone— then to an act of reparation—the imagining of an old woman whose subhuman stillness qualifies her (along with other Wordsworthian solitaries) as what Kristeva would term a nonobject or "abject." The lines with which the verse paragraph concludes rehearse, in narrative form, the burden of the emblematic lines (ll. 27–33) that preceded them, playing out the energies that had been momentarily "tranquillized" into abeyance. We should ask now what those energies are, and where in the poem they would seem to be coming from.

The descent of the "tranquillizing spirit" seems to have been triggered by the lines just preceding 27–33, lines that first present the Hawkshead children's boisterous games, then pause to ask some elaborately phrased rhetorical questions about the relations of the energies of youth to the morally serious concerns of their elders:

From week to week, from month to month, we lived
A round of tumult. Duly were our games
Prolonged in summer till the daylight failed:
No chair remained before the doors, the bench

And threshold steps were empty, fast asleep
The labourer and the old man who had sate
A later lingerer, yet the revelry
Continued and the loud uproar. At last,
When all the ground was dark and the huge clouds
Were edged with twinkling stars, to bed we went
With weary joints and with a beating mind.
Ah, is there one who ever has been young
And needs a monitory voice to tame
The pride of virtue and of intellect?
And is there one, the wisest and the best
Of all mankind, who does not sometimes wish
For things which cannot be, who would not give,
If so he might, to duty and to truth
The eagerness of infantine desire?
A tranquillizing spirit presses now . . .   [2.8–27]

The initial contrast is between the noisy mobility of youth and
everything that is sedentary, not to say recumbent, about age. (This
is a contrast that will be repeated in the lines on the later visit to
Hawkshead, where the screaming fiddle takes the place of the children's revelry and the old woman ["who there had sate / . . . / Assiduous through the length of sixty years"] sits in for the "old man
who had sate / A later lingerer"). But the rhetorical questions offer
another set of abstractions—the reiterated honorific doublets of
maturity (virtue and intellect, the wisest and the best, duty and
truth) versus that remarkable phrase, "the eagerness of infantine
desire"—and frame the contrast as irreducible: "who does not
sometimes wish / For things which cannot be . . . ?" And it would
seem to be the poet's sense of irreducibility, of the split between the
thoughtless energies of youth and the values "of virtue and of intellect," that brings on the "tranquillizing spirit."

The poet, apparently, is firmly located in the world of maturity:
he might wish for "things which cannot be," but he knows better.
Perhaps; but an odd turn of phrase in these lines suggests that the
poet's position is less determined than that account would suggest.
The children's "revelry" ends with them finally going off to bed,
"with weary joints and with a beating mind." We may not have

237

expected the children to be credited with minds at all, still less with minds like Prospero's. I quote the famous speech from *The Tempest:*

Our revels now are ended. These our actors
As I foretold you, were all spirits and
Are melted into air, into thin air;
And, like the baseless fabric of this vision,
The cloud-capped towers, the gorgeous palaces,
The solemn temples, the great globe itself,
Yea, all which it inherit, shall dissolve,
And like this insubstantial pageant faded,
Leave not a rack behind. We are such stuff
As dreams are made on, and our little life
Is rounded with a sleep. Sir, I am vexed.
Bear with my weakness: my old brain is troubled.
Be not disturbed by my infirmity.
If you be pleased, retire into my cell
And there repose. A turn or two I'll walk
To still my beating mind.[14]

If the "beating mind" has migrated from Prospero to the tumultuous children, it is by way of Wordsworth's own awareness of a strenuous imaginative effort—not to conjure up a masque, as Prospero has, but to "fetch / Invigorating thoughts from former years" (11.648–49). There is a potential for confusion here of his current autobiographical project with "the eagerness of infantine desire," as he finds himself invigorated by this reading of the past, and it is that confusion of positions that is warded off by the ternary structure set in place in lines 27–33. Past and present identities, "some other being" and "myself," are named as such and stabilized.

But it may not be the stability of those identities that matters so much as the momentary fixity of the difference between them. Just as in the encounter with the Blind Beggar, where Wordsworth finds, at the end of the line, the almost meaningless (but meaning-producing) difference between a "face" and a written "label," so here the objects of this tranquillizing consciousness ("myself," "some other being") are presented in as spare and abstracted a way as possible, drained of biographical substance but located over

238

against each other as different. A feeling of arbitrariness always clings to the irreducible; in these scenarios of self-reading it may be assimilated—as Kristeva has argued—to the arbitrary nature of the Saussurian sign. Here, I believe, it is that sense of the arbitrary, of the way in which the grounds of meaning resist consciousness, that prompts Wordsworth's figure of material recalcitrance, the "stone of native rock," a figure that is then rewritten as the stolid, assiduous old woman. The possibility of misogynistic scapegoating is not taken up in these lines, even though it hovers around the gesture of assigning a gender to a stone. But the movement of the passage— from the "eagerness of infantine desire" to the tranquillizing formulation of a "vacancy," from there to the splitting of the stone and its restoration as the thought of an old woman—is comparable to the movement, in *Daniel Deronda,* from the polemical energies of "history" to Daniel's apprehension of "double darkness" and on to the appearance of "the mother." Both texts exhibit the involution and subsequent exfoliation that marks the turn at the end of the line.

NOTES

1. A READING OF LONGINUS

1. *"Longinus" on Sublimity,* trans. D. A. Russell (Oxford: Clarendon, 1965), 9.2, 7.2; all further references to this work will appear in the text, though I have changed a word or two of Russell's translation in the interests of a more literal rendering of the Greek. I am indebted to another recent translation, G. M. A. Grube's *Longinus on Great Writing* (New York: Bobbs-Merrill, 1957), and more particularly to the ample and intelligent introduction and notes accompanying Russell's edition of the Greek text, *"Longinus" on the Sublime* (Oxford: Clarendon, 1964).

2. W. K. Wimsatt, Jr., and Cleanth Brooks, *Literary Criticism: A Short History* (New York: Random House, 1957), p. 101.

3. See also 32.5, where Longinus selectively condenses Plato's allegorical account of the body (*Timaeus* 65c–85c), ostensibly as an illustration of "a continuous series of tropes," and 36.2, where Homer, Demosthenes, and Plato are praised as deserving to keep their prize "so long as waters flow and tall trees flourish." The line quoted in the text is from the quatrain recited by Socrates as an instance of bad, that is, *in*organic, discourse, because "it makes no difference what order the lines come in." It would be a mistake to see in this either inadvertence or irony on Longinus' part; it is, rather, an example of the persistent play throughout the treatise of the paired terms "body"/"fragment."

4. One index of Longinus' attraction for eighteenth-century readers can be found in the reappearance of this image among the precepts of that theoretician of passion and of *la vraisemblance,* Laclos's Mme de Merteuil: "Relisez votre letter: il y regne un ordre qui vous décèle à chaque phrase. Je veux que votre Présidente est assez peu formée pour ne s'en pas apercevoir: mais qu'importe? l'effet n'en pas moins manqué. C'est le défaut des romans; l'auteur se bat les flancs pour s'échauffer, et le lecteur reste froid" (*Les Liasons dangereuses,* letter 33).

5. Risks and perils abound in the treatise, both in the passages quoted and in Longinus' own prose. Especially marked is the figure of the perilous, because apparently uncontrolled, flight—the motif of Phaeton. In 22.3, for example, Demosthenes is praised for his use of the trope *hyperbaton* in these terms: "His transpositions produce not only a great sense of urgency but the appearance of extemporization, as he drags his hearers with him into the hazards of his long hyperbata. He often holds in suspense the meaning which he set out to convey and, introducing one extraneous item after another in an alien and unusual place before getting to the main point, throws the hearer into a panic lest the sentence collapse altogether and forces him in his excitement to share the speaker's peril." Russell shrewdly places this passage in apposition with 10.7, where the dominant figure, rather than that of the trajectory of a risky flight, is of the building up of a structure without "gaps" or "crevices," continuous in the way a wall is continuous (see *"Longinus" on the Sublime*, p. 139). A third continuous figure, that of the organically unified human body, is itself apposite here. All three turn out to conceal imperfections or to risk fragmentation.

6. The division of the treatise into chapters did not occur until the sixteenth century and does not always correspond to the stages of Longinus' official argument. In this case, however, the break between 15.12 and 16.1 is marked very clearly.

7. "A healing specific" = *alexipharmakon*. See also 17.2 and 32.4: "strong and appropriate emotions and genuine sublimity are a specific palliative [= *alexipharmakon*] for multiplied or daring metaphors." Readers of Jacques Derrida's "La Pharmacie de Platon" (*La Dissémination* [Paris: Seuil, 1972]) will not be surprised to find a rhetorical treatise by an admirer of the *Phaedrus* invoking a term like *alexipharmakon,* nor will they be surprised to discover Longinus at one point applying the term to figurative language itself (Demosthenes' oath, for example) while at another point applying it to those aspects of discourse (pathos or sublimity) that act to *counter* the effects of figurative language.

8. Werner Jaeger, *Paideia,* trans. Gilbert Highet, 3 vols. (New York: Oxford University Press, 1944–45), vol. 3, bk. 4, chap. 11.

9. See Walter Benjamin, "On Some Motifs in Baudelaire," *Illuminations,* trans. Harry Zohn (New York: Schocken, 1958).

10. Ibid., p. 194.

11. Walter Benjamin, *Schriften,* 2 vols. (Frankfurt: Surhkamp, 1966), 1:571 (cited by Hannah Arendt in her introduction to the New York edition of *Illuminations*).

12. Russell, citing Aristotle's *Rhetoric,* notes that the "observation that important people sometimes take offense at what they regard as deceitful cleverness was naturally nothing new. . . . So it is not this which L claims as original, but the proposition that *hupsos* defends figures as figures assist *hupsos*" (*"Longinus" on the Sublime*, p. 131).

13. See Angus Fletcher, *Allegory: The Theory of a Symbolic Mode* (Ithaca: Cornell University Press, 1964), chap. 5, and Harold Bloom, *The Anxiety of Influence: A Theory of Poetry* (New York: Oxford University Press, 1973), chap. 4.

14. See Russell, *"Longinus" on the Sublime*, p. 132.

15. Edward Burnaby Greene, "Observations on the Sublime of Longinus," *Critical Essays* (1770; New York: Garland, 1970), p. 143.

16. Henri Lebègue, ed., *Du sublime* (Paris: Editions "Les Belles lettres," 1939), p. 53; my trans.

17. Grube, *Longinus on Great Writing*, p. 50.

18. Russell, *"Longinus" on the Sublime*, p. 171.

2. WORDSWORTH AND THE TEARS OF ADAM

1. Quotations in this article are from *The Poetical Words of William Wordsworth*, ed. E. de Selincourt and Helen Darbishire, 5 vols. (Oxford: Clarendon, 1963–66); William Wordsworth, *The Prelude: 1799, 1805, 1850*, ed. Jonathan Wordsworth, M. H. Abrams, and Stephen Gill (New York: Norton, 1979); and *The Poetical Works of John Milton*, ed. Helen Darbishire (Oxford: Clarendon, 1958). Line references will be given in the text.

2. On the transformation of the scene, see David Ferry, *The Limits of Mortality* (Middletown: Wesleyan University Press, 1959), pp. 30–31; and James Kissane, "A Night-Piece: Wordsworth's Emblem of the Mind," *MLN* (1956), 71:183–86.

3. "Composed on the road between Nether Stowey and Alfoxden, extempore. I distinctly recollect the very moment when I was struck, as described, — 'He looks up at the clouds, etc.' " *The Poetical Works*, 2:503.

4. In *Table Talk*, May 12, 1830; reprinted in *Coleridge on the Seventeenth Century*, ed. Roberta Florence Brinkley (Durham: Duke University Press, 1955), p. 587.

5. Louis L. Martz, *The Paradise Within* (New Haven: Yale University Press, 1964), p. 153.

6. A brief summary of critical opinion on books 11 and 12 followed by a perceptive and informed account of their significance can be found in Barbara Keifer Lewalski, "Structure and the Symbolism of Vision in Michael's Prophecy, *Paradise Lost*, Books XI–XII, *Philological Quarterly* (1963), 42:25–35. See also George Williamson, "The Education of Adam," and Lawrence A. Sasek, "The Drama of Paradise Lost, Books XI and XII," both articles available in Arthur E. Barker's anthology, *Milton: Modern Essays in Criticism* (New York: Oxford University Press, 1965).

7. The other moments occur when Milton addresses Adam and Eve at 4.773 ("Sleep on, / Blest pair . . ."), and Eve at 9.404 ("O much deceived, much failing, hapless *Eve* . . .").

8. In *The Literary Remains of Samuel Taylor Coleridge* (London: Pickering, 1836–39), 1:172 f.; reprinted in Brinkley, *Coleridge*, p. 578.

9. I am indebted to Geoffrey Hartman's discussion of "The Ruined Cottage" in *Wordsworth's Poetry 1787–1814* (New Haven: Yale University Press, 1964), pp. 135–40, 302–6, and to his remark à propos of "Michael" that "the poet is Michael's true heir" (p. 266). I should also record the degree to which Hartman's article "Milton's Counterplot," *ELH* (1958), 25:1–12, has encouraged me to read *Paradise Lost* book 11 as I do.

10. *Journals of Dorothy Wordsworth,* ed. E. de Selincourt (New York: Oxford University Press, 1941), 1:106.

3. The Notion of Blockage in the Literature of the Sublime

1. Immanuel Kant, *Critique of Judgment,* trans. J. H. Bernard (New York: Hafner, 1966), p. 83.

2. Ibid., p. 91.

3. Thomas McFarland, "Recent Studies in the Nineteenth Century," *Studies in English Literature* (1976), 16:693–94.

4. William Wordsworth, *The Prose Works of William Wordsworth,* ed. W. J. B. Owen and Jane Worthington Smyser, 3 vols. (Oxford: Clarendon, 1975), 2:355.

5. Samuel Monk, *The Sublime: A Study of Critical Theories in Eighteenth-Century England* (1935; rpt., Ann Arbor: University of Michigan Press, 1960), p. 58.

6. Ibid., p. 6.

7. Ibid., pp. 3–4.

8. Thomas Weiskel, *The Romantic Sublime: Studies in the Structure and Psychology of Transcendence* (Baltimore: Johns Hopkins University Press, 1976), pp. 22–23.

9. David Hume, *A Treatise of Human Nature,* ed. L. A. Selby-Bigge (Oxford: Clarendon, 1888), p. 436.

10. Angus Fletcher, *Allegory: The Theory of a Symbolic Mode* (Ithaca: Cornell University Press, 1964), pp. 234–35.

11. Alexander Gerard, *An Essay on Taste,* 2nd ed. (Edinburgh, 1764; rpt., New York: Garland, 1970), p. 12.

12. Kant, *Critique of Judgment,* p. 91.

13. Weiskel, *Romantic Sublime,* p. 21.

14. Ibid., p. 41.

15. Ibid., pp. 92 ff.

16. Ibid., pp. 99 ff.

17. Ibid., p. 106.

18. This may be the moment to acknowledge some other people's ideas. Henry Abelove pointed out to me the nice irony, no doubt conscious

on McFarland's part, of his selecting Schopenhauer for this particular role. Schopenhauer is the occasion for a peculiarly devious development in Proust's essay "On Reading." (Originally published as the preface to Proust's translation of Ruskin's *Sesame and Lilies* in 1906, the essay has been reprinted, in a bilingual edition, ed. and trans. Jean Autret and William Burford [New York: Macmillan, 1971].) On p. 51, Proust offers Schopenhauer as "the image of a mind whose vitality bears lightly the most enormous reading"; on the next page, Schopenhauer is praised for having produced a book "which implies in an author, along with the most reading, the most originality"; between these two accolades Proust quotes a series of fifteen or so passages, taken, he says, from one page of *The World as Will and Representation,* which he strings together so as to produce a rapid, abbreviated, reiterative, and finally comical parade of bits of Voltaire, Byron, Herodotus, Heraclitus (in Latin), Theognis (in Latin), and so on, down to Byron (again) and Balthazar Gracian. The effect is like that of riffling the pages of Curtius; the whole run-through is punctuated by Proust's repetition of "etc." as he cuts off one citation after another. Josué Harari has drawn my attention to a fine reading of this essay by Barbara Harlow in *MLN* (1975), 90:849–71.

19. William Wordsworth, *The Prelude: 1799, 1805, 1850,* ed. Jonathan Wordsworth, M. H. Abrams, and Stephen Gill (New York: Norton, 1979). Henceforth, references to *The Prelude* will appear in the text; unless otherwise indicated, line numbers refer to the 1850 version of book 7.

4. FLAUBERT'S CONVERSION

1. *L'Idiot de la famille: Gustave Flaubert de 1821 à 1857* 3 vols. (Paris: Gallimard, 1971–72). Page references will appear in the text. Translations are my own.

2. The interview appeared in the *New Left Review,* no. 58. An abridged version was reprinted in *The New York Review of Books,* March 26, 1970. The entire text, in French, may be consulted in *Situations IX* (Paris: Gallimard, 1972).

3. *La Première education sentimentale* (Paris: Seuil, 1963). Page references will appear in the text. Translations are my own.

4. *The Words,* trans. Bernard Frechtman (New York: Braziller, 1964), pp. 152–53.

5. RECOGNIZING CASAUBON

1. George Eliot, *Middlemarch,* ed. Gordon S. Haight (Boston: Houghton Mifflin, 1956). Page numbers are given in the text.

2. J. Hillis Miller, "Narrative and History," *ELH* (1974), 41:466. Miller's account of the novel is further developed in "Optic and Semiotic in

Middlemarch," in *The Worlds of Victorian Fiction,* ed. Jerome H. Buckley (Cambridge, Mass.: Harvard University Press, 1975), pp. 125–45.

3. *The George Eliot Letters,* ed. Gordon S. Haight, 7 vols. (New Haven: Yale University Press, 1954–55). Volume and page numbers are given in the text.

4. *George Eliot: A Biography* (New York and Oxford: Oxford University Press, 1968), p. 552. The notebook itself may be seen in the Beinecke Library at Yale.

5. Richard Ellmann, "Dorothea's Husbands," in *Golden Codgers: Biographical Speculations* (London: Oxford University Press, 1973), pp. 28, 38.

6. In "The Natural History of German Life" (1856), reprinted in Thomas Pinney, ed., *Essays of George Eliot* (New York: Columbia University Press, 1963), p. 270.

7. Pinney, *Essays,* pp. 320–21.

8. George Eliot, *Romola* (Edinburgh and London: Blackwood, n.d.), chapter 38 ("The Black Marks Become Magical"), pp. 291–92.

9. Immanuel Kant, *Critique of Judgment,* trans. J. H. Bernard (New York: Hafner, 1966), p. 83.

10. Kant, *Judgment,* p. 91.

11. Richard Holt Hutton, review of book 2 of *Middlemarch, Spectator,* February 3, 1872, reprinted in *George Eliot: The Critical Heritage,* ed. David Carroll (London: Routledge, 1971), p. 291.

12. George Eliot, "Janet's Repentance," in *Scenes of Clerical Life* (1858), ed. David Lodge (Harmondsworth: Penguin, 1973), p. 343.

13. "Janet's Repentance," p. 322.

14. George Eliot, "The Lifted Veil," in *Silas Marner—The Lifted Veil—Brother Jacob* (Edinburgh and London: Blackwood, n.d.), p. 301.

15. John Locke, *An Essay Concerning Human Understanding,* ed. Alexander Campbell Fraser (1894; rpt., New York: Dover, 1959), 1:403.

6. FREUD AND THE SANDMAN

1. Cited by Paul Roazen in *Brother Animal: The Story of Freud and Tausk* (New York: Knopf, 1969), p. 92.

2. *The Standard Edition of the Complete Psychological Works of Sigmund Freud,* 24 vols., trans. James Strachey (London: Hogarth, 1953–74), vol. 17. References to this and other writings of Freud will be given in the text by volume and page in the *Standard Edition.*

3. Philip Rieff, introduction to S. Freud, *Studies in Parapsychology* (New York: Collier-Macmillan, 1963), p. 7.

4. See Hélène Cixous, "Fiction and Its Phantoms: A Reading of Freud's *Das Unheimliche,*" in *New Literary History* (Spring 1976), 7:525–48, a translation of an article originally published in *Poétique* (1972), 10:199–216. "The Uncanny" has drawn to it a series of remarkably acute interpretations in the

NOTES: FREUD AND THE SANDMAN

last few years. See Jacques Derrida, "La Double séance," in *La Dissémination* (Paris: Seuil, 1972), pp. 300–1; Samuel Weber, "The Sideshow, or: Remarks on a Canny Moment," *MLN* (1973), 88:1102–33; Jeffrey Mehlman, "Poe Pourri: Lacan's Purloined Letter," *Semiotext(e)* (1975), 1:51–68; and Sarah Kofman, "Le Double e(s)t le diable," in *Quatre Romans analytiques* (Paris: Galilée, 1974), pp. 135–81.

5. For clarification of psychoanalytic theory, see J. Laplanche and J. B. Pontalis, *The Language of Psycho-Analysis*, trans. Donald Nicholson-Smith (New York: Norton, 1973), esp. the entries "Compulsion to Repeat" and "Death Instincts."

6. On the relation between Freud's theorizing and his figurative language, see the superb reading of *Beyond the Pleasure Principle* provided by Rodolphe Gasché in "La Source métapsychologique," *digraphe* (1974), 3:83–122.

7. *Selected Writings of E. T. A. Hoffmann*, ed. and trans. Leonard J. Kent and Elizabeth C. Knight, 2 vols. (Chicago: University of Chicago Press, 1969). "The Sandman" is printed in 1:137–67. Henceforth, references to the story will be given parenthetically in the text.

8. For an account of the use of this term by Freud and, in its French version—*après-coup*—by Jacques Lacan, see the entry "Deferred Action" in Laplanche and Pontalis, pp. 111–14.

9. Hoffmann's account of the plot and scenic effects of Nathanael's poem, like Freud's account of "The Sandman," serves as a powerfully convincing substitute for a text, in this case a poem in meter which we never get to read. Unlike Freud, however, Hoffmann calls attention to this play between a literary object and its lurid double by stressing the wild alternation in Nathanael's response to what he had written.

10. On the conflict of psychoanalytic and "literary" texts, see Jacques Derrida, "Le Facteur de la vérité," *Poétique* (1975), 21:96–147.

11. See note 1.

12. I say this despite the objections raised by K. R. Eissler in *Talent and Genius: A Psychoanalytic Reply to a Defamation of Freud* (New York: Quadrangle, 1971). Eissler corrects Roazen on a number of points of detail, and objects, often quite rightly, to the tone and the tendentiousness of Roazen's account, but Eissler's own interpretations are hardly compelling. Other material on Freud and Tausk can be found in Ernst Pfeiffer, ed., *Sigmund Freud and Lou Andreas-Salomé: Letters*, trans. W. and E. Robson-Scott (New York, 1972), and in *The Freud Journal of Lou Andreas-Salomé*, ed. Stanley A. Leavy (New York: Basic Books, 1964). For other interpretations of the Freud-Tausk affair, see the essays by Th. Neyraut-Sutterman and Jean Gillibert accompanying the French translation of Tausk's articles, *Oeuvres psychanalytiques* (Paris: Payot, 1975).

13. A comparable gesture can be found in Tocqueville's account of the events of 1848 in France. Writing of the February Revolution he states,

"This was something completely new in our history. It is true that similar revolutions had taken place in other countries at other times; however new and unexpected contemporaries may find the particular events of any age, including our own, they are always part of the age-old history of humanity." His editors note the following words marked for omission in the manuscript: *"For what we call new facts are most often only forgotten ones,"* next to which, in the margin, Tocqueville had added *"Has not this been said by others?"* The passage is translated by George Lawrence in J. P. Mayer and A. P. Kerr's edition of the *Recollections* (New York: Anchor-Doubleday, 1971), pp. 89–90.

14. Gilles Deleuze, *Différence et répétition* (Paris: Presses Universitaires de France, 1968), pp. 1–30 and 128–68.

7. DORA'S SECRETS, FREUD'S TECHNIQUES

1. Henry James, preface to "What Maisie Knew," in *The Art of the Novel,* ed. R. P. Blackmur (New York: Scribner's, 1934), pp. 148–49. Further page references to this volume will appear in the text.

2. Sigmund Freud, "Fragment of an Analysis of a Case of Hysteria," in *Dora: An Analysis of a Case of Hysteria,* ed. Philip Rieff (New York: Collier, 1963), p. 66. Unless otherwise indicated, references to Freud will be to this edition of this work.

3. Philip Rieff, *Fellow Teachers* (New York: Harper and Row, 1973), p. 84. Rieff was the first to point out, as far as I know, the resemblance of Maisie and Dora: "Alas, poor Dora: there were no longer truths strong enough in her resistances to fight off, unsupported, the assaults of experience. Dora had no protector against the deadly competitive erotic circles that drew themselves around her. Unlike Maisie's author, the spiritual author of Dora could think of everything except to support those resistant, self-perpetuating truths by which Dora's neurotic, self-divided and socially isolated resistances were once chartered. Freud's special mission was to point out to Dora the fact (which is changeable, like all facts—changeable, not least, by the authority of his interpretation) that her truths had become neurotic, mere resistances signaling their opponents, her desires" (p. 85). These sentences convey some sense both of Rieff's central concern—the erosion of moral authority, an erosion accelerated by Freud's "interpretations"—and of the densely ironical style in which this strange book is elaborated.

4. Jacque Lacan, "Intervention sur le transfert" in *Écrits* (Paris: Seuil, 1966), p. 220.

5. It is worth noting the vicissitudes of this word in Freud's writings. Most often it is used in phrases like "the technique of dream interpretation" or "the technique of psychoanalysis" to suggest certain procedures available to the analyst. But in Freud's book on *Witz,* published in 1905, the year he

was revising the "Fragment of an Analysis" for publication, he uses "technique" and its cognates steadily to mean the mechanisms that produce the joke, not the means of its interpretation; so the word crosses the line and becomes synonymous with "joke-work" (a term Freud employs much less frequently) and homologous with "dream-work" and the work of producing symptoms, that is, with "the internal structure of the neurosis." At this point, "techniques" and "secrets" begin to look alike.

6. Steven Marcus, "Freud and Dora: Story, History, Case History," in *Representations: Essays on Literature and Society* (New York: Random House, 1975), pp. 301–3.

7. Luce Irigaray, *Ce Sexe qui n'en est pas un* (Paris: Minuit, 1977), pp. 205–17.

8. Sigmund Freud, *The History of the Psychoanalytic Movement,* ed. Philip Rieff (New York: Collier, 1963), p. 47. Further page references will appear in the text.

9. Sigmund Freud, *Jokes and their Relation to the Unconscious,* ed. James Strachey (New York: Norton, 1963), p. 115.

8. Two Extravagant Teachings

1. Harold C. Martin, *The Logic and Rhetoric of Exposition* (New York: Holt, 1958).

2. "Such, such were the joys . . .", in George Orwell, *A Collection of Essays* (Garden City: Doubleday, 1954), p. 37.

3. In *JEGP* (1966), 65:422–44. Page references to this article will be given parenthetically in the text.

4. "Introduction" to Geoffrey Tillotson, ed., *The Rape of the Lock and Other Poems,* vol. 2 of *The Twickenham Edition of the Poems of Alexander Pope* (London: Methuen and New Haven: Yale University Press, 1954).

5. "Introduction" to William K. Wimsatt, Jr., ed., *Alexander Pope: Selected Poetry and Prose* (New York: Rinehart, 1951), pp. xxxvi f.

9. Medusa's Head: Male Hysteria under Political Pressure

1. Sigmund Freud, "Fetishism," in *Sexuality and the Psychology of Love,* ed. Philip Rieff (New York: Collier-Macmillan, 1963), p. 215.

2. Edmund Burke, *Reflections on the Revolution in France,* ed. Conor Cruise O'Brien (Baltimore: Penguin, 1968), pp. 181, 166 and 165.

3. Victor Hugo, *Oeuvres complètes,* 35 vols. (Paris: Martel, 1955).

4. My source for this biographical information was the *Album Hugo,* ed. M. Ecalle and V. Lumbroso (Paris: Gallimard, 1964), pp. 188–96.

5. Compare the following account from *The Examiner,* a London weekly: "One of the females, a young woman, neatly dressed, picked up

the flag, and leaping over the barricade, rushed towards the national guards, uttering language of provocation. Although the fire continued from the barricade, the national guards, fearing to injure this female, humanely abstained for some time from returning it, and exhorted her to withdraw. Their exhortations, however, were in vain, and at length self-preservation compelled them to fire, and as the woman was in front of the barricade a shot reached her and she was killed. The other female then advanced, took the flag, and began to throw stones at the national guards. The fire from the barricade had become feeble, but several shots were fired from the sides and from the windows of houses, and the national guards, in returning the fire, killed the second female."

This appeared in the issue of July 1, 1848 and is described as a translation of an eyewitness account which had appeared earlier in Paris.

6. Freud, "Medusa's Head," in *Sexuality and the Psychology of Love*, pp. 212–13.

7. This combination of offenses—against property and decency—reappears in an American National Guardsman's recollections of his participation, ten years earlier, in the encounter with protesters at Kent State during the Vietnam War:

"James W. Farriss admits he was excited when he heard his National Guard unit was going to Kent State. He had never been on a college campus.

"He recalls now that when he got to campus he was repelled by the students' obscene gestures and filthy language. As a soldier sent to protect property, he was outraged to see it destroyed.

"'It seemed like all the young women were shouting obscenities or giving obscene gestures. I had never seen that before,' said Farriss. 'I've heard a few men talk like that, but not women.'

"There were 75 guardsmen besides Farriss on the hill alongside Taylor Hall, according to Guard reports. A 13-second fusillade stilled the din of an anti-war protest."

(From an Associated Press story published in the Ithaca *Journal* May 4, 1979.)

8. Jean Laplanche, *Problématiques II/Castration-Symbolisations* (Paris: Presses Universitaires de France, 1980), p. 66.

9. The *politically* apotropaic effects of the Medusa's head derive from its reappearance on Minerva's shield and from the use of representations of that shield as symbols of the State's power to defend itself against its enemies. See, for example, the ceremonial use of the shield in Rubens' *Philip IV Appoints Prince Ferdinand Governor of the Netherlands* (Figure 66 in John Rupert Martin, *The Decorations for the Pompa Introitus Ferdinandi* [London and New York: Phaidon, 1972]). In *Détruire la peinture* (Paris: Galilée, 1977), Louis Marin discusses a notorious instance, Caravaggio's *Medusa's Head* painted on a circular shield, a work commissioned by a cardinal as a present

to the Grand Duke of Tuscany. Marin's analysis is detailed and fascinating and should be read—especially the section entitled "Intermède psychanalytique"—as a counterirritant to the argument of this essay. Marin notes the ways in which thinking about matters of representation can lead one into the thematics of castration, but he is leery of what he takes to be the pathos—or bathos—of Freud's reading of the Medusa's head.

10. The details of Courbet's involvement in the Commune, his trial, and his exile are summarized in Marie-Thérèse de Forges's *Biographie* in the catalogue of the centenary exhibit of his work in Paris, 1977–78, *Gustave Courbet (1819–1877)* (Paris: Éditions des Musées Nationaux, 1977), pp. 46 ff. A longer account may be found in Gerstle Mack, *Gustave Courbet* (New York: Knopf, 1951).

11. Maxime du Camp, *Les Convulsions de Paris*, 4 vols., 5th ed. (Paris: Hachette, 1881), vol. 2, chap. 5 ("La Colonne de la Grande Armée"), p. 190 (my translation). Further page references will appear in the text.

12. Burke, *Reflections*, p. 230.

13. This may seem like a gratuitous slur, but Norman Podhoretz is, in fact, the interesting contemporary analogue and his book, *Breaking Ranks* (New York: Harper, 1979), takes a position in relation to "The Movement" remarkably like that of du Camp in relation to the Commune. Compare du Camp's sexual-political fulminations with this, from Podhoretz's "Postscript" (addressed, instructively, to his young son): "But if the plague [of the sixties] seems for the moment to have run its course among these groups [i.e., "the young, the blacks and the intellectuals"], it rages as fiercely as ever among others: among the kind of women who do not wish to be women and among those men who do not wish to be men. . . . [T]here can be no more radical refusal of self-acceptance than the repudiation of one's own biological nature; and there can be no abdication of responsibility more fundamental than the refusal of a man to become, and to be, a father, or the refusal of a woman to become, and be a mother" (p. 363). Peter Steinfels, in *The Neoconservatives* (New York: Simon and Schuster, 1979) offers a measured but deftly witty discussion of the sociology as well as the intellectual background of writers in Podhoretz' group and indeed sees their dependence on a tradition that extends back through Tocqueville to Burke. For a less scholarly but even funnier discussion, see Gore Vidal's "Pink Triangle and Yellow Star," in *The Second American Revolution and Other Essays* (New York: Random House, 1982).

14. Alexis de Tocqueville, *Oeuvres complètes*, ed. Luc Monnier (Paris: Gallimard, 1964), 12:159–60. *Souvenirs* has been translated, by George Lawrence, under the title *Recollections*, ed. J. P. Mayer and A. P. Kerr (Garden City: Doubleday, 1970), where this passage appears on p. 145. I have generally quoted Lawrence's translation, occasionally modifying it to produce a more literal rendering. Page references will henceforth be given in the text, in both French (S) and English (R) editions.

15. G. W. F. Hegel, *The Phenomenology of Mind* (1807), trans. J. B. Baillie (New York: Harper, 1967), pp. 342–50. "In content," Hegel remarks of insights based on physiognomic laws, "such observations cannot differ in value from these: 'It always rains at the annual fair,' says the dealer; 'And every time, too,' says the housewife, 'when I am drying my washing.'" A whiff of misogyny, perhaps, in this *anti*-physiognomical stance?

16. See Judith Wechsler's *A Human Comedy: Physiognomy and Caricature in 19th Century Paris* (Chicago: University of Chicago Press, 1982) for an account of the persistence of Lavater's notions in France.

17. Burke, *Reflections,* p. 140.

18. Jennifer Harris, "The Red Cap of Liberty: A Study of Dress Worn by French Revolutionary Partisans 1789–94," *Eighteenth-Century Studies* (1981), 14:283–312. Similar remarks can be found in Jules Renouvier's *Histoire de l'art pendant la révolution,* 2 vols. (Paris: Renouard, 1863), 2:394–96, and in the introductory pages of the most recent sophisticated discussion of the iconography of Liberty in France, Maurice Agulhon's *Marianne into Battle: Republican Imagery and Symbolism in France, 1789–1880* (Cambridge: Cambridge University Press, 1981).

19. A. F. von Pauly et al., *Paulys Real-Encyclopädie der classischen altertums Wissenschaft* (Stuttgart: Druckenmüller, 1894–), *s.v.* Pilleus. A variant spelling is *pileus.*

20. *Ibid., s.v.* Tiara.

21. John H. Young, "Commagenian Tiaras: Royal and Divine," *American Journal of Archaeology* (1964), 68:29 ff.

22. François Boucher, in his encyclopedic survey, *Histoire du Costume en Occident de l'Antiquité à nos Jours* (Paris: Flammarion, 1965), describes the *pileus* as "a felt cap of diverse forms, worn in Rome by men: the Phrygian cap had a folded-down point, the Greek style was ovoid in form, and that of Roman freed slaves was tubular" (p. 124). Leonardo Olschki, in *The Myth of Felt* (Berkeley: University of California Press, 1949), insists that one should not confuse the "cap of freedom," which is semi-oval, like those worn by Castor and Pollux, with the Phrygian cap, that "headgear of slaves" (p. 39).

23. Eleonore Dörner, "Deus Pileatus," in *Études Mithräiques,* ed. J. Duchesne-Guillemin (Leiden: Brill, 1978), pp. 115–22.

24. In *The Death of Classical Paganism* (New York: Scribner, 1976), John Holland Smith lists six "great mysteries" active and spread throughout the empire in the second and third centuries: those of Cybele-Attis, of Mithra, of Demeter, of Dionysus, of Isis, and of Orpheus (p. 11).

25. Henri Graillot, *Le Culte de Cybèle* (Paris: Fontemoing, 1912), p. 193. This is the classic monograph. Graillot goes on to contrast the austerity of Mithraic practice with the "sentimental and sensual" aspects of the cult of the Great Mother, a religion "made for tender and passionate souls" and particularly popular among women.

26. A handsome marble head of a young man with his hair radiating out in waves from beneath a *tiara,* found near a sanctuary of Cybele in Ostia and thought, by one scholar, to be a head of Attis, has recently been reidentified as that of Mithra. See entry 396 (and plate 246) in M. J. Vermaseren, *Corpus Cultus Cybelae Attidisque (CCCA): III Italia-Lattum* (Leiden: Brill, 1977), p. 124. Other such instances may be found in Vermaseren's collection of the remains of the cult, part of the multivolume project of which he is the editor, *Études préliminaires aux religions orientales dans L'Empire Romain,* 93 vols. (Leiden: Brill, 1961–81). Vermaseren's more popular account of his research—*The Legend of Attis in Greek and Roman Art* (Leiden: Brill, 1966)—has been helpful in preparing this article. I am particularly grateful to him for referring me to Dörner's article.

27. Graillot devotes a chapter to the *galli* in *Le Culte de Cybèle* (pp. 287–319). A more recent summary of scholarship can be found in G. M. Sanders' article *Gallos* in vol. 8 of the *Reallexicon für Antike und Christentum* (Stuttgart: Hiersemann, 1972), cols. 984–1034.

28. Edith Weigert-Vowinkel, in "The Cult and Mythology of the Magna Mater from the Standpoint of Psychoanalysis," *Psychiatry* (1938), 1:347–78, offers a speculative account of the relation between matriarchal religions and the practice of self-castration.

29. See, for example, Ascanius' tirade in *Aeneid* 9.598–620. These lines, along with *Aeneid* 4.216 are those discussed by Servius and cited by Dörner ("Deus Pileatus," p. 119).

30. Harris, "The Red Cap of Liberty," pp. 290–91.

31. Agulhon, *Marianne into Battle,* p. 16.

32. Lynn Hunt, in "Hercules and the Radical Image in the French Revolution," *Representations* (1983), 2:95–117, offers a more nuanced account of this development than Agulhon's. See also her *Politics, Culture, and Class in the French Revolution* (Berkeley and Los Angeles: University of California Press, 1984).

33. Agulhon, *Marianne into Battle,* p. 84.

34. Esprit-Antoine Gibelin, *De l'Origine et de la forme du bonnet de la Liberté* (Paris: Buisson, 1796), pp. 24–26. Renouvier (see n. 18, above) draws on this pamphlet for his discussion of the *bonnet rouge;* he gives a brief sketch of Gibelin's career in the first volume of his *Histoire,* pp. 132–34.

35. Agulhon, *Marianne into Battle,* p. 82 and n. 73.

36. That these sexual associations would be repressed and would surface only in oddities of phrasing or of iconographical development is one of the (conventional enough) assumptions of this essay. But there are likely to be exceptions that serve as proof of this rule, occasional acts of explicitness, marginal voices more apt to be ignored than suppressed. One of these voices is that of Joel Barlow, the Connecticut poet (and friend of Tom Paine) who was living in Paris during the 1790s. Barlow left behind a brief, un-

dated manuscript entitled "Genealogy of the Tree of Liberty" which is now in the possession of the Houghton Library of Harvard University (bMS Am 1448). Barlow traces the festive use of the Liberty Tree back to Bacchic and, beyond that, Egyptian worship of the phallus, "The *liberty cap*," he adds, "is precisely from these [?] origins. It is taking a part for the whole, as the *Ear of Wheat* is used, in some planispheres, to represent the *harvest* Virgin or Ceres in the Constellations. The Liberty Cap is the head of the Penis, an emblem of Liberty. The first civil or political use that was made of it was by the Romans when they gave liberty to a Slave. They put a Red Cap upon his head, which he wore ever after, to denote that he was a Freed Man.— Neither master nor man knew the origin of this curious emblem" (p. 13, recto). I'm grateful to the Houghton Library for permission to reprint the text, and to Robert Dawidoff and Eve Kosofsky Sedgwick for help in tracking it down.

37. See Maurice Agulhon, "On Political Allegory: A Reply to Eric Hobsbawn," *History Workshop* (1979), 8:169: "Certainly such areas need exploring, and the (only recently abandoned) reluctance to explore them was undoubtedly misguided. However, now that the taboo on the history of sexuality has been lifted, there is much danger in attaching undue importance to it, as in the past there was error in ignoring it altogether." This is sensible enough and, in the context of Agulhon's quarrel with Hobsbawm, very much to the point. But consider this more elaborate expression of his scepticism, from the Conclusion of *Marianne into Battle*. He is speculating on why "the Republic" was given a woman's name and he notes that "a number of subtle writers have meditated upon similar themes." From one such meditation, by Jean Giraudoux, Agulhon cites the following sentence—"He felt that to change a country from a kingdom (*un* royaume) into a Republic (*une* Republique) was to change its very sex . . ."—then continues: "The sex of a Nation! . . . One can imagine how far up the garden path of socio-psychoanalytical meditation one could be led if one pursued that track. We must admit that we would put no great faith in such a venture, believing that to apply categories of individual psychology to collective concepts could lead one to make the mistake of taking metaphors for realities" (p. 185). Neither of the distinctions relied on here—between "categories of individual psychology" and "collective concepts," or between "metaphors" and "realities"—seems refined enough to justify a serious methodological *parti pris*.

38. Agulhon, *Marianne into Battle*, p. 159. The painting is reproduced on p. 160.

Response from Joel Fineman

1. "It is to be anticipated that male analysts with feminist sympathies, and our women analysts also, will disagree with what I have said here. They

will hardly fail to object that such notions have their origins in the man's 'masculinity complex,' and are meant to justify theoretically his innate propensity to disparage and suppress women. But this sort of psychoanalytic argument reminds us here, as it so often does, of Dostoevsky's famous 'knife that cuts both ways.' The opponents of those who reason thus will for their part think it quite comprehensible that members of the female sex should refuse to accept a notion that appears to gainsay their eagerly coveted equality with men.. The use of analysis as a weapon of controversy obviously leads to no decision. . . ." Sigmund Freud, "Female Sexuality" (1931), in *The Standard Edition of the Complete Psychological Works of Sigmund Freud*, 23 vols., ed. James Strachey (London: Hogarth, 1961), 21:230. The editor notes that "The actual simile used by Freud and in the Russian original is a 'stick with two ends,'" p. 230.

2. The development of Renaissance emblematics and its correlation of word with picture—away from iconic allegory and toward more narratively and discursively conceived tableaux, toward a kind of Shaftesburyan "Characteristick"—prepares the way for specifically historicist painting; see Rosemary Freeman, *English Emblem Books* (New York: Octagon, 1970). This background is relevant to Courbet's place, on the one hand in Hertz's paper and on the other in the painting tradition that begins with David.

3. Roland Barthes discusses the power of photography to present a vivid absent in *Camera Lucida: Reflections on Photography,* trans. R. Howard (New York: Hill and Wang, 1981), originally published as *La Chambre claire* (Paris: Gallimard/Seuil, 1980). Barthes's late concern with photography exemplifies the evolutionary direction of recent French literary theory, which, speaking very generally, has developed itself through a phenomenology first of the seen, then of the spoken, then of the written. Current critical interest in photography manifests a turn away from language, speech being elided in the photo-graph.

4. *Egypte, Nubie, Palestine et Syrie, dessins photographiques recuellis pendant les années 1849, 1850 et 1851, accompagnés d'un texte explicatif et précédés d'une introduction par Maxime Du Camp, chargé d'une mission archéologique en Orient par le Ministère de l'instruction publique* (Paris: Gide et Baudry, 1852). It has often been noted that du Camp's photographs, taken frontally and without reference to scale, become somewhat abstract, and for this reason convey less archeological information than they might. For example, referring to du Camp's plate 39, a photograph of the pillar of Tuthmosis III, Richard Pare remarks, "Du Camp's photograph presents the pillar without reference to scale or context, a view that transforms the object into an emblematic image of Pharaonic Egypt. . . ." *Photography and Architecture: 1839–1939,* ed. Richard Pare (Montreal: Canadian Centre for Architecture, 1982), p. 246. Ian Jeffrey makes the same general point in *Photography: A Concise History* (New York: Oxford University Press, 1981), pp. 18–20. The abstract realism of du Camp's photography is similar to, though less subtle than,

that of Auguste Salzmann: see Abigail Solomon-Godeau, "A Photographer in Jerusalem, 1855: Auguste Salzmann and his Times," *October* (1981), 18:90–107. Blanquart-Evrard, who printed 125 calotypes for *Egypte, Nubie,* also printed Salzmann; for details, see Helmut Gernsheim, *The Origins of Photography* (London: Thames and Hudson, 1982), pp. 240–41.

5. Gisèle Freund makes this point in *Photography and Society* (Boston: Godine, 1982), p. 108.

6. Throughout this paragraph I am indebted to the excellent essay by Gen Doy, "The Camera Against the Commune," in *Photography/Politics* (London: Photography Workshop, n.d.), pp. 13–26.

7. Walter Benjamin, "A Short History of Photography," trans. P. Patton, *Art Forum* (February 1977), 15:46–51; originally published as "Kleine Geschichte der Photographie," in *Literarische Welt,* September 18, 25, October 2, 1931. Benjamin also discusses the relationship of a photograph to its caption.

8. Du Camp, who took up photography because he was very bad at architectural sketching, complained about the time required—two minutes—to photograph his oriental pictures. See Beaumont Newhall, *The History of Photography* (Boston: New York Graphic Society, 1982), p. 50.

9. I am told by John Richardson of New York City that Courbet's lesbian *Paresse et Luxure*—also commissioned, as was *L'Origine du monde,* by Khalil Bey—was part of a series of three such paintings, these nicknamed "Avant," "Pendant," and "Après." Of this series only *Paresse et Luxure,* "Pendant," survives. Such a series suggests that specifically female sexuality is for Courbet—as also, if my suggestion above is correct, for du Camp and Hertz—an image of time, a chronotope of temporality. If so, this opens up the possibility of a genuinely historical, as opposed to historicist, painting.

10. I am told by John Rajchman, also of New York City, that Lacan possessed, if not the first, at least a version executed by Courbet of *L'Origine du monde;* Lacan's painting is a kind of double exposure, however, since its original Courbet image is covered over (re-covered?) by a Masson drawing.

11. Octave Mannoni, "Je sais bien, mais quand même . . . ," in *Clefs pour l'imaginaire* (Paris: Seuil, 1969), pp. 9–33.

IN REPLY

1. *The Discourses of Niccolò Machiavelli,* trans. Leslie J. Walker, 2 vols. (London and Boston: Routledge, 1975), 1:487.

2. For a more extended analysis of the language of this anecdote, see John Freccero's "Machiavelli and the Myth of the Body Politic," forthcom-

ing in *The Stanford Literary Review.* See also his earlier article, "Medusa: The Letter and the Spirit," *Yearbook of Italian Studies* (1972), 2:1–18.

3. One reader of this paper, Margaret Ferguson, has suggested that the narcissism implicit in these texts might be that of nineteenth-century literary types, and that men of different historical periods, or of different social rank, may play out their sense of women's difference in less specular, less voyeuristic ways. She had in mind the discussion of popular transvestism and the figure of "the unruly woman," a phenomenon discussed in Natalie Zemon Davis's *Society and Culture in Early Modern France* (Palo Alto: Stanford University Press, 1975), pp. 124–51.

4. For a superb moment of high Romantic self-representation (and of high Romantic disillusionment) see act 3, scene 3 of Alfred de Musset's *Lorenzaccio* (1834): "I had begun to say aloud that my twenty years of virtue were a stifling mask: O Philippe! I then entered the world and I saw that, at my approach, everyone was doing the same as I; all their masks fell before my glance; Humanity lifted up her dress, and displayed to me, as to an adept worthy of her, her monstrous nudity. I have seen men as they are, and I have said to myself: For whom, then, do I work?" John MacInnes, who drew my attention to this passage, suggests that its language may have informed that of Hugo's anecdote.

5. Discussions of Marcel Duchamp's homage to *L'Origine du monde*, his construction *Étant donnés: 1° la chute d'eau, 2° le gaz d'éclairage* (1946–66), can be found in the Duchamp *Catalog raisonné*, ed. Jean Clair (Paris: Musée National d'Art Moderne, 1977), pp. 137–40, and in articles by Jean Clair (pp. 52–59) and Jean-François Lyotard (pp. 87–109) in *Marcel Duchamp: Abécédaire*, also edited by Clair and published at the same time and under the same imprint.

6. *Gustave Courbet (1819–1877)*, ed. Hélène Toussaint (Paris: Ed. des Musées Nationaux, 1977).

7. Courbet's alertness to distinctions of rank and status, and the often disturbing use he made of these, is discussed in T. J. Clark's *Image of the People: Gustave Courbet and the Second French Republic, 1848–1851* (Greenwich, Conn.: New York Graphic Society, 1973). A fuller account of modes of differentiation in Courbet, and especially of his fascination with the difference between a painter and his self-representation on canvas, can be found in Michael Fried's recent work, in particular his "Painter into Painting: On Courbet's *After Dinner at Ornans* and *Stonebreakers*," *Critical Inquiry* (1982), 8:619–49, and "The Structure of Beholding in Courbet's *Burial at Ornans*," *Critical Inquiry* (1983), 9:635–83.

8. Gustave Flaubert, *L'Éducation sentimentale*, in *Oeuvres*, 2 vols., ed. A. Thibaudet and R. Dumesnil (Paris: Gallimard, 1936), 2:81. Trans. Perdita Burlingame (New York: New American Library, 1972), p. 53.

9. Gaius Valerius Catullus, *The Complete Poetry*, trans. Frank O. Copley (Ann Arbor: University of Michigan Press, 1957), p. 69.

10. Afterword: The End of the Line

1. In a series of recent articles Michael Fried has developed a persuasive account of Courbet's obsessive self-representation. See, in particular, "Representing Representation: On the Central Group in Courbet's *Studio*" in Stephen J. Greenblatt ed., *Allegory and Representation* (Baltimore and London: Johns Hopkins University Press, 1981), pp. 94–127.

2. The expression recurs in the section titled "On Methodology" in Kenneth Burke, *The Philosophy of Literary Form: Studies in Symbolic Action,* rev. ed. (New York: Vintage Books, 1957), pp. 56–75. When *The Philosophy of Literary Form* was first published, in 1941, the term *mise en abyme* had not yet become current in France; Burke uses "the end of the line" sometimes to indicate such effects of embedding, sometimes to point to related turns: "One may get the pattern in Coleridge's line, 'Snow-drop on a tuft of snow.' And in *Moby Dick* there is an especially 'efficient' passage of this sort, prophetically announcing the quality of Ishmael's voyage: after walking through 'blocks of blackness,' he enters a door where he stumbles over an ash box; going on, he finds that he is in a Negro church, and 'the preacher's text was about the blackness of darkness'" (p. 74).

3. William Wordsworth, *The Prelude 1799, 1805, 1850,* edited by Jonathan Wordsworth, M. H. Abrams, and Stephen Gill (New York: Norton, 1979), p. 172. All references to *The Prelude,* which henceforth will appear in the text, are to this edition. Unless otherwise noted, they will be to the 1805 version of the poem.

4. Gustave Flaubert, *L'Education sentimentale* in *Oeuvres* 2 vols., ed. A. Thibaudet and R. Dumesnil (Paris: Bibliothèque de la Pléiade, 1936), 2.81–82.

The passage is translated by Perdita Burlingame in *The Sentimental Education* (New York: New American Library, 1972), p. 53: "He was no longer aware of his surroundings, of space, of anything at all, and, stamping his heels on the pavement and rattling his stick against the shutters of the shops, he moved blindly forward at random, distracted, overwhelmed. A breath of damp air enfolded him and he realized he had reached the quays.

"The street lamps stretched away to infinity in two straight lines, and long, red flames wavered in the depths of the water. The river was slate-colored while the lighter sky seemed to rest on two great walls of shadow which rose on either side of the flow. The darkness was deepened by unseen buildings. Farther off a luminous mist floated above the roofs; all the sounds melted into one murmur; a light breeze blew.

"He had paused in the middle of the Pont-Neuf and, bareheaded and with his coat open, he breathed deeply. At this moment he felt an inexhaustible spring welling up within him, a flood of tenderness which undid him like the movement of the waves before his eyes. A church clock struck the hour, slowly, like a voice calling to him.

"Suddenly he was gripped by one of those moods when one seems to have been transported to a higher world. An extraordinary ability, whose purpose he did not know, had come upon him. He considered seriously whether he should become a great painter or a great poet—and decided on painting, as the demands of that career would draw him closer to Madame Arnoux. So he had discovered his vocation! The goal of his existence was clear now, the future infallible.

"When he shut the door behind him he heard someone snoring in the small dark closet next to his bedroom. It was his friend. He had forgotten all about him.

"He noticed his face, reflected in the mirror. He found it handsome—and stayed there for a minute gazing at himself.

5. See my discussion of "A Night-Piece" above and the early drafts of the Boy of Winander episode reproduced in Stephen Parrish's edition of *The Prelude, 1798–1799* (Ithaca, N.Y.: Cornell University Press, 1977), pp. 86–87.

6. Paul de Man, "Autobiography as De-facement," in *The Rhetoric of Romanticism* (New York: Columbia University Press, 1984), pp. 67–82.

7. See, in particular, "Excuses (*Confessions*)," in Paul de Man, *Allegories of Reading: Figural Language in Rousseau, Nietzsche, Rilke, and Proust* (New Haven and London: Yale University Press, 1979), pp. 278–301; and, in *The Rhetoric of Romanticism*, both "Autobiography as De-facement" and "Shelley Disfigured" (pp. 67–82 and 93–124).

8. See Nina Auerbach, *Woman and the Demon: The Life of a Victorian Myth* (Cambridge and London: Harvard University Press, 1982), p. 205; Ruby V. Redinger, *George Eliot: The Emergent Self* (New York: Knopf, 1975), pp. 359–60; and Sandra M. Gilbert and Susan Gubar, *The Madwoman in the Attic: The Woman Writer and the Nineteenth-Century Literary Imagination* (New Haven and London: Yale University Press, 1979), p. 455.

9. George Eliot, *Daniel Deronda*, 3 vols. (Edinburgh and London: Blackwood, n.d.). Page references will appear in the text.

10. Julia Kristeva, "L'Abjet d'amour", *Tel Quel* (1982), 91:17. Further page references will appear in the text. The translation is my own. I'm grateful to Cynthia Chase for pointing this article out to me, and for her discussion of it in her review of Kristeva's recent work, in *Criticism* (1984), 26:193–202.

11. See, among others, my own discussion of these lines on pp. 25–26 above, which lingers over the pathos of consciousness. The wish to read these lines in isolation, as a peculiarly moving "epitome," is coordinate with that essay's mournful-pious, teacherly tone.

12. Thomas Weiskel, *The Romantic Sublime: Studies in the Structure and*

Psychology of Transcendence (Baltimore and London: Johns Hopkins University Press, 1976), p. 143.

13. See William Wordsworth, *The Prelude of Growth of a Poet's Mind,* ed. Ernest de Selincourt and Helen Darbishire, 2d ed. (Oxford, Clarendon, 1959), p. 44.

14. William Shakespeare, *The Tempest,* ed. Northrop Frye (Baltimore: Penguin, 1959) IV.i.148 ff. Another echo of Prospero, this time his summoning of his magical collaborators to dismiss them (V.i.33 ff.: "Ye elves of hills, brooks, standing lakes, and groves . . .") appears in the First Part of the 1799 *Prelude,* 11. 186 ff.

INDEX